1001
FISHING TIPS

THE ULTIMATE GUIDE TO FINDING AND CATCHING MORE AND BIGGER FISH

EDITED BY
LAMAR UNDERWOOD

ILLUSTRATED BY
JOHN RICE

FOREWORD BY
STU APTE

Skyhorse Publishing

T0063778

Skyhorse Publishing books may be purchased in bulk at special discounts for sales promotion, corporate gifts, fund-raising, or educational purposes. Special editions can also be created to specifications. For details, contact the Special Sales Department, Skyhorse Publishing, 555 Eighth Avenue, Suite 903, New York, NY 10018 or info@skyhorsepublishing.com.

www.skyhorsepublishing.com

10 9 8 7 6 5 4 3 2 1

Library of Congress Cataloging-in-Publication Data

Underwood, Lamar.
 1001 fishing tips : the ultimate guide to finding and catching more and bigger fish / Lamar Underwood.
   p. cm.
 Includes bibliographical references.
 ISBN 978-1-60239-689-0
 1. Fishing--Miscellanea. I. Title.
 SH441.U53 2010
 799.1--dc22

                          2010012651
 ISBN: 978-1-5107-6679-2

Cover design by Kai Texel

Printed in the United States of America

"Doubt not therefore, sir, but that angling is an art, and an art worth your learning."

—Piscator, in *The Compleat Angler*, 1653

"There is no short cut, no quick and easy way to become a successful fisherman. I've met men who think so. But then these fellows never fished. Talk to the man with the full stringer and you'll find out fishing 'luck' is really not luck as much as it is knowing how and when and where to fish."

—Dick Kotis, who was President of Fred Arbogast Co., makers of the famed Jitterbug and other legendary lures.

" . . . But I know many tricks and I have resolution."

—The Old Man, in Ernest Hemingway's *The Old Man and the Sea*, Scribners, 1952

Contents

PART ONE
BEFORE YOU GO . . .

PART TWO
ON THE WATER FOR LARGEMOUTH AND SMALLMOUTH BASS

1001
FISHING TIPS

Introduction

LAMAR UNDERWOOD

Somewhere along the way, "tips" have left many folks with a bad taste in their mouths. They have been burned by tips, ending up buying the wrong stocks and mutual funds; seeing the wrong doctors and dentists; driving the "garage queen" SUVs; and spending their hard-earned vacations at Destination Disaster. That's to say nothing of heeding the tom-toms and chants urging them to buy products they don't really need or that don't really work.

Fishing tips are different. They are always out there, and, it would seem, we're pretty much always ready to lend an ear and hear the latest on the creek where the trout are as long as your leg; the lure so deadly you have to tie it on while hiding it from the murderous eyes of nearby fish, least risk a collision with the hurtling body of a prowling bass; the knot so strong you could tow the Queen Mary with it; and the deft retrieving motion that turns a tiny topwater lure into a creeping, crawling, wounded tidbit no predator can resist.

You might say, with considerable bite and accuracy, that this editor has had his proper turn at bat as a tip-provider. As a former editor-in-chief of both *Sports Afield* and *Outdoor Life*, in addition to other publications, and as a writer of both magazine articles and books on fishing, with the help of my collaborating publishers I have sent countless numbers of tips, dancing and singing and begging to be taken, under noses of readers. Some of them must have gotten a few strikes, or I would have been fired. Editors do not remain editors very long when their products are ignored.

Despite their sometimes tawdry reputations, fishing tips keep coming along with enough promises to attract the attention of anglers—while at the same time allowing editors to keep their jobs. This particular fusillade of tips, however (and if 1001 isn't a fusillade, there never will be one), has been unleashed by this editor neither to test the strength of the marketplace nor to provide temporary employment. My goal is much more selfish, a deep personal desire to get more fun out of my fishing by spreading the word on ways to be successful.

There is a great quote from the legendary naturalist and nature-story writer Ernest Thompson Seton. One of his characters says, "Because I have known the agonies of thirst,

I would dig a well so that others might drink." While not catching fish cannot be reasonably compared to the "agonies of thirst," the state of mind where one reaches out to others with a helping hand has rewarded generations of anglers. And now that I find myself fishing the "Seniors Creek," I have discovered, along with multitudes of my limping, gray-haired colleagues, that one can enjoy the catches and fishing pleasures of other anglers with all the joy and fervor of one's own—even more-so when you're in the boat or on the stream with a partner and see their smiles produced by trying one of your tricks or suggestions.

So confident am I of the tips presented in this book that I can anticipate the smiles and joy they are going to bring. Not every one of them will work; I know that. But so many of them will bring new fun to your fishing that I am already enjoying the idea of your success. I wish we could be in a boat or on a stream together when you try them. That not being possible, I present the best tricks, tackle, destinations, and information sources I have found that will help you catch more fish. Some of them, I can honestly say, will change the way you fish forever.

Sometimes the tip I have for you will be a certain lure, other times ways to fish certain lures. There will be tips on rewarding Web sites and tips on destinations. You'll find tips on every knot you need, plus ways to get help tying them. There are all kinds of tips about the habits of gamefish, and even lots of useful tips on the habits of your fellow anglers that will enable you to outfish them.

Saltwater anglers will especially be interested in a special section of tips from legendary angler and flats guide Stu Apte. A true pioneer of flats fishing from the sport's fledgling days when he guided Joe Brooks, Curt Gowdy, Ted Williams, and many others (between flying jets for PanAm), Stu is still a familiar sight in flats boats today and ranks as a true Hall of Fame angler with his big-fish records and guiding experience. He grew up in the Florida Keys, has lived there all his life between flying U.S. Navy fighters and Pan Am 747s, and still lives there now—with journeys to the Rocky Mountain high country for trout. A long-time friend, Stu did me a great honor when he agreed to write a foreword for this book.

It's coming up right now, and leaves me nothing else to say about what's ahead except, "Good luck, and good fishing wherever you are!"

—**Lamar Underwood**, *March, 2010*

Foreword

STU APTE

In the mountain man movie *Jeremiah Johnson*, the storekeeper who sold Johnson his gear for trapping answers Johnson's question on where he should go to start trapping critters whose skins he can sell. The man tells Johnson: "Ride due west to the sunset. Turn left at the Rocky Mountains."

Johnson thanks him and rides on . . . and within a week is a starving pilgrim.

That's not much of a tip the man gave Johnson, is it? Tips are like that. If I said to you, "Fishing is usually better early in the morning or late in the afternoon," that would be a tip. And certainly true. Pretty empty tip, though—and that's the way many "tips" turn out to be.

To qualify for a "tip" in my boat, the advice has to be something that can actually effect the way you fish. And bring more fun to your fishing. I deliberately said *can*, instead of *will*. Because no tip, no matter how good it is, is going to work every time you go out. The world of fishing is mostly gray, not black and white.

Want to know what kind of tip I respect sounds like? I'll show you a couple: 1) Before wading into a trout stream or river and casting to midstream, fish the water close to the bank. Otherwise you'll be wading into fish and spooking them; 2) The best time of the year to catch a big tarpon is April in the lower Florida Keys, within three days of each side of a full moon and new moon; 3) In largemouth bass water, if your cast to a stump or a shadowy pocket lands 2 or 3 feet away from the target, it's a wasted cast.

Those are tips you can do something with—two tips that will help you catch more fish and another tip that could start you planning a successful trip. Those are my kind of tips. Starting when I was a kid using a safety pin and thread to catch shiners, to my trips today for just about everything that swims, I have always been a passionate angler with the goal of catching fish. Yes, I enjoy all the gifts of Mother Nature while I'm on the water—the dawns and sunsets, the birds we see and hear, the forests in bloom or aflame with color. They are all part of my fishing day, but, frankly, they are not enough for me. I want to catch fish. When I fail to do that—and, believe me, I've had my share of days I've been skunked or nearly skunked—I'm not a happy camper.

    I know all about those days when you come in and manage to say, with a half-baked grin accompanying your words: "Well, they just weren't biting today, but it sure was great out there on the water." Yeah . . . sure. I got a boat ride, or a hike in the woods, but not many fish, or even *any* fish.

    If you have this book in your hands because you want to put more fun into your fishing day by catching more fish, or if you're a beginner out to learn the ropes, you will not be disappointed by the many tips you'll be hearing here. Whether you're a bass angler with a super-rigged boat and interested in tournaments, or a bank-sitter with a long pole out for

crappie, or a spinning or fly fisher wading the flats for bone-fish, the tips pulled together by Lamar Underwood will be like a coach sending you into the game with a new play to run. And some of those plays are going to pay off—big time!—with better catches and more fun.

Lamar Underwood has been a good friend and one of my most trusted editors since the early 1970s when he was editor of *Sports Afield.* (As a Pan American 747 pilot, I once obtained permission for him to ride in the cockpit jump seat on one of my flights.) Lamar has always been an aviation buff and wrote about that experience in his "Adventures in Editing" columns. Then, and later as Editor of *Outdoor Life* and with other magazines, Lamar has guided a great deal of my editorial output through publication. He most certainly helped guide my memoir, the book *Of Wind And Tides,* into being the great read that it is now. I know from personal experience that attaining reward for the readers has been Lamar's highest priority and life's great work. In addition to his magazine work, he has edited many books and is a good writer himself, as you will see here.

Despite our friendship and long working relationship, Lamar and I have never fished together. Some sort of bad luck always seemed to interfere with the trips we wanted to do. We did, however, hunt quail together on a fantastic trip in the mountains of Arizona with the late Pete Brown, who was shooting editor of *Sports Afield* for so many years.

My years of leaning on a push-pole as a guide on the Florida flats, with the good fortune of fishing virtually all over the world while piloting for Pan Am, have presented me with countless occasions to give other anglers some good tips and advice on improving their fishing. Those occasions, when the things I've learned and shared with others—particularly youngsters—have brought them great joy and have been as much fun to me as fishing myself. I feel the same way now about introducing you to these pieces of fishing wisdom. I wish I could see the smile that's going to be on your face when you're trying one of these tips and your rod goes into a big, trembling loop. Because that's what's going to happen, All you have to do is to keep this book close at hand so that you can dip into it from time to time—then go out and run one of the new plays the coach has for you. They work! I guarantee it!

—**Stu Apte**, *The Florida Keys, March, 2010*

PART ONE

BEFORE YOU GO . . .

CHAPTER 1

Reflections on Angling: Inspiration and Information You Can Use

1. Best Fishing Tip Ever Heard

"There is only one theory about angling in which I have perfect confidence, and this is that the two words, least appropriate to any statement about it, are the words 'always' and 'never.'"

—Lord Grey of Fallodon, 1899, as referenced in the book,
The Trout Fisherman's Bedside Book, by Arthur R. Macdougall, Jr., 1963

2. Confidence: Fishing's Great Leveler

"The man who consistently catches fish *knows* that each cast will get a strike. If, by some mystery, it doesn't, he is equally confident that the new one will. Consequently he makes each cast a little better, fishes it out a little more carefully, and puts a little more effort into the manipulation of his fly or lure. The line between catching fish and not catching them is often very thin."

—Ted Trueblood, *Field & Stream,* February 1961,
"Faith, Hope, and Success"

3. The Thing About Fishing Is . . .

Some years ago I wrote something in a magazine article that I'm still proud of remembering after many years. I said that the thing about fishing is that on any given day, things can happen that you will remember the rest of your life. Events like that don't happen on most days of our lives. But they can—and they do!—when we go fishing.

4. It's Not Just Luck

It happens all the time: two men in a boat, one keeps catching fish, the other doesn't, even though they're using the same lures or bait. The reason may not be luck, as Grits Gresham explains in his *Complete Book of Bass Fishing* (1966): "It may be the way he casts, how he retrieves, or even the way he has the lure attached to his line."

5. One to Remember

Give a man a fish, and you have given him a meal. Teach a man to fish, and you have given him a lifetime of meals.

—Old Proverb

6. A Creed for Visiting Anglers

"If, like so many of us, you have to do your fishing away from home, do not forget that you are a stranger and that you are coming among those who have lived there all their lives, and their fathers before them, and who regard you as an invader of something which they look upon as their own. Be courteous, offend no prejudices, and when you have the opportunity, perform little actions of kindness."

—The legendary English writer John Waller Hills in his classic book
A Summer on the Test (1924, republished in later editions)

7. Time to Go Fishing

"Son . . . when your heart is sick and you got some thinking to do, there ain't no substitute for a boat and a fish pole. Water eases the mind, soothes the eyes, calms the nerves, and you can always eat the fish."

—The Old Man, in Robert Ruark's *The Old Man and the Boy*,
Field & Stream (1953)

8. Fishing Knowledge Simplified

"Ninety percent of all fishing knowledge is local knowledge."

—Lefty Kreh

9. The "Fightinist" Quote About the "Gamest" Fish

Dr. J.A. Henshall's *Book of the Black Bass*, first published in 1881, is an icon in American bass fishing, so much so that it was republished by the Bass Anglers Sportsman Society (B.A.S.S.) in

1970 and is still available today. One remark by Dr. Henshall has become one of the most often quoted in all angling literature. "I consider him (the Black Bass), *inch for inch* and *pound for pound*, the gamest fish that swims. The royal Salmon and the lordly Trout must yield the palm to a Black Bass of *equal weight*." The italics are used where Dr. Henshall placed them. Although a great many of today's anglers would agree with Dr. Henshall, many others would be ready to put up an argument for fish like tarpon, bonefish, bluefish, even bluegills. Don't forget: Dr. Henshall said "inch for inch, pound for pound." That leaves room for a lot of argument.

10. Why a Fishing "Rod" Is Not a "Pole"

"A thoroughly good and well-balanced rod is the angler's especial joy and pride. A true and tried rod of graceful proportions and known excellence, which has been the faithful companion on so many a jaunt . . . I doubt if rifle, shot-gun or fowling-piece ever becomes so dear and near to the sportsman as the rod to the angler, for the rod really becomes a part of himself, as it were, through which he feels every motion of the fish when hooked, and which, being in a measure under the control of his will, and responsive to the slightest motion of his wrist, seems to be imbued with an intelligence almost life-like."

—James A. Henshall, MD, *Book of the Black Bass,* 1881,
republished and available today from B.A.S.S.

11. A Tip on Staying Young

"Time may alter the kind or quantity of angling we do, but it never ends our opportunity. The old man casting over a darkening pool and the white-haired lady watching her sand-spiked rod nod to the surf are only variations to the little boy who once chased suckers in the shallows or the little girl who collected shells along the beach."

—George Reiger, *A Single Step, The Gigantic Book of Fishing Stories,*
edited by Nick Lyons, Skyhorse Publishing, 2007

12. The Call of the River

"Once I got hooked on these 'ol river bream, I gave up the bass. Now if I've got water moving under me, I'm happy. Sometimes, if it gets too long since I've been on the river, I'll sit on the toilet and flush a few times, just to make myself feel better."

—Angler Ron Morris, in the article "1000 Miles of Panfish,"
by T. Edward Nickens, *Field & Stream,* March 2008

13. The Reason Why

"Some people will tell you that the point of fishing is to escape from daily worries, so if the fish do not cooperate, who cares? (I care.) People say, too, that fishing for brook trout is just an excuse to get out and look at nature. But I don't want to be a spectator; I want to play the game."

—Datus C. Proper, *Field & Stream*, April 1992

14. A Fly-Fisher's Confession

"My vest weighs ten pounds, and I never have all the stuff along that I need. I'm an authority on high water, low water, bad tides, and wind knots, I'm never convinced I've got on the right fly—unless there's a fish attached—which is seldom. I know everything there is to know about landing fish—except when I get too excited to remember—which is always. I can't double haul, tie more than two knots, or recognize much more than a mayfly. But I'm a fly fisherman."

—Gene Hill, *Sports Afield*, February 1975

15. Presidential Advice

"Fishing is the chance to wash one's soul with pure air; with the rush of the brooks, or with the shimmer of sun on blue water. It brings meekness and inspiration from the decency of nature, charity toward tackle makers, patience toward the fish, a mockery of profits and egos, a quieting of hate, a rejoicing that you don't have to do a darned thing until next week. All these put a discipline in the quality of men."

—Herbert Hoover

16. The Lure of Fly Fishing

"So, basically, I wake up in the morning to find that life is strange but simple, and fly fishing is still as important to me as it was a few decades ago, even though I still can't tell you exactly why, and even though I'm glad it's no more important than it is. It just turns out to be the one part of my life where things are right, or where it seems worth the trouble to *make* them right, or maybe the only place where the possibility of rightness even exists. Something like that."

—John Gierach, *Another Lousy Day in Paradise*, Simon & Schuster 1996

17. Portrait of a Perfect Trout Stream

"The trout stream was utterly unlike the lukewarm shallows of the lake, tumbling clear and cold from the springheads in its cedar-swamp headwaters. Watercress thrived in the seepage places below the bridge, and the passage of the river only briefly touched the sunlight. Its ephemeral moments in the sun were quickly lost again in its sheltering cedars and willows. Its bright currents seemed startlingly alive there, collecting its rich palette of foliage and sunlight in its swiftly changing prisms, until their lyric threnodies seem to promise a world of half-understood secrets."

—Ernest Schwiebert, *Thoughts at Coltsfoot Time* in *Death of a Riverkeeper,* Dutton, 1980

CHAPTER 2

Set for Success: These Tips Can Make Your Day—Or Even Your Trip

18. Going on Vacation? Hire a Guide

Fishing vacations to unfamiliar locations often turn into big disappointments, and we're not talking about bad luck with the weather. Especially when your time on the trip is shared with family activities, you need to sort out local conditions and information as fast as possible, and the best way to do that is to hire a guide—at least for a day or two. Even hiring a guide for even one day can make a big difference in your vacation fishing success. Budget for it.

19. Google Has the Answers

Although this tip may seem rather obvious to computer-savvy readers, I am including it because it will help those who have not gotten the word yet. At www.google.com, you can find the answers to any fishing subject under the sun you're curious about. It will even take you to videos on sites like www.YouTube.com. Type in simple subjects, then add the words to expand them. Like this: Type "Yellowstone Park Fishing" or "Yellowstone Park Fishing Videos." Type "Drop-Shot Fishing Rigs." Type "Fish Hooks." Then type "Plastic worm hooks." Type "Bonefishing." Then type "Bonefishing in the Bahamas." I'm sure you get the idea now. You can go to the subject, then start digging into the specifics of the subject. You'll find Google—and some other Web .sites—to be of amazing help.

20. Saltwater Reel Protection

When I was editor of *Sports Afield* in the 1970s, Saltwater Editor Tom Paugh consistently came up with how-to info and tips that helped our readers immensely. This one was right on target, from February, 1972: "A reel does not have to be dunked in saltwater to be subjected to its corrosive effects. Salt spray and water coming in on the line as it is retrieved will get to metal parts in time." Paugh went on to describe how hosing down reels with fresh water is not the correct clean-up method. Doing that forces water into the innards of the reel, taking salt with it. "Instead, wipe the surface of your reels clean with an oily rag. Next oil all external moving parts and work them to get the oil down as deep as possible." Paugh recommended using de-moisturizing lubricating agents in spray cans. These sprays don't hurt your lines.

21. Boat Rides Need Raingear

Never forget this one: It doesn't have to be raining for you to need raingear. You may be headed for a special cove where walleyes are waiting, or a bass fishing honey hole across a reservoir, or along an Alaskan river where the salmon are running, but to get there you're going to have to take a boat ride. You may need to wear some of your raingear, or even a full set. Your eyes may need protection from the wind and spray. Your baseball hat may be blown overboard. And all your stuff—camera, tackle, thermos, snacks—needs to be in a wet bag. That's a boat bag that can withstand splashes, as well as rain. Years ago, I messed up a day's bonefishing in the Bahamas because I wasn't prepared for the long, splashy, and very wet ride to get to the flat the guide wanted to fish. My eyes, clothes, and gear bore the brunt. Lesson learned.

22. If Your Boat Turns Over . . .

This is a tip that you may already know. If you don't, learning it could save your life. So here goes: If your boat, or canoe, or whatever, turns over, STAY WITH IT! Hang on for dear life. DO NOT try to swim to safety. Try to maneuver your craft into shallow, safer waters and live to fish another day.

23. Busting Open Those Painted-Over Jig Eyes

A troublesome frustration that arises when you buy and use a lot of jig heads is that they come painted-over. Using another hook to punch out the paint in the eye often doesn't get the job done. Cabelas has a Jig Fisherman's Eyebuster that will knock the paint right out and cut your line if you wish. It's $2.49 as of this writing. Available at www.cabelas.com.

24. Those Best Times to Fish Gimmicks

Every year or so a new gimmick on fish feeding times hits the market. . . . It appears that anglers are every bit as gullible as dieters.

—Leonard M. Wright, Jr., The Ways of Trout 1985

25. Foggy Weather Fishing: Forget About It!

I have never, anywhere, anytime, been able to catch fish when dense fog covers the water. My choice is to wait until it clears, or at least starts to clear.

26. Minnow Bucket Helper

Use a common tea strainer to lift minnows out of your minnow bucket. Saves a lot of messy and time-wasting fumbling around.

27. Enjoying the Gentler, Kinder Bass Fishing

As a son of a father and soldier during Tom Brokaw's "Greatest Generation" in the 1940s, I grew up in a world of bass fishing largely forsaken (but not completely) today. For a day's fishing the needs were simple: first a good companion, next a small boat. Add in rods and reels, lures and live bait, a good lunch box with something to drink (cool or otherwise), and you were ready to go. Your boat eased silently along the bank as you and your buddy (or dad) cast to shoreline targets like stumps and logs and into shadowy nooks under overhanging branches. Sometimes you caught fish, sometimes you didn't. You saw and heard birds and snakes along the banks and squirrels in the trees. You smelled the blossoms and the lake or river itself. You finished the day with stiff muscles, a little sunburned, tired, and full of memories. That's the way many people still fish today. If you've never tried it, brother, I pity you.

28. Rivers vs. Reservoirs

Reservoirs are big and perplexing. Somewhere near 90 percent of the reservoir water will have no fish. Did you get that? I repeat: *Somewhere near 90 percent of the water will have no fish.* Where are the magic spots making up the other 10 percent? Tough question. You need charts, local knowledge, and a lot of exploring on your own. Rivers are easy to read, since the fish will be lying mostly along the banks, or by rocks and logs breaking the mid-stream flow. In reservoirs, you'll need a good boat, trolling motor, and lots of electronic gear. In rivers, a canoe or johnboat will work, as will a float tube. You can also wade in certain spots. In some rivers, you'll need a trolling motor to help with positioning. In rivers you'll have to be able to get up- or downstream, or have someone drop you off and meet you at a designated spot. In reservoirs, you can launch and go fishing and come back to your vehicle anytime you want.

29. Old Impoundments Mean Tougher Fishing

The older the impoundment you're fishing, the more likely you are to get skunked or catch very few bass . . . unless you know the bottom very well. As the bass have grown larger, they have gathered into schools, and, as A.D. Livingston, *Fishing for Bass: Modern Tactics and Tackle*, (1974), says: "They have selected their feeding areas and have established migration routes. Blind trolling and random casting become less productive." Livingston says you may catch a few small bass around the shoreline cover or stickups in the lake, but unless your depth finder, charts, or the local "experts" have put you on the spots where the fish are, you're in for slim pickings.

30. Farm Pond Fishing 101

Farm ponds, of which there are millions, are great places to catch bass and panfish. Be aware, however, that many of them are virtually fished-out because of the overpopulation of runt bluegills. As the populations of tiny bluegills increase, the bass spawn decreases. Bass are still there, however, and they can be caught. Look for them in holes or on structures where they have cover and can ambush the bluegill prey when hungry. When you find a farm pond with the bass and bluegill populations in balance, rejoice and enjoy. You'll catch big bluegills perfect for the pan and lots of battling bass.

31. Get That Hook Out

It can happen at any time, even when you're home and messing around with your tackle: You're hooked, and past the barb. You've got to get the thing out, and you don't want to head in for first aid or doctors. What to do? Well, this system works like magic, but you've got to have some nerve to pull it off. First, press down on the eye of the hook. Next, wrap a piece of string or cloth around the curve of the hook. Finally, while pressing down hard on the eye, give the shank a quick jerk. Put some antiseptic on the wound and go back to fishing. Caveat: Don't try this when hooked in vulnerable areas like the face. If you want to see technique done visually before you try it, Google the words "fish hook removal." That will take you to several sites.

32. Good Time to Go Fishing

"I have always observed that the pleasantest days for the angler's comfort, were usually the most propitious and successful days for angling."

—James A. Henshall, MD, *Book of the Black Bass,* 1881, republished and available today from B.A.S.S.

33. Asking the Right Question

When two anglers meet, the first question invariably goes, "What are they hitting?" Or, "What are you getting them on?" All anglers tend to think in terms of a magical lure or bait. The more important question should be, "How are you fishing that bait?" Or worm, or plug, or spinner . . . whatever.

34. The Most Useless Thing in All Fishing Is . . .

. . . raingear you've left behind because you thought you would not need it that day.

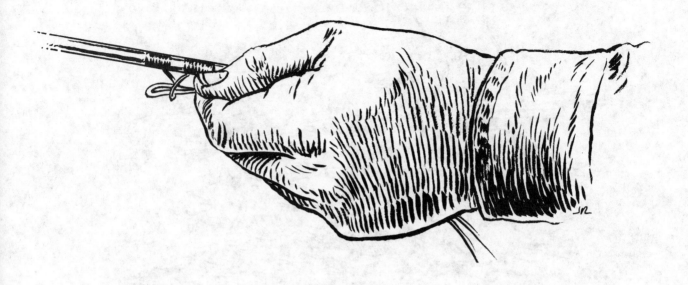

35. Stringing Up Your Fly Rod

If ever there was a "fool's errand," it's the act of trying to thread your leader and line through the guides of your fly rod by pushing the point of the leader through the ferrules first. It's like threading a needle. Instead, grasp the end of the fly line, where it's tied to the leader, and the leader itself with your thumb and forefinger and then thread the bow of leader/line through the ferrules. You'll be fishing a lot sooner.

36. Carrying Your Rod: Tip First or Butt First?

When carrying your rigged-up rod from one fishing hole to another, sometimes through brushy and rocky terrain, is it best to hold the rod tip first or butt first? The question deserves thought and debate. Tip first catches more snags and brush, and the tip is exposed to being rammed into the ground or a tree during a lax moment. Butt first seems to avoid more snags, but if you have companions coming up behind you, they may walk right into your tip. My preference, butt first, stems from seeing too many tips broken on the ground or obstructions in front of the angler.

37. Visit Kaufmanns Streamborn

One of fly fishing's most interesting and information-packed sites for gear, flies, and destinations is Kaufmanns Streamborn at www.kman.com or www.kaufmannsstreamborn.com. This is a Pacific Northwest company, but their interest and services are fly-fishing worldwide.

38. Waders and Drowning: The Big Myth

Despite long-time and widely held myths, waders and/or a wading belt cannot be the sole cause of you drowning if you fall into the river. The extra weight and cumbersome gear may make them feel as if they're dragging you down, but they're actually not dragging you down any more than your trousers or shirt. Swift currents, especially white water, can force you under, whether you're wearing waders or not. Lee Wulff proved all this by diving off a bridge into a river back in 1947 wearing full waders. He let the waders fill with water and floated downstream with his head up without a problem. If you fall in with waders on, keep your head up, get your footing as soon as you can, and slosh out of the water. Repeat: Keep your head up and don't panic. The waders will not drown you. If you're still not convinced, wear your waders and hop into a swimming pool to see what it's like. Of course, we're assuming you know how to swim.

39. Is the "Bad East Wind" Outlook a Myth?

In his classic *Book of the Black Bass* (1881), republished and available today from B.A.S.S., Dr. James A. Henshall opines that the legend that an east wind is bad for fishing might have been handed down for generations from our English forefathers. He states, " . . . in the humid climate of Great Britain, an east wind is exceedingly raw, chilly, and disagreeable, and is held to be productive of all manner of evils . . . "

40. Terrific Guide to Fishing Hooks

One of the best guides to understanding the different types of fishing hooks and their purposes is Tim Allard's "Fishing Hook Buyer's Guide" on the Bass Pro Outdoor Site Library, www.basspro.com. Allard's presentation has both the quick-read text and visual images that will help you know how to pick and use the best hooks for every situation.

41. The Same Spot Trap

The spot where you caught fish a week before—or even a day or two—might not deliver the goods your next time out. Fish move; sometimes a lot. Devoting all your time and effort to your now-favorite spot may not pay off as well as seeking out new strike zones and honey-holes—spots that fit the changing conditions.

42. Fishing Clubs: Give One a Try

Even though you may never have considered tournament fishing, you might want to expand your horizons by joining a fishing club. There's only so much you can learn on your own and from reading and surfing the internet. Clubs of abundant variety are out there: bass, walleye, salt water, you name it. Once you start making new friends—some of whom will have far more experience—you'll find your own skills and success growing rapidly. And you'll be having more fun.

43. Fourteen Ways to Fish Better Fast!

No matter how good a fly fisher you are, you will become much better by using the handy-sized, quick-read, superbly illustrated *Orvis Pocket Guides* and *Streamside Guides*. Those little books, on every aspect of fly fishing, are written by proven experts and are available from Orvis (www.orvis.com), Amazon (www.amazon.com), and Barnes and Noble (www.barnesandnoble.com). They cost about $17 apiece and feature compelling illustrations on how things should look and how you should cope with each situation. Find the one that fits your favorite fishing, and you'll find yourself fishing with much more confidence. The *Orvis Pocket Guides* and *Streamside Guides* cover Striped Bass and Bluefish; Leaders, Knots and Tippets; Dry Fly Fishing; Great Lakes Salmon and Steelhead; West Coast Steelhead; Bonefish and Permit; Caddisfly Handbook; Trout Foods and Their Imitations; Flyfishing for Bass; Streamer Fishing; Mayflies;

Terrestrials; Stillwater Trout; and Nymphing. Orvis full-size books include guides to almost every form of fly fishing.

44. Fishing Travel Facts

If you're in the financial position to travel to fish wherever you wish, whenever you wish, consider subscribing to "The Angling Report" newsletter and information service. It is extremely well presented, like a "mini-magazine," and gives you the absolute latest on angling destinations around the world. The reports and comments come writers of the highest integrity, and from readers who have visited the fishing resorts, paid their own money, and now tell you everything about what they encountered—good and bad. The "Report" has been published since 1988 and has a full archive on places you might want to visit. As with its companion newsletter, "The Hunting Report," you can get the monthly "The Angling Report" for about $50 a year; $2 more per month will get you into their exclusive database of thousands of reader reports of various destinations. Go to www.anglingreport.com.

45. Binoculars Pay Big Dividends

When boat fishing in fresh or salt water, you'll never regret stowing a good pair of binoculars in the bag holding your gear. (It should be a wet bag, to keep your stuff dry.) During a good day on the water, you'll see lots of sights that deserve closer viewing. When trout fishing or otherwise walking and carrying everything you need, consider a pair of pocket binocs.

46. The Mid-Current Is Just Right

One of the best Web sites for fly-fishing information and videos is www.midcurrent.com. The information on flies, techniques, and destinations is bountiful, and the videos are fascinating. Prepare to spend some real time here. If you think you haven't yet mastered the Double-Haul, check out the video with Joan Wulff.

47. Learn to Fly Cast An Easier Way

If you can't attend a fly-fishing school and are having trouble with your casting, don't forget the videos available from many sites listed in this book. For instance, you'll find the sometimes-difficult Double Haul a lot easier when you watch Joan Wulff do it on www.midcurrent.com. There are many others out there. Watch them, then practice. You'll become a much more accomplished fly fisher.

48. Fly Reels: Direct Drive or Anti-Reverse?

Once you get the hang of fly fishing, you'll enjoy casting, fishing, and playing fish much more if you have a direct drive reel. Heavier, more-complex anti-reverse reels help novices who are inexperienced in playing fish, but they have a lot less "feel" and seem strange when you're reeling like mad and the spool's not turning (or is even going backward) because it's locked on a drag setting that's too soft for the fish you're playing. I don't think you'll ever regret going with a direct drive reel.

49. *Fish & Fly:* A Treasure Trove

Although I do not know Thomas Pero personally, I do know his magazine, *Fish & Fly*, and I consider it to be one of the most interesting and rewarding being published today. I say this as one who has spent his life in the outdoor editing field and thinks he knows a good thing when he sees it. *Fish & Fly*, with Thomas Pero as editor and publisher, is loaded with engaging prose on all forms of fly fishing, interviews with the most interesting anglers and guides out there, and destination tips that will have you wanting to buy a plane ticket. I never miss an issue, nor should you. Look for it among the fishing magazines on selected newsstands and go to their Web site, www.fishandflymagazine.com.

50. Fish Superlines Where Pickerel and Pike Roam

Even though bass or walleyes may be your target, when you're fishing waters where pickerel and pike roam, your line may meet sharp teeth. When that happens, say good-bye to your expensive lure. When I'm fishing for bass in waters that hold pike and pickerel, I've had good luck using Berkley's Fireline. There are other choices of superlines out there, of course. Some anglers do not like the feel or casting characteristics of the superlines, but I'm not in that group.

51. Frayed Superlines Won't Last

Even though superlines are very strong and resist breaking or being cut by toothy fish, they are not indestructible. If the line becomes frayed, perhaps on a snag or rock, it's going to fail at a critical moment—like when a big pike has hit your expensive swimbait.

52. More on Those Braided Superlines

The braided superlines such as FireLine, SpiderWire, and Tuf-Line, and others are getting a lot of attention from anglers these days. My experience with FireLine and SpiderWire has convinced me they are strong as all get-out and will not stretch. I like them. They are so strong that when you hang on the bottom or something, they are hard to break free. Some Internet reports I've seen have warned that these lines can cut you if handled the wrong way, bare-handed. Sometimes there are complaints of the line biting down into the line spooled on the reel. There are also caveats about which knots to use with braided lines. [See the "Knots" chapter.]

53. How Braided Lines Can Break Your Rod

The braided superlines are so strong that if you try to use the force of your rod to break a hang-up, you are going to break your rod.

54. Put a Fillet Knife to Work

If you've been cleaning and filleting your fish with the same pocket or carry knife you use for everything else, you might consider parting with a little cash for a specialized knife that's going to make cleaning your fish a lot easier. Fillet knives have thin, sharp blades that let you cut down to the fish's backbone and follow it smoothly. You can find fillet knives and accessories, including Rapala's excellent knives, under "Fish & Fillet Knives" in the "Sport & Outdoors" section of www.amazon.com.

55. Rule for Fighting Big Fish

"When he pulls, you don't. When he doesn't, you do."

—Jerome B. Robinson, *Field & Stream*, March 1992

56. Why Be Patient?

"Beginners often believe the myth of patience. The best anglers I know are somewhat impatient. If they aren't catching fish, they try something different."

—John Barsness, *Field & Stream,* March 1992

57. The Wrong Stuff

"I'm continually astounded by budding anglers who show up at the water's edge with a heap of stuff, having no idea what to do with it. Buying a scalpel doesn't make you a surgeon."

—Jim Bashline, *Field & Stream,* March 1992

58. Twelve Best Places to Retire and Fly Fish

In a *Fly Rod & Reel* magazine special issue focusing on retirement and fly fishing, November/December 2005, an article by Jim Reilly named the magazine's top twelve choices for "Fly-

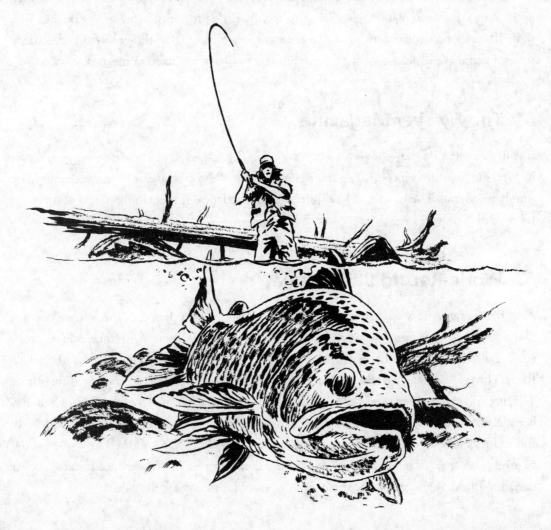

Fishing Retirement Towns." The winners were Hanover, New Hampshire; Traverse City, Michigan; State College, Pennsylvania; Asheville, North Carolina; Mountain Home, Arkansas; Key West, Florida; Bozeman, Montana; Durango, Colorado; Park City, Utah; Bellingham, Washington; Bend, Oregon; and Ashland, Oregon.

59. Fly Casting Reality Check

When two anglers are fly fishing from a drift boat, they quickly come up against the demands for either casting with both hands or making a good backhand cast. Suppose you are in the front of the boat, fishing the right bank. You either have to throw it left-handed, or backhanded. If you have been practicing, you'll be ready.

60. Casting Practice: The Absolute Necessary Evil

All athletes, from stickball to the pros, know they have to practice to master the skills they need. Why is it that so many anglers refuse to spend a little time outside practicing their casting skills? If lack of casting practice is an issue for you, consider fixing the problem and actually trying to enjoy your practice. Your fishing fun will soar as your casting improves.

61. The *Fly Tyer* Magazine

If you're an active fly tyer—or even a wannabe—*Fly Tyer* magazine will be a treat for you, as will its Web site (www.flytyer.com). The color photography of the flies, and the ideas exchanged, are simply wonderful. There's a lot of free spirit and camaraderie out there in the world of fly tying. It's refreshing to see.

62. World-Record Bass Mania

As of this writing, the world-record largemouth bass dates back to June 2, 1932, when a twenty-two-year-old Georgia farm boy named George Perry landed a 22-pound 4-ounce monster from a spot called Montgomery Lake, which may have been part of an oxbow bend of the Ocmulgee River. The fish was weighed and certified in the *Field & Stream* records caretaking of that time. The lure said to have been used was a "Creek Chub," but the exact model of the Creek Chub has been lost in controversy and lost records over the years. Today, thousands of anglers passionately fish to break Perry's record, especially in California where transplants of the Florida bass grow to prodigious sizes. Many of these anglers believe that they really have a chance to catch such a bass, and that doing so will make them wealthy. Just like buying a lottery ticket!

63. Fishing Those Golden Autumn Days

When the weather is clear and gorgeous in autumn, expect trout to be even spookier than usual—especially where the fish are running into the river from a lake or reservoir. The autumn days that bring the best fishing are *not* the calendar type. You want cloudy, rainy conditions for ripping streamers.

64. Long-Handled Nets for Shoreline Fishing

British anglers, who love shoreline fishing for all sorts of species, learned long ago that it's easier to land a fish from shore with a long-handled net that can reach out and do the job. Many are available at shops like www.cabelas.com, www.bassprshops.com, and others.

65. Batter Up! Ted Williams on Fly Fishing

"Spinning or casting with lightweight equipment for salmon, trout, bass, walleyes, panfish, northern pike, and muskies is great fun. I even go for trolling the deep with medium-weight tackle for great tuna, marlin, and sails, but for the greatest thrill in fishing, I like to take my gamefish on a fly rod."

—Ted Williams, Boston Red Sox Slugger, *Field & Stream*, April 1951

66. Women's Flyfishing: Good Idea, Great Execution

The company, Women's Flyfishing, not only sells gear, runs guided fly-fishing trips around the world, and conducts schools and seminars on fly fishing. It also has an excellent Web site, www.womensflyfishing.net, that is dedicated to helping women enjoy fly fishing. You'll find instruction here, schools, destination ideas, news, tackle, and articles of interest. Cecilia 'Pudge' Kleinkauf, who owns and operates Women's Flyfishing, has also just produced a new book on Arctic grayling, a fish like no other and one she loves dearly from her years as a guide in Alaska. The book, *Fly-Fishing for Alaska's Arctic Grayling, Sailfish of the North,* was published by Amato Press. Look for it at the Women's Flyfishing site or www.amazon.com.

67. Florida's Winter Fishing: Cold Front Woes

You're not alone in wanting to go to Florida during the winter to get into warm weather and good fishing. And it can be done, if you're lucky. However, when cold fronts move into Florida during the winter months, the fishing shuts down just as tight as your ice-bound lake back home in Michigan. Cold fronts, particularly the extreme versions, and Florida fishing do not mix.

68. When Guides Give You a Bonus

The money you invest in a day's fishing with a good guide isn't just paying for the trip to his favorite hotspots. If he's any good, he *knows* stuff, lots of stuff. Watch him and learn his techniques. Ask questions. Consider him your professor for the kind of fishing you're doing.

69. Rods Belong in the Bag

Avoid the bugaboo of long fishing rod cases requiring special handling in the airport baggage area by using three-piece spinning rods and four-piece fly rods. They will fit into your duffle bag or other bags, and today's models cast superbly. The experience of waiting for your long rod case to emerge from the little door behind the baggage belts is not fun. The caveat is that many expert anglers, including Stu Apte, consider three-piece fly rods to be much better casters than four-piece rods. Unfortunately, three-piece rod tubes won't fit into a regular-size duffle bag.

70. Snoring Is Serious

Sharing a room with a loud snorer can wreck your trip. A night or two in camp without sleep is a terrible ordeal. Always carry earplugs, no matter where you go, because they'll help. Request to be moved to another room, if one is available. Trips are too expensive and short to have to put up with this problem.

71. What the Writers Say

People who write articles and take photographs for outdoor magazines and Web sites are generally dependable and take their reputations seriously. When they write glowingly about a place they've fished—with a free ride from the owners, of course—you can bet they're telling the truth about what they saw and experienced. When most writers visit a place, and it turns out to be a bummer, they don't write pieces knocking it. They just don't write anything at all. Regrettably, there are a few writers who may feel indebted to a place where they've had lavish treatment, and even though the fishing stank, they'll make it sound like Fishing Heaven. Because of this, you owe it to yourself to check out everything about the place—from the reputation of the writer and the place where the article was published, from other articles, if they're available; references; and Web sites. Check everything out. If the place is really good, it will stand up to your inquiries.

72. Fly-Out Fishing Camps

Fly-out fishing is great, especially in places like Alaska and Canada, but keep in mind that the weather can be so lousy that you won't be flying. What then? Is there fishing near camp you can get to by walking or by boat or canoe? Are fly-out fees extra? Check out *all* the facts before you book your fly-out trip.

73. How to Not Ruin Your Trip

If you're coming off an injury, or perhaps you're at an age when your legs might be a little shaky, never underestimate the maneuvers of getting into or out of a boat, or negotiating steep banks, or docks. Grab hold of something—or somebody! It's nothing to be ashamed of. You've earned a helping hand. Use it and avoid the fall that can ruin your day—or your trip.

74. The Lure of the Salt

"Saltwater fish are much stronger than their freshwater counterparts. The freshwater fly rodder worries that a fish may break his leader—the saltwater man occasionally wonders if he owns enough line to hold the fish streaking through the water with his fly in its mouth."

—Lefty Kreh, "The Fly Rod and Big Game—The Basic Techniques and Tackle for Salt Water," *Sports Afield*, February 1975

75. Improving Your Light-Tackle Fishing Skills

Although writer and angler Mark Sosin is perhaps best known for his saltwater experiences and know how, because of television exposure, he is also a freshwater angler with few peers in ability. Among his videos and books (some, such as *Practical Fishing Knots*, done in collaboration with the legendary Lefty Kreh), Mark's *The Complete Book of Light-Tackle Fishing* is a master work that will make you a better angler in every department. Sosin shares with engaging prose knowledge and experience gained world wide. Available at www.amazon.com.

76. When a Light Rod Is the Right Rod

Light rods that come alive in your hand, practically trembling with feeling while both working a lure or fly or fighting a fish, are irresistible. But whether fly fishing, spinning, or baitcasting is your game, one must remember that rod tip strength and lifting power are essential to good casting and fish fighting. Rods with tips that are too limp or whippy won't give you the quickness and strength you need to pop a good cast or set a hook. Repeat: You will regret ignoring tip quickness and power in all types of casting and fishing. Other than specialized situations, "slow tip" rods are not the way to go in my opinion. And remember, I'm not a casting champion, I'm just a guy trying to get a lure or fly out there, set the hook, and play the fish.

77. Spinning Tackle vs. Fly Tackle: An Early View

Back in 1942, when spinning gear and techniques were just coming over the horizon, the legendary writer Burton L. Spiller (*Grouse Feathers* and others) wrote in *Field & Stream*: " . . . the spinning rig . . . materialized in response to a very special need. It will put a minnow or a spinner or a weighted fly down—and it will put it there with a minimum of effort . . . I am a fly fisherman with an elastic conscience, and I hate days of inactivity. For that reason when I go north again after landlocks, I shall probably take a spinning outfit along."

78. Polaroid Glasses: The Absolute Essential

No matter what kind of fishing you do, you shouldn't be out there without polarized glasses. Not only will they protect your eyes from any errant hooks, but they will cut the glare so you can see what's happening in the water. You can buy economy models that cost $20 to $50. With some of these, you may feel as if you need two pair, one with dark lenses for bright days and one with the lighter lenses for dull days. Personally, I like the more expensive models with copper photochromatic lenses. They adjust to any light all day long. The really good ones, like Action Optic's Guide Choice (The Fly Shop), cost around $150.

79. Saltwater Fishing: What You're Missing

"No one can really describe the run of a bonefish, the slugging battle of a jack crevalle, the mighty leap of a tarpon; these things have to be experienced. Once they are, the freshwater angler is never the same."

—Lefty Kreh, "The Fly Rod and Big Game—The Basic Techniques and Tackle for Salt Water," *Sports Afield*, February 1975

80. The Ding That Breaks a Rod

When a graphite fly rod breaks unexpectedly, say during a routine cast or while playing a small fish, the cause is often a cast that went wrong sometime before. It happened when a fly or lure dinged the rod on a Backcast or Forward Cast. Graphite can take a lot of stress and bending, but it hates dings.

81. Bass Resources Galore

One of my favorite bass-fishing sites has become www.bassresource.com, which calls itself "The Ultimate Bass Fishing Resource Guide." They back up that claim with a site loaded with information, news, and just about everything you can wish for on bass fishing. The how-to information here is massive, and it's well organized so that you can find what you're looking for. This is not a mail-order lure and tackle site, but it will direct you to whatever you need.

82. Good Fishing at Gander Mountain

Gander Mountain is an outdoor gear and information resource center with outlets about the country and a huge mail-order operation via their Internet site, www.gandermountain.com. The site's Resource Center has fine articles and tips on fishing and other outdoor subjects. Its walleye and ice-fishing coverage is some of the best I've seen.

83. Fly Fishing Without Casting

If you're just dying to get on the water and do some fly fishing, even though you haven't practiced casting yet, remember that you can have fun and catch fish by trolling streamers or wet flies while you paddle. Canoes, kayaks, and jonboats will all work fine—without trolling motors and expensive gear. Let out your line and troll your flies slowly past good shoreline cover and drop-offs in small lakes and ponds, or in sheltered coves of larger waters.

84. Great Maps Show the Way

As a confessed map junkie, I cannot resist poring over them every chance I get, dreaming of the trails to great fishing in the backcountry. Some of the best topo versions are the DeLorme's Topo USA. GPS users will find them a helpful way to download a track. Available at www .delorme.com.

85. Try Bank Fishing With Poles—Yes . . . *Poles*!

As the British have known for centuries, sitting on the bank with a long pole and fishing with hook, line, and bobber is as relaxing and productive a way of fishing as you can enjoy. You don't need a great deal of money, and you can do it on lakes, ponds, rivers, and streams. The popular image of this type of fishing is of the southerner fishing with a long canepole. The best way to go about it, however, is with today's long graphite rods and poles, available through tackle outfitters such Cabelas and Bass Pro Shops. These beautiful sticks come in lengths out to 16 feet, plenty long enough for you to hoist your bait out from the bank, even over the tops of bushes. You can add a reel and have yourself a rig that can easily flip or toss your bait into productive water.

86. Tournament Anglers Are Having a Blast

While many anglers would rather spend their time on the water relaxing, others prefer to compete in tournaments such as those run by the B. A. S. S. And even though you may not care for tournaments yourself, know this: These guys and gals are good when it comes to understanding and catching fish. Watch one of the tournaments on television; you'll see what I mean.

87. Bank Fishing: Working the *Real* Hotspots

Bank-fishing spots that offer open views of the water, and where the brush has been worn down by other anglers, are inviting and may, or may not, be good places to fish. The real hotspots, however, are the tough places to fish, the ones the crowds never touch. Watch for good holes and runs of water beyond the screens of bushes and tangled bank vegetation. Use crappie rods or long graphite poles that come in lengths to 16 feet. Wear knee-high rubber boots so you can maneuver freely. Reach out and drop your bait into water most people never fish.

88. Try Bank Fishing the British Way

You have to hand it to the Brits for enjoying bank fishing to the max. They spend hours, sometimes entire days, just sitting on the bank along interesting stretches of water, watching their bobbers. They move occasionally, trying different spots, enjoying the anticipation and scenery at the same time. Birds and flowers, the stream's or lake's surroundings, are duly noted and appreciated, in lazy-seeming, unhurried fishing. These anglers carry along food and snacks, beverages, and portable stools to sit on. They wear knee-high rubber boots so they won't be constantly worried about mud and water. They use long graphite crappie rods or poles. Another thing the Brits do that you seldom see in America is they use extra-long-handled landing nets so they can reach out over weeds and obstructions to pull in their catch.

89. Stools for Bank Fishing

Be aware that when selecting a portable stool for bank fishing, you do not want the kind with long narrow legs. They will sink into the mud and soft earth unevenly, causing you to tumble. Your stool needs wide, flat support.

90. The Greatest Snakebite Kit

The best snakebite kit in the world is a set of car keys. Get to the hospital promptly, without panic or killing yourself or someone else on the way. If possible, carry the dead snake with you for certain identification that the bite is poisonous.

91. The Fish-Catching Method Banned in Tournaments

Does trolling catch fish? It's a method banned in most tournaments. I guess it would create chaos among the boats, but it would also show the pros where the fish are. Enough said?

92. Help from the Pros

You don't have to fish in tournaments to let the pros help you catch more fish. Their days on the water are exalted in publications, the Internet, and on TV. Learn what you can, then apply the knowledge to your favorite local fishing.

93. Which Size Sinker?

The best sinker size is to use no sinker at all. The next best choice is to use the smallest you possibly can to get your bait down to the fish.

94. Lightning and Fishing

You can read a lot about lightning, learning interesting stuff, like the fact that instead of the old bromide of "never striking twice in the same place," it usually *does* strike twice in the same places. The thing to remember is that lightning can, and will, kill you very quickly if you're caught in a storm—or even on the edges of a storm—waving your rod around. No fish is worth the consequences. Take cover when a storm is approaching.

95. The Wind Behind the Rain

When the rain that has been plaguing your region for a day or two is coming to an end, and you're cheering the prospect of going fishing, be aware that with the passing front will come the wind. Be ready to fish in windy conditions. On big water, fresh or salt, you might not even be able to fish the way you want to—or even get out.

96. How to Treat a Fishing Guide

Believe it or not, there are some people out there who become idiots and jerks when they hire a fishing guide. Having lots of money never taught them manners. Hopefully, you'll never be in camp with one. Don't join their ranks. You already know how to treat a fishing guide, even if you've never hired one before. Treat him—or her—the same way you would like to be treated if your roles were reversed.

97. Plastic Tubs Can Hold Your Gear

Those plastic tubs commonly used for carrying laundry can be a great asset for your fishing. Use them in your boat and vehicle to hold your waders and other gear and tackle in organized, separate compartments. They're easy to put into your vehicle and to put away when your outing is over. Your truck and home don't get wet or muddy.

98. It's a Great Day to Go Fishing

The best time to go fishing? That's easy. It's always *today*. If you wait until tomorrow, you'll hear the often-repeated chant, "You shoulda' been here yesterday." That's *today*.

99. Keeping a Logbook

Shoulda . . . woulda . . . coulda . . . didn't! That old notion sums up this angler's broken promise to himself to keep a logbook of all fishing days: the weather, the lures, the friends, the fish—it would all be there. Now that I'm in what they call the twilight years, I see what a mistake I have made. How I wish I had such a book to sit with, remembering. But I don't have it. I hope you don't make the same mistake.

100. The Joys of Night Fishing

My brother is a private pilot who never flies at night. I asked him why? "It's because you can't see anything," he said, laughing. Well, that's not exactly true. You can see lots of things when your eyes become accustomed to the dark. And you can hear plenty, if you're listening: a fox barking, an owl hooting, ducks and geese passing overhead, the splashes of marauding fish on the prowl. No, don't knock night fishing until you've tried it.

101. How to Have a Night to Remember

It's summertime, and the livin' may be easy, but the fishing becomes hard—especially in big lakes and impoundments where the fish go deep. Now's the time to focus on night fishing, and one of the deadliest techniques is to find a deep-water ledge or hotspot—say about 40 feet deep for trout, anchor your boat about sunset, and put out floating lights. As the darkness deepens, the lights will attract the bugs, and then the baitfish will come to eat the bugs, and the fish you want will eventually be right under the baitfish. Fish deep with jigs or live bait such as shrimp. You'll catch trout, walleyes, and panfish the daytime anglers never see.

102. Two Rods Are Better Than One

Where legal, you should have two rods rigged and ready in your fishing boat. One will be on duty fishing the banks and shoreline cover. Rig the second for deep-water operations on the ledges and points.

103. Right Way to Put Your Rod Together

When putting any two sections of a rod together, start by offsetting the guides about 25 degrees. Twist sections in order to align guides while pulling them together. This creates a suction that will keep them from coming apart while casting or playing a big fish. Be sure not to grip any of the guides while twisting the rod to align the guides. To take the rods apart, simply reverse the process.

—Stu Apte

104. Locking Down Your Reel

To save the embarrassment of fishing your fly reel, or any reel, out of the water, rock it gently back and forth while tightening the reel seat locking ring, making sure it is properly seated.

—Stu Apte

105. Stringer Danger!

In the deep South, where fishing in the black-water streams and swamps might yield a hefty stringer of bream, bass, and crappies, leaving that stringer waiting at the edge of the stream or lake while you make camp requires a note of caution. Before you reach down to pull it up, make sure a big moccasin or water snake hasn't paid your fish a visit. The cottonmouth is venomous, poison to you and me, while the non-venomous water snake can have a lousy disposition at times and ruin your day.

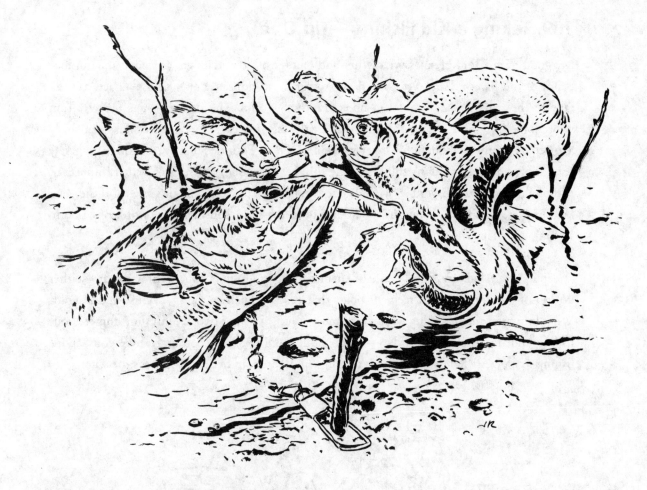

106. Wobblers Need Swivels

To get the best action out of your wobbling spoons and lures (and to prevent line kinking), connect them to the line or leader with snap swivels.

107. Fill That Spool With Line

No, I'm not on the take from fishing line companies. But I want you to fill your spinning and baitcasting reels with line, and backing if necessary, for the simple reason that they can't deliver smooth casts without being completely filled. Less-than-full spools also make your drag inefficient. And I know you don't want to lose that big one!

108. Camp Cooks Get Special Treatment

Fishing camp is a great place to be with all your buddies. Usually there's one guy who does the cooking, or at least supervises the chow preparation. Sometimes the boys need to be reminded: The cook doesn't do the dishes!

109. Taking a Kid Fishing—Tip One

My good friend Tom Hennessey, a writer and painter of great renown, as well as the outdoor editor of the *Bangor Daily News,* is a down-to-earth, no-nonsense man whose advice you can take to the bank. In his wonderful book, *Feathers 'n Fins,* The Amwell Press (1989), Tom wrote some tips on taking a kid fishing that are the best I've ever read, and Tom has graciously allowed us to reprint them in full excerpts from his book. Four tips on taking a kid fishing may seem a bit much, but I don't think so. The tips are that good; the subject is that important. Although Tom used the word "boy" as a generic name, his tips apply to girls as well. If there is a kid out there whom you know and would like to take fishing, consider these words of wisdom, starting with Tip One:

"Keep in mind, kids are kids. Names of far-flung fishing grounds don't impress them. Neither do top-of-the-line rods and reels, or boats that cost as much as the first house you bought. What impresses them is being with you—and catching a fish or two . . . . In short forget about fishing and, for one day—his day—think about guiding . . . Accordingly, take your 'sport' fishing in a place where you know his rigging will tighten up frequently. That's the secret."

110. Taking a Kid Fishing—Tip Two

"It's not the end of the world if your boy tips the bait bucket over, or drops your tacklebox. Tell me you haven't. You know he'll step on your flyline, sit on the knapsack containing the sandwiches, lose his paddle in the swiftest part of the stream, and leave the insect repellent on a rock back where you put in. And you can bet your best reel that sometime during the day he'll go in over his boots—but won't dump them out until he's back in the canoe. Years later, you'll laugh at all that. Why not laugh at it then? It'll mean more."

—Tom Hennessey, *Feathers 'n Fins,* The Amwell Press, 1989

111. Taking a Kid Fishing—Tip Three

"A boy's curiosity and competitive nature make him an eager student. You'll be surprised at how quickly he'll learn knots, the names of flies and lures, and how to rig tackle. If he were half as attentive in school, he'd be on the honor roll. The courses offered in the classroom of the great outdoors are, however, infinitely more interesting and challenging, and the teachers far less demanding."

—Tom Hennessey, *Feathers 'n Fins,* The Amwell Press, 1989

112. Taking a Kid Fishing—Tip Four

"Most of all, don't let catching fish take precedence over the little things that, to a boy, make goin' fishin' so much fun. Show him how to make a whistle from a piece of willow, see who can skip rocks the farthest, catch frogs, and maybe a turtle to take home and keep in a washtub. Teach him to row or paddle. What difference does it make if you go around in circles for a few minutes. You've been doing that all your life. Ask him what pattern of fly he thinks you should use. Let him net a fish for you, and although you've stressed the importance of 'catch-and-release,' let him take a couple home. Aside from making him feel like a man, and you feel like a boy, it'll guarantee that next time you pick up your tacklebox he'll ask, 'Can I go?'"

—Tom Hennessey, *Feathers 'n Fins,* The Amwell Press, 1989

113. Tackle Shop Advice on Hotspots: What's It Worth?

There's a great old pleasant thought (it's been around in fishing lore forever) that if you spend some time in a tackle shop, buying a few things and perhaps having a cup of coffee, the proprietor will share the latest and greatest information on hotspots you should be fishing. Perhaps this is true in a broad sense at saltwater and big-lake destinations, where the holes the crowds have been fishing are well known, but don't expect it to put you on bass fishing "honey holes" or the stretches of trout streams and creeks where the action is really hot. In today's competitive, crowded fishing atmosphere, you'll find most free advice to be worth just what it cost: nothing!

114. Respect for Other Anglers

In today's pressured fishing environment, good angling spots are hard to find and hard to keep. Don't expect other anglers to tell you the exact locations of their "secret" spots. Keep your questions general in nature, and make up your mind to look for, and find, your own.

115. Carry a Hook Sharpener

Of all the gizmos you can carry in your tackle kit or wading vest, a hook sharpener is one of the plainest and simplest. It can really pay off, however, For an excellent visual guide to getting the most from your hook sharpener, go to the Orvis Web site, www.orvis.com.

116. Want a Really Big Bass? Try Landlocked Stripers

Landlocked stripers, common in impoundments and rivers throughout North America, are the best way for landlocked anglers to tangle with a truly giant bass. If you're not heading for the coasts where the salty stripers swim, your best chance at a fish topping 15 and 20 pounds could come in a reservoir or river not far from your home. Don Wirth reported in the May 2008 issue of *Field & Stream*, " . . . nine new state records have been set since 2000. The current freshwater world record, from O'Neill Forebay in California, is 67 ½ pounds." At the rate things are going, that record may be broken by the time you are reading this.

117. Easy Way to Get Started in Fly Fishing

The name of the site is very long, but try to get it right because it's worth the trip: www .associatedinternet.com/flyfishing101/. This takes you to "The Beginner's Netguide to Flyfishing," one of the best sites I've seen for everything fly fishing, including Internet links, books, tackle—you name it! If you're just getting into fly fishing, or even if you're experienced, this site is a winner.

118. One of the Greatest Fishing Books Ever Published

This is a tip not about catching big fish, but on landing hours and hours of fishing pleasure through reading. The book is Tom McGuane's collection of fishing stories that he has written during his lifetime as a novelist, filmwriter, rancher, and worldwide angler. The title is *The*

Longest Silence: A Life in Fishing. The story "The Longest Silence" is a permit-fishing story originally published in *Sports Illustrated*, and is but one article of many that were published first in prominent magazines. The articles cover everything from trout fishing, to flats fishing, to salmon, and are mostly fly-fishing stories. McGuane has the ability to take you with him wherever he goes fishing and, trust me, you're going to enjoy the trip. It's available in paperback at www.amazon.com and other booksellers.

119. Rigging Up the Right Way

To have the best ways to set up your bait rigs, knots, and tackle right at your fingertips, a paperback copy of Vic Dunaway's *Baits, Rigs & Tackle* will do the trick. Dunaway, a respected veteran writer and editor of Florida fishing fame, is the kind of no-nonsense expert you can depend on to tie up the rig to match the fish and the conditions. Look for it, and similar books, on www.amazon.com.

120. The Amazon Is Not a Jungle!

In this book, you'll hear a lot about going to www.amazon.com for all the books and publications on fishing you could possibly need. If you don't consider that to be a fishing tip, I'm sorry, but I must tell you that Internet resources are a miracle, and you might as well take advantage of them. There are other sites besides Amazon, of course, but it's the one I have relied on the most and am confident will deliver what you need. Where-to guides, how-to, specific subjects—it's all there.

121. Two Hemingway Stories for Young and Old Readers

In case you haven't read them, two Ernest Hemingway tales you owe it to yourself to start reading as soon as possible are his classic *The Old Man and the Sea* and the short story "Big Two-Hearted River." The fame of *The Old Man and the Sea* precludes any need for an introduction, but "Big Two-Hearted River" is easy to miss unless you've gotten into collections of Hemingway short stories. You'll find it in any of the Hemingway short story collections at your library. It's written in two parts, and is the simple narrative of a young man, Nick Adams, who has returned to his beloved Michigan backcountry to camp and fish for trout. The original version has some very sex-explicit stories; if that offends, try to get a copy of *Hemingway on Fishing*, a collection of some of his best fishing stories, including "Big Two-Hearted River," published by the Lyons Press. It will pass inspection by everyone, from your parents to your teachers.

122. Don't Miss Prime Time

As the sun is setting and the shadows deepening, the idea of heading home or to camp before darkness descends is perfectly natural. By doing so, however, you might miss out on the day's best fishing time—those precious minutes between sunset and darkness. That's when fish will be on the move, more likely to strike than at any time since dawn. If your gear includes a small flashlight or headlamp, you'll have no reason to dread the dark. Keep on fishing! It may pay off between sunset and darkness.

123. Houseboat Fishing: What a Great Idea

Imagine being with your family or a bunch of friends on a comfortable, easy-to-steer-and-run boat that chugs along anywhere you want to go on big waters like the TWA lakes, the Boundary Waters area of Minnesota and Ontario, or the high desert lakes of the West. You're not just out for a swim or a boat ride here: You're going fishing. Big time! Along with the houseboat

that you'll live on, you'll also have a good fishing boat in tow. Consider the houseboat as your movable base camp. You can stop and fish anywhere you please, and in the evenings pull into quiet coves for a relaxing dinner and night anchored in a safe spot. The Internet, of course, is one place to make this kind of fishing vacation start to happen. Check out www.houseboating.org.

124. Fishing's Critical Water Temperature

"The rate of digestion in largemouth bass and most other species is very slow below 65 degrees. Lower energy consumption and growth cessation reduces the fishes' need for food."

—Oklahoma Department of Wildlife Conservation, "Reservoir Fishing Tips,"
www.wildlifedepartment.com/fishing.htm

125. They're On the Bite!

"Fish that are actively feeding are generally more susceptible to being caught than those not feeding. However, the assumption 'the hungrier the fish, the easier to catch' is not always true."

—Oklahoma Department of Wildlife Conservation, "Reservoir Fishing Tips,"
www.wildlifedepartment.com/fishing.htm

126. Fishing the Spawning Beds

"During the spawning period of certain species, the spawning activity is the dominant biological drive and feeding activity may be reduced. However, some spawning fish may defend their territories by striking a lure placed in their area."

—Oklahoma Department of Wildlife Conservation,
"Reservoir Fishing Tips,"
www.wildlifedepartment.com/fishing.htm

127. When Sight-Feeders Turn Off

"The catches of fish species which feed primarily by sight can be difficult when water visibility is less than two feet."

—Oklahoma Department of Wildlife Conservation,
"Reservoir Fishing Tips,"
www.wildlifedepartment.com/fishing.htm

128. Give 'Em What They Want

"Bait or lure selection, placement and action should approach the natural food organism of the species sought. Learn more about forage species such as crayfish or aquatic insects by turning over rocks in the water."

—Oklahoma Department of Wildlife Conservation, "Reservoir Fishing Tips,"
www.wildlifedepartment.com/fishing.htm

129. Fly Fishing Made Easier

A great Internet spot to learn more about the details of fly fishing—for everything from panfish to salmon, from tackle to tactics—is Robert Yacullo's "Beginner's Netguide to Flyfishing" at www.associatedinternet.com/flyfishing101/.

130. Bank Fishing Made Easier

Fishing from the bank can bring great rewards. It's much easier, though, when you invest in a pair of rubber boots, called "wellies," that come up near your knees. Without such boots, even though you're not going to wade the stream, you're bound to get your feet wet and muddy at some point during the day.

131. Before You Release That Fish . . .

There's so much attention paid to the ethics and techniques of releasing fish these days that sometimes a simple, important moment is overlooked. That is, the short time it takes you to really look over the fish you've caught. Really appreciate its colors and beautiful shape. Stoke your memory bank first, *then* release your catch. You've got time to do both, despite the "Hurry!" cries you hear about releasing fish today.

132. Forceps, Please

If you're fishing without forceps or a tool to remove your hook from a fish's mouth, you're just making things hard for yourself . . . and the fish.

133. Handling the Midday Lull

It's completely normal for freshwater fishing action to slack off during the midday hours, especially in high summer. Don't fight it or wear yourself out, especially when you've been out there since the crack of dawn. Take some time out for your lunch, a shady spot, perhaps even a nap or something to read. You'll be primed and ready when things pick up again later in the afternoon.

134. Don't Forget the Crawfish

"We were quitting when I got an idea: crawfish . . . We went back to one of the places which had looked ideal but had yielded nothing. And . . . just as fast as I could bait a hook with craw-fish, drop it overboard . . . I landed three good bass."

—Ray Bergman, *Fresh-Water Bass,* 1946

135. The Never-Ending Joys of Fly Fishing

One of the most experienced fly fishers in the world on his love of fishing: " . . . even today, if someone were to point out a truly big fish and ask me to try for it my hands would still tremble as I tried to tie on a fly he may accept. Apart from anything else, one of the greatest aspects of angling is that no matter how old or experienced you become, you never stop learning."

—John Goddard, *A Fly Fisher's Reflections,* 2002

136. Autumn Action: Too Good to Miss

If you've been giving football and baseball a lot of your free time in September, October, and early November, you might benefit by doing a reappraisal. These months are prime time for fishing in both fresh and salt water. While there's never a guarantee of action in fishing, the weeks of autumn are your best bet.

137. What's In a Name?

Growing up mostly in Georgia (with other travels as an "Army brat" accompanying my Army officer father), I was brought up on a strange assortment of fish names. Other areas of the country will vary, but here's what the folks called all the local fish in southeastern Georgia: A bass was called a "trout." Bluegill, "brim." Pickerel, "jack." Striped bass, "rockfish." Rock Bass, "warmouth" or "stump-knocker." Crappie, "speckled perch." The fish with the correct name was the red-breast sunfish, called, "redbreast." We didn't have to worry about what to call a real trout. There weren't any down there.

138. Got Any Clouser Minnows?

"In fact, the Clouser minnow has probably been the most popular fly designed in the last fifteen years. It's still useful in both fresh and salt water and appropriate for any type of fish. It

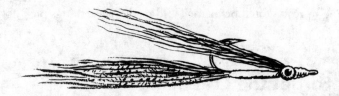

offers size flexibility; that is, it can be effective at 10 inches long or 1 inch long. By adjusting the weight of the eyes you can customize the swimming depth of the fly. I have to date caught eighty-six species of fish on versions of that lure, about a third of which were caught using a combination of either chartreuse and yellow or chartreuse and white on the wing."

—Lefty Kreh, with Chris Millard, *My Life Was THIS BIG and Other True Fishing Tales,* Skyhorse Publishing, 2008

139. Make Mine Chartreuse!

"There's an old saying among fishermen: If it ain't chartreuse, it ain't no use."

—Lefty Kreh, with Chris Millard, *My Life Was THIS BIG and Other True Fishing Tales,* Skyhorse Publishing, 2008

140. Why Rising Water Isn't All Bad

"In rising water, most species of fish move toward shore or upstream. A rise can be associated with increased oxygen, more favorable water temperatures and an influx of food organisms."

—Oklahoma Department of Wildlife Conservation, "Reservoir Fishing Tips," www.wildlifedepartment.com/fishing.htm

141. The All-Important Temperature

"Every species has a temperature preference, the temperature at which they are most comfortable. They will seek this temperature all during the year."

—Oklahoma Department of Wildlife Conservation, "Reservoir Fishing Tips," www.wildlifedepartment.com/fishing.htm

142. Night Feeders, Prowling in Daylight

"Turbid water or cloudy days cut down light penetration, encouraging nocturnal feeders to forage during daylight hours. Also, many predatory fish will feed throughout the day in shallow water, even in hot summer weather."

—Oklahoma Department of Wildlife Conservation, "Reservoir Fishing Tips," www.wildlifedepartment.com/fishing.htm

143. How Barometric Pressure Affects Fish

"Barometric pressure seems to provide fish with the same stimulation as water fluctuations. Falling pressure influences fish to become more active along shorelines, whereas rising pressure leads to a decrease in fish activity and poorer fishing."

> —Oklahoma Department of Wildlife Conservation, "Reservoir Fishing Tips,"
> www.wildlifedepartment.com/fishing.htm

144. Side-Arm Casting Rewards

Fish grow old lying in the deep, shadowy pockets protected by overhanging branches and brush. The only way to get a cast in there is side-arm, with the rod horizontal. Every moment you spend practicing the Side-Arm Cast can bring you huge rewards when you're fishing.

145. Casting: The Real Art of Fishing

No matter what kind of fishing you're doing, making a good cast has a huge bearing on the results. Other than dropping your bait straight over the side, putting your lure, fly, or even live-bait rig into a precise spot is critical. Almost always, the best casters are the best fishermen. Spend as much time practicing your casting on your lawn or a nearby lake as you possibly can, and you'll catch more fish and enjoy your fishing a lot more.

146. Catching Those Night Crawlers

You'll catch night crawlers easier and faster by taping some red tissue paper over your flashlight.

147. Wind Action Can Be Good for Fishing

"Wind action creates alternatives in the fish's environment. On a cool, windy summer day, the windward bank may present temperatures and oxygen levels more favorable to his disposition. Wind may also concentrate forage."

> —Oklahoma Department of Wildlife Conservation, "Reservoir Fishing Tips,"
> www.wildlifedepartment.com/fishing.htm

148. Wind Direction: Breeding Bad Weather

"Wind direction does seem to affect fishing. The phrase '. . .winds in the east, fish bite least. . . .' seems generally true, although the wind direction itself may not be as important as the accompanying climatic factors."

> —Oklahoma Department of Wildlife Conservation, "Reservoir Fishing Tips,"
> www.wildlifedepartment.com/fishing.htm

149. Beating the Heat

"Cloud cover, turbidity, rain and cooler air masses will all cause cooling, stimulating fish movement in summer. Weather that has a warming effect on water may also set off increased activity."

—Oklahoma Department of Wildlife Conservation, "Reservoir Fishing Tips," www.wildlifedepartment.com/fishing.htm

150. Spinning Reels and Ultralight Baits

Although most advice on putting your line on spinning reels stresses filling the spool, writers like Don Wirth have recommended that when using lighter lures such as floating worms, a large-diameter spinning reel eliminates line twists better than ultralight, smaller-diameter reels. Do not fill the spool. Leave the last quarter unfilled to prevent troublesome loops.

151. Going Ultralight

One of the most interesting arrays of ultralight and soft-plastic baits I've seen comes from Southern Tackle Company in Columbia, Mississippi. Their Scum Frogs and others look great. Check them out at www.southernlure.goodbarry.com/.

152. Understanding the Thermocline

"A 'thermocline' is a layer of water that usually develops in reservoirs during the summer where the temperature rapidly falls with an increase in depth. Water temperatures above and below the thermocline change more gradually. Because there is often little oxygen below the thermocline, it is generally accepted that fishing is frequently poor below this layer."

—Oklahoma Department of Wildlife Conservation, "Reservoir Fishing Tips," www.wildlifedepartment.com/fishing.htm

153. Predators Hunt in the Shadows

"Large predators are most effective in lower light conditions, when their greater size is easier to conceal while foraging."

—Oklahoma Department of Wildlife Conservation, "Reservoir Fishing Tips," www.wildlifedepartment.com/fishing.htm

154. Fishing the Spring Warm-Up

"During early spring the northern portion of ponds and reservoirs tend to warm faster and will stimulate more activity than other areas. Turbid water will warm faster and cool slower than clear water. In early spring, look for fish to move out of clear water into turbid water. In summer, find fish in clear water during morning and evening."

—Oklahoma Department of Wildlife Conservation, "Reservoir Fishing Tips," www.wildlifedepartment.com/fishing.htm

155. Reading the Pattern

"A common thread that links all good anglers is their ability to establish a fishing pattern. Factors such as water temperature, water depth, weather conditions, habitat type, bait type, and presentation can be used to establish a pattern. Accomplished anglers will keep a mental, or even a written, diary of these factors each time they catch a fish. But duplicating a successful angling technique, lure type, and fishing depth in a similar area with similar climatic conditions, anglers can often establish a successful pattern that will produce fish year after year."

—Oklahoma Department of Wildlife Conservation, "Reservoir Fishing Tips," www.wildlifedepartment.com/fishing.htm

156. Be Optimistic! It Will Pay Off!

"Don't leave confidence and optimism out of your tackle box. Since casual anglers cannot select the perfect day, they must align the factors on a given fishing day with a positive attitude."

—Oklahoma Department of Wildlife Conservation, "Reservoir Fishing Tips," www.wildlifedepartment.com/fishing.htm

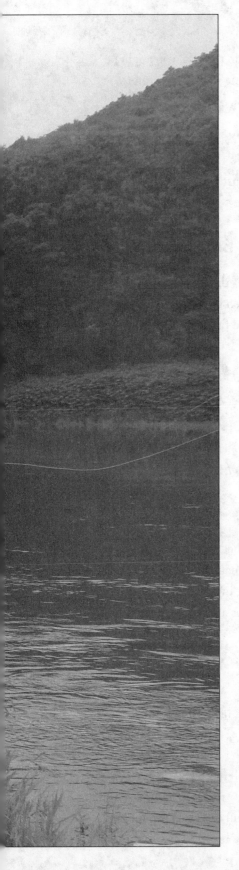

CHAPTER 3

Beyond the Basics:
A Mixed Bag of Essential Skill Tips

157. The Backlash Retrieve: Deadliest in All Fishing

If you had $1 for every fish that has been hooked—quite unexpectedly—while an angler was trying to untangle the line on his reel after a backlash, you'd be very wealthy. Backlashes with baitcasting tackle and tangled line with spinning divert the angler's attention long enough for the lure being used to sink all the way to the bottom. Then, when the retrieve finally begins, bottom-hugging fish zero in for a strike. There's a lesson here, but most anglers never heed it. Simply allow your jig or bait to sink all the way to the bottom, however agonizingly long it takes, then slowly ease it up while twitching it a little. You'll catch lots of fish.

158. The Dock That Produces More Fish

If you can find a dock that sits alone, providing the only shade and cover in the area, you might be onto something special. Look for bass, panfish, and pickerel to be waiting in the dark waters.

159. Betting on the Outside Bend

In most river situations, at any significant curve in the river's flow, it's the outside bend you should give special time and attention. The push of all the water against the turn can dig out undercut banks and holes where fish will be waiting in ambush for prey.

160. The Windy Side Is Where You Want to Be

Although it seems perfectly natural to seek the calm and quiet water of the lee side of the lake when the wind is blowing, you ought to be doing just the opposite. Fish the windy side, hard. Bait will be blown against the windy shore and pinned there, and the fish will be feeding in those waters.

161. Turning Nibbles Into Bites

"When a fish nibbles indecisively or shows only a lackadaisical interest, I start withdrawing my lure with tantalizing twitches to make him think he is about to lose it."

—Havilah Babcock, *Tales of Quails 'N Such*, 1951

162. It's Not Just the Lure

No matter how effective the lure or bait you're using is supposed to be, there's a lot more to fishing it well than merely casting it out and reeling it back. Use your imagination, think about what you can be doing to the lure to make it look alive. Fast, slow, wiggling, shaking, stopping, dipping, sinking: Put your mind out there in the water where the bait is and put it to work for you.

163. You Have to Be Sneaky to Catch Fish

"The first principle in all fishing is simple: Never let the fish know he's being fished for."

—Havilah Babcock, *Tales of Quails 'N Such*, 1951

164. Use the Deadly Slingshot Cast in Tight Places

One of the best casts when using fly tackle doesn't look like a cast at all, but can catch fish for you when no one else is catching a thing. In places on streams or lakes where brush makes it impos-

sible to get a cast into one of those shady, dark holes where you just know a fish is waiting, try the Slingshot Cast. Ease into and lean over the brush as carefully as you can. Slowly get your rod pointed out over or through the brush toward your target. With the fly or bug in your hand and your line the same length as the rod, pull back smartly, get a nice bow in the rod tip, and let it fly. You can hook a lot of fish with this sneaky tactic. Your problem will be playing them, once they're on. You may end up getting wet, but that's fishing.

—James A. Henshall, MD, *Book of the Black Bass*, 1881

165. Minnows Will Wake Up Sluggish Feeders

"As a weather-beaten old bass fisherman said to me: *'A minnow is the only thing in the world you can catch a fish with when he doesn't want to bite.'*"

—Havilah Babcock, *Tales of Quails 'N Such*, 1951

166. Making the Cast: Rule One

"It is better to cast a short line well, than a long one bunglingly."

—James A. Henshall, MD, *Book of the Black Bass* 1881,
republished and available today from B.A.S.S.

167. Why Suspended Fish Are Tough

When walleyes, bass, and panfish are suspended, holding at a certain depth where oxygen levels and water temperature suit them just right, working your lure at exactly the right depth becomes critical—and difficult to do. Lures that yo-yo up and down through the critical zone won't be as effective as those that swim and fish at one level. That's a reason trolling is so effective for suspended fish.

168. Rx for Line Twists

When spin fishing without a swivel, your line is bound to develop twists after hard use. You can get rid of this flaw by trolling your line, without a lure, behind the boat for a while.

169. Change Locations and Baits Often

"Be persistent, vary your lures, colors and baits, keep them moving and do not spend more than 15 minutes in one location unless you are catching fish. Do these things, and you'll increase your chances for success."

—Oklahoma Department of Wildlife Conservation, "Reservoir Fishing Tips,"
www.wildlifedepartment.com/fishing.htm

170. Colors That Make Fish Bite Most

"Fish vary in their capability to distinguish color, but most have some ability. Red is the color to which fish are most sensitive but it is visible only at close distances. Blue and purple are most visible in deep water."

—Oklahoma Department of Wildlife Conservation, "Reservoir Fishing Tips,"
www.wildlifedepartment.com/fishing.htm

171. Why Live Bait Works So Well

"Combining an appeal to the taste, smell, feel and sight will increase the catch of any species. It has been suggested that live bait emits an 'injured' odor and distress signal."

—Oklahoma Department of Wildlife Conservation, "Reservoir Fishing Tips,"
www.wildlifedepartment.com/fishing.htm

172. In Deep Water, Fish Look *Down*

"Fish in deep water look for food on their own visual plane or lower, whereas fish feeding near the surface tend to blend vertical and horizontal movement."

—Oklahoma Department of Wildlife Conservation, "Reservoir Fishing Tips," www.wildlifedepartment.com/fishing.htm

173. Checking Out Your Lure's Action

"Practice working lures in shallow water to observe their action."

—Oklahoma Department of Wildlife Conservation, "Reservoir Fishing Tips," www.wildlifedepartment.com/fishing.htm

174. When Snagged Lures Snap Loose

When your lure is snagged on a tree trunk or stump above the water, pulling it as hard as you can in a direct line with your position on the bank, or your boat, is asking for big trouble. If the lure pops loose, it and all those treble hooks will be flying your way as if shot from a gun. Somebody is going to get hurt. To free a lure when you think such a dangerous moment is possible, take the time to get over to the lure and pry it loose.

175. Putting Your Lures to Work

"Subtle changes in speed and retrieval techniques can be important. Experts claim technique makes the difference in 90 percent of bass catches. Generally, work lures faster in warm water and slower in cold water."

—Oklahoma Department of Wildlife Conservation, "Reservoir Fishing Tips," www.wildlifedepartment.com/fishing.htm

176. When the Water's Falling

"During falling water, fish movement is downstream or toward deeper water. During changing, unstable weather and dramatic temperature changes, fish feed sparingly."

—Oklahoma Department of Wildlife Conservation, "Reservoir Fishing Tips," www.wildlifedepartment.com/fishing.htm

177. Inside the "LureNet"

The home page for some of the best lures in all bass fishing is www.lurenet.com. You'll find tons of information and videos on lures and tackle from all these great makers: Arbogast, Bomber, Booyah, Smithwick, YUM, XCalibur, Heddon, Cotton Cordell, Creek Chub, Lazy Ike, Rebel, and Silver Thread.

178. Trying the Mepps Timber Doodle

The famed spinner-bait company has a spoon lure I'm dying to try next spring when the bass fishing starts for me. It's the Timber Doodle, pre-rigged with a Mister Twister Split Double Tail, and made to fish weedless. Throw it right into the thick stuff and let its flashing, wobbling action go to work. The lure comes with three Mister Twister tails and is available in ¼- and ½-ounce sizes and a choice of colors. All the big lure shops have it. Like I said, I haven't tried it yet, but it looks deadly.

179. Freeing a Bottom-Hung Jig or Blade Bait

In his blog "Charley Hartley's Bass Wars," Jan. 8, 2009, on the B.A.S.S. site at www.sports.espn.go.com/outdoors/bassmaster/index, veteran pro Hartley says his favorite technique for freeing a blade bait hung on the bottom is to grasp the line between the reel and the first rod guide and pull it back like a bow and arrow.

180. Putting Depth Finders to Work the Right Way

It's always fun—and sometimes rewarding—to use your depth finder (aka: fish finder) to look for fish. Many successful anglers also use the depth finder to seek out structure and baitfish. Either one can be the key to finding schools of fish.

181. Live Minnow Hook-Up

When fishing a live minnow, insert the hook in the back between the head and dorsal fin. Not too deep. Fish attack their prey headfirst. As mentioned elsewhere, when attaching a live minnow to a jig or grub, hook it upward through the lip. The jig itself will be the target of the fish.

182. Less Line, Tighter Drag!

The lesson was very painful for me when I learned that the smaller the diameter of the line on your reel, the tighter the drag. This occurs without you touching a thing! In the Virginia surf for channel bass, I watched as a big fish was melting the line from my reel. I panicked, tightening the drag. The sound of the line breaking was like a shot.

183. Fighting a Fish with "Sosin's Law"

When fighting a fish, Sosin's Law says, "Wherever the head of the fish goes, the tail is certain to follow." If you're going to move that head, you most have lifting power in the rod to lift the fish.
—Mark Sosin, *The Complete Book of Light-Tackle Fishing*, Lyons Press, 1979

184. Riding High, Down Deep

At the Cabelas site, www.cabelas.com, the Todd's Wiggle Minnow is listed under the Warm Water section of Fly Fishing. This is a foam-bodied floater for bass and pike on the surface. What I like about it, however, is that it's a perfect fly for the bottoms-up fly-fishing trick we've covered earlier. Use a sinking fly line, or heavy fly such as a Czech nymph, with 7 feet or so of leader attached to your Wiggle Minnow. It will ride behind and above your line or weight pulled over the bottom. You'll catch fish.

185. Jigging with the Fuzz-E Grub

The Fuzz-E Grub from Lindy, www.lindyfishingtackle.com, comes in several colors, $1/32$ to 1 ounce, and has wonderful jigging action that takes walleye, bass, crappies, even trout. Fish it plain, or tip it with a minnow, worm, or leech.

186. The Fly-Rod Grip That Sets More Hooks

When your fly or bug is on the water, grip your fly rod by sliding your thumb down the side and allowing all your knuckles to show on top—as opposed to a grip more like a handshake. When you get a strike, simply roll you knuckles back to the right and you lift the rod tip as you pull on the line. You'll set more hooks this way.

187. Baitcasting: Hand Position for Better Casting

It may look funny from the side, but the proper position for the reel when making a cast with a baitcasting rod and reel is to have your hand turned to the left and the handles of the reel on top of the spool in a perpendicular position. The reel will turn with less friction, and your wrist will be looser, delivering easier power.

188. Casting Sink-Tip and Full-Sinking Lines

You can't pull sink-tip and full-sinking lines out of the water and get a decent backcast. They must be retrieved and be almost completely out of the water before you begin your cast and shoot them out again.

189. Fish Jigs for Spring Panfish

For crappies, bluegills, and perch, fish tiny jigs with soft-plastic grubs deep and slow. Let them sink until you find the bottom, then adjust the sink-depth to avoid the weeds and/or lighten up your jig size and weight. Remember that these baits, with their fluttering action, are fishing for you on the way down as well as when being retrieved. Cabelas and Bass Pro Shops have zillions of them. I like yellow and white best.

190. You Have to Find 'Em First

For walleyes and lake trout, troll to find the ledges where suspended fish are holding. For lake trout, use the original Eppinger Dardevle or Dardevle imitations. Top choices for walleyes include Rapala's Jointed Minnow and Shallow Shad Rap, and the Smithwick Mister Walleye Deep Rogues. Lake trout will be most active immediately after ice-out.

191. Where to Fish Early, Pre-Spawn Bass

Expect largemouth bass to be moving onto flats and lake edges that catch the sun early and often. (They're as tired of Old Man Winter as you are.) Fish the headwaters where rivers and creeks flow into impoundments. These tributaries will warm up before the main, colder lake waters. Bass move into the areas fed by the warming flow of waters. Be there to meet them with swim baits, such as Berkley's soft-plastic Gulp Minnows and Mann's Hard-Nosed Jerkbaits. There are many other swimbait choices to check out at Cabelas or Bass Pro Shops. Many experienced and well-known anglers prefer crankbaits for this type fishing. I do not. I've found they're tough to fish with the slow action I want at this time of the year. Fish swimbaits very, very slowly.

192. Best Bet for Mixed Bag Action

For a mixed-bag springtime catch of crappies, bluegilsl, perch, walleyes, bass—you name it!—fish a ⅛- or ¼-ounce jig, sweetened with a minnow hooked through the lip, and use a sliding bobber. Experiment with the bobber until you find the depth where you're getting strikes.

193. The "Touch" That Catches Fish

"To become an effective light-tackle angler with bait, you must understand the concept of fishing it and develop a feel that no writer can put into words. . . . My father described this feel as 'keeping in touch' with your bait. You had to know what your bait was doing every second it was in the water."

—Mark Sosin, *The Complete Book of Light-Tackle Fishing*, Lyons Press, 1979

194. Best Trolling Speed

Experiment with your trolling speed, of course, but follow this basic premise: the colder the water, the slower you go.

195. Don't Waste Time on Early-Season Top Water

Despite some exceptions, it's a mistake to spend your fishing hours searching for top-water action in early season. Sure, we all want top-water action when we can get it, but on these first cold spring outings, I'll go down (even deep!) for action and fish.

196. Watch Those Weather Fronts

When you're having one of those springtime "teaser" spells of warming weather for two or three days, and a new cold front is predicted to be moving in, try to fish just before the front arrives. In a posting on Cabelas Web site, "Contending with Spring Weather Fronts," pro bass expert Denny Brauer says several days of consistent, warming weather should give you the best springtime fishing. After the next cold front passes, fishing will be tougher, with the fish holding tighter to cover or in deep water. Fish your crankbaits, jigs, or worms much slower now, in the cover, or outside on channels, drop-offs, creek beds, and points. "The jig is probably the best for this situation because the lure's at its best in the springtime after the passage of a cold front."

197. Hot Flies and UltraLight Spinning Lures

Many of today's best-looking flies and ultralight spinning baits are being produced by B-17 Swimsuit Fishing Lures (www.b-17swimsuit.com). I first ran across these folks in an ad beside Gary LaFontaine's landmark article on his "Yo-Yo" retrieve in the November-December, 1996, issue of *Fly Rod & Reel* magazine. As we explain in a separate tip coming right up, the Yo-Yo retrieve still works its magic. And we're happy to report that the B-17 product line is still going strong. Founder Thom Hnizdor tells you all about their stuff and has a wonderful catalog at their site. Going there can open new horizons in your fly fishing and ultralight spinning.

198. The Deadly "Yo-Yo" Retrieve (Don't Miss This One!)

In a landmark article in the November-December 1996 issue of *Fly Rod & Reel* magazine, the late Gary LaFontaine described in detail one of the most important techniques discovered in

his entire career. Due to a mix-up, he was sold a sinking fly line instead of a floating version when he was a young man going after smallmouth bass. Without noticing the kind of new fly line he was using, he tied his favorite floating Gerbubble deerhair bug to a long leader. After his initial amazement that his bug was sinking as the line pulled it toward the bottom, he started catching serious amounts of smallmouths. He let the line go to the bottom, and used a slow retrieve, with the floating fly riding just off the bottom. The technique is deadly, with a combination of sinking lines and floating bugs and long leaders. In trout fishing, particularly lakes, the results proved to be the same. LaFontaine later experimented with scuba divers watching the line, leader, and floating fly do their thing underwater. He discovered that the line, scraping across the bottom, was churning up all kinds of trout "goodies." In other words, the line was creating a chum line for the trout. Experiment for yourself. Some of the best floating flies you can get for this type of fishing are available from B-17 Swimsuit Flies (www.b-17swimsuit .com.) In his article, LaFontaine credited the late Ted Trueblood with first writing about the technique in a *Field & Stream* article in the 1950s.

199. Float Fishing's Top Tip

In float fishing, whether the boat is moving slowly or whipping right along, you'll have much more success with this simple tip: While fishing out a cast, watch the water ahead, where you're

going to make your next cast. You'll be ready to make a good cast into a likely pocket instead of making a quick, clumsy, indecisive chunk that goes to barren water.

200. Use Gulp Baits for Spring Action

Berkley's Gulp soft-plastic baits come in a variety of forms, sizes, and colors. Two are on the top of my go-to tactics for spring. For mixed-bag action on everything from crappies to bass, use the 2-inch Gulp Minnow Grub on $\frac{1}{16}$- or $\frac{1}{8}$-ounce jigs. I prefer the yellow or the white. Let 'em sink, swim, or jerk them very slowly. For more action when bass are the targets, fish the Gulp 3-inch Minnow in yellow/green or white.

201. Fine-Tuning Your Jigging Techniques

If you aren't getting any strikes jigging spring waters for panfish or bass using some of the techniques outlined above, try jigging slower and deeper until you find the fish. If you've had trouble getting your bait into the strike zones on a consistent basis, consider buying a reel with a line-counter system that lets you know how deep your jig is fishing every time.

202. It's Woolly Buggers for Spring Trout

When there's no hatch to match, and the water is running high, cold, and off-color—and you're on fly-fishing-only water—you can bet your day's fishing on an olive Woolly Bugger fished slow and deep. Choose a bead-head model large enough to get down to the fish. You may prefer the jazzed-up crystal Bugger, but make no mistake: Nothing catches spring trout like a well-fished Woolly Bugger.

203. A Lesson from Bird-Feeders

In all the enjoyable hours I've spent watching bird-feeders, a notion that relates to fishing has occurred to me. Somehow, it seems important. No matter how many birds are interested in the feeder, and are in the area around it, actual feeding seems to come in spurts, in waves of activity. There are quiet feeding periods, with the occasional bird showing up, then sudden bursts when all the birds in the area try to get to the food at once. Are fish the same way? Probably. Perhaps that's why we have those lulls when they seem to have gone off the bite.

204. "String" Your Fish to Stay Fresh

By stringing your caught fish through only one lip, you'll drown them when you move your boat around. Fish need to move their lips to breath. String them through both lips to keep them alive and kicking.

205. Nervous Water Means Action

When a patch of water seems to be shimmering or jiggling, while all the water around it is calm, it may not be a gust of wind hitting it. You might have a nervous water situation, with tiny baitfish struggling on the surface to escape the predators zeroing in for the kill. Get your bait into the water now!

206. Side-Arm Casts for Live-Bait Fishing

When fishing live-bait rigs with bobbers and small sinkers, it's usually easier to get a good cast by using a smooth side-arm motion. It's more of a lob than a normal cast. Don't hurry it; go smooth and easy.

207. Live Bait in Current: Let It Ride

When bobber fishing with live bait in a stream, if your bobber goes under, but there's no hook-up when you react, don't pull in your line and bait. Instead, let out more line and let the bobber float on downstream a bit. Chances are the interested fish will hit your bait again, before it escapes.

208. When the Wind's in Your Favor

When your boat is positioned on the side of a lake, or when you're fishing from shore, and you've got a strong wind in your face, consider yourself lucky. Microorganisms are carried downwind by the push of the water, tiny baitfish follow, and the larger fish are right behind them. Look for fishing to be best on the *downwind* reaches of the lake.

209. Gripping Fish During Filleting

A couple of handy gizmos to help you grip the fish and keep your hands clean during filleting are the Hypark Fish Grabber and the Premier Products Grip 'N Fillet Wizard. The Hypark may be found at www.amazon.com and the Wizard at www.premierplasticsinc.com.

210. Setting That Rod Aside

Before you lay down a rod you're not going to use for a while, especially in a boat where many rods are on hand, place the hook in the keeper, then wrap the line around the rod twice and hook it over the middle ferrule. You'll have far fewer foul-ups this way.

211. Plastic Storage Boxes in Your Boat

Those plastic storage boxes they sell just about everywhere—the kind with the snap-on tops— are perfect bins for raingear, first-aid items, tools, cameras—even your lunch.

212. Treating Cuts and Scrapes

When tackle, fins, or teeth put cuts or scrapes in your hand, you can't just let them go, because they probably will get infected. Peroxide or a simple antibiotic ointment—Neosporin is my favorite—should be in your first-aid kit, which you should carry in your boat or in your truck at all times.

213. Micro Jigs for Fly-Rod Action

Some fly rodders are creating a bit of a revolution by going to micro jigs, $1/64$-ounce and smaller. They're sold by Cabelas, www.cabelas.com, and Bass Pro Shops, www.basspro.com. No, they are not legal in fly-only waters, but everywhere else they catch crappies, bluegills, trout, and just about everything else. I like the Cabelas Whip'r Snap micro jigs, but they're all worth checking out if you like using a fly rod and catching lots of fish.

214. Ready for Action? Go to Drop-Shot Fishing

The Drop-Shot methods that have been the rage in bass fishing for some time now can not only help you catch more bass, but panfish, walleyes, and other species as well. They work because they get your lure or bait down to where the fish are. The rig and techniques are many and varied, but at its simplest form, you tie on a swivel clip weight between $1/16$- to ¼-ounce, the clip giving you the ability to change the weight as you wish to experiment in getting down. Tie a Palomer Knot (see our Knots section on page 75) about 12 to 14 inches above the weight, leaving the tag (loop) end rather open. Pull the tag end around and through the hook eye to keep the bait or lure straight. The hook should be pointed up and on the rod tip side of the line. Most anglers fish the rig in a vertical jigging fashion, but you can also cast it out, let it sink, and fish it back along the bottom. Many anglers prefer to make the business end of the rig a leader, say 6- to 8-pound test, when their line seems too big for finesse fishing.

215. The Twenty Best Fishing Towns in America

In an article with the dramatic blurb, "The Places to Live If You Live to Fish," the February 2008 issue of *Field & Stream* magazine named "The Best Fishing Towns in America." The article by Kirk Deeter is still on the *Field & Stream* Web site, www.fieldandstream.com, last time we looked. The towns (not cities, mind you) getting the nods in the Top 10 were: Glenwood Springs, Colorado; Mountain Home, Arkansas; Traverse City, Michigan; Bozeman, Montana; Minocqua, Wisconsin; Apalachicola, Florida; Nantucket, Massachusetts; Bend, Oregon; Guntersville, Alabama; and Morehead City, North Carolina. In the Second Tier were Missoula, Montana; Ely, Minnesota; Page, Arizona; Driggs, Idaho; Jasper, Texas; Tahlequah, Oklahoma; Beaufort, South Carolina; Euraula, Alabama; Redding, California; and Montauk, New York.

CHAPTER 4

The Portable Angler:
Fishing with Kayaks, Float Tubes, and Pontoon Boats

216. Self-Propelled, Go-Anywhere Fishing Crafts

Somewhere between sitting on a stool on the bank, floating comfortably with a professional-type float boat, and racing about the lakes in a $30,000 bass boat, a form of fishing has evolved and is spreading like wildfire. Fishing from kayaks, float tubes, and kick-boats has turned angling for everything from bluegills to blue-finned tuna into fishing adventure and freedom. These crafts are affordable, can be stowed with ease, and are immensely portable. Once launched on the water of your choice, they allow you to fish with stealth and precision, working the holes, depths, and structure that bank anglers can't reach, and the big boats barely explore, before they race away. Fishing methods that may once have been considered offbeat and extreme are now the subjects of Web sites, books, DVDs, and clubs.

217. Float Tubes Become U-Boats

Float tubes—often called belly boats—for fishing have been around so long that they have evolved into veritable

fishing machines far advanced from the original doughnuts that were used in the pioneering days of float-tube angling. Today's tubes have strong, puncture-free covers shaped in the form of a U for better entry and exiting—and also for faster movement. The tubes are loaded with storage pockets for tackle and refreshments, and even back rests and rod holders. The kick-fins have been modernized to be stronger, and are either floatable or come with safety straps to prevent loss. Stow your gear, pull on your waders (preferably neoprene if it's going to be chilly or cold), and away you go for fishing adventure in hard-to-reach spots the crowds never touch. Sites like www.basspro.com and www.cabelas.com are loaded with products and accessories you need to get into this exciting fishing.

218. The Spider Boats Are Coming

Pontoon boats have become such familiar sights on lakes and rivers that they've already earned an affectionate nickname—"Spider Boats." When fitted with rod holders and with rods poking skyward, ready for action, pontoon boats do look like spiders from a distance, as they creep

along the water, powered by oars or feet with fins. Once thought of as a craft for kids to mess around with, pontoon boats now boast models exclusively designed and built with anglers in mind. You can get them as sparse or as tricked-out as you want and your wallet can stand, Some of them come with chairs, electric motors—the works. The kick models will let you use your feet as well as the oars as you sit in a sling, in your waders, float-fishing in comfort as you drift in rivers like the Missouri in the West and the Delaware in the East. Even if you've considered kayaks and belly boats, a pontoon boat may be the one that's right for you.

219. Belly-Boat Fishing Clubs

As an example of the popularity of specific-subject fishing clubs, consider the Sonoma Belly Boat Bass Club in California. Their web site, www.scbbbc.com, showcases float-tube bass fishing in a lively, informative manner that covers everything from tournaments to just plain old fishing for fun. There are links galore, FAQs, news, and reports from members on their experiences and observations. For more clubs on the internet, Google the "Belly-Boat Fishing Clubs." You'll find a lot of suggestions to surf through and find the club that fits your fishing and area.

220. Kayak Fishing: The New Angling Frontier

Kayak fishing has undergone an explosion of interest in recent years, and with good reason: They're easy to store and transport to the waters of your choice, and they can get you into fishing action as fast as you can paddle there. You can use them in lakes, streams, big rivers, bays, and even the ocean. They are available in shapes for running rapids, or for stable paddling with fishing and camping gear for extended trips. As an example of the popularity and diversity of kayak fishing today, I cite the article in the *New York Times* of November 23, 2009 covering the feat of Dave Lamoureux in landing a 157-pound bluefin tuna off Yarmouth, Massachusetts. The fish took Lamoureux for a Nantucket sleigh ride, as Melville called it in the Moby Dick whaling days. Now that's kayak fishing adventure. From bluegills to bluefin tuna, you'll find kayak fishing that's right for you.

221. Choosing a Fishing Kayak—Step One

A lot of thought goes into picking the right kayak for fishing. Right up front, you have to make the critical choice of whether to get a SOT (Sit on Top) or a SINK (Sit Inside Kayak). There are pros and cons of both types and many considerations in every kayak feature. There are many great sources of information, as you will see in some of my suggestions to come, but a solid place to start is with Tim Allard's article "Choosing a Kayak" in the Bass Pro Shop Outdoor Library, www.basspro.com.

222. Try a Kayak Fishing Club

Typical of the kayak fishing clubs that have flourished in the wake of kayak fishing interest is the Northern California Kayak Anglers, NorCal, an internet community of kindred spirits. The site has articles, information, and news, and is far from the only one of its kind. See www.ncka.org or Google the words "Kayak-Fishing Clubs" to find others.

223. Kayak Fishing Books and DVDs

Once you've decided you're serious about getting into kayak fishing, you can't go wrong by a visit to www.amazon.com for books and DVDs covering the subject in detail. Even though I have been fully aware of the popularity of the spread of kayak fishing, I was astonished at the number of quality books and DVDs on the subject.

224. Kayak Sportfishing Has It All

A Web site that has just about everything one could wish for on kayak fishing is www.kayak-sportfishing.com. It has 120 links that take you directly to sites of interest, including destinations.

225. A Pair of Kayak Fishing Aces

Two magazines of intense focus on kayak fishing are *Kayak Angler* and *Kayak Fishing*. You'll be in the midst of kayak-fishing enthusiasts at both of them. Check them out at www.kayakan-glermag.com and www.kayakfishingmagzine.net.

226. A Kick-Boat Hard to Beat

The Water Strider One-Man Inflatable Raft Kickboat won a *Field & Stream* magazine "Best of the Best" award for Fishing Craft and has been getting a lot of attention on Internet sites reviewing it. Water Strider also has a DVD that shows the craft being put together and how it is used in steelhead fishing. A terrific and detailed review of the Water Strider craft and DVD was done by Rob O'Reilly on the www.hipwader.com. Check it out, and also see the Water Strider home site at www.waterstrider.com. Whether or not the Water Strider is the craft for you, you'll learn a lot about the state of the art in kick-boat crafts today.

227. The Most Stable Kayaks

Some kayaks come in double-hull models, so wide and stable you can even stand up for a while, such as when you're playing a fish. They'll even carry your favorite cooler.

228. How Great Is Kayak Fishing?

In an article called "The Birds and the Kayak" in the September 2005 issue of *Fly Fisherman*, writer-teacher Arnold Sabatelli describes his experiences kayak-fly fishing for stripers and blues on the Connecticut shore of Long Island Sound. He says he keeps his kayak on his car most of the summer and can launch it, rigged, in seven minutes. He likes to fish for stripers at night and says, "I probably catch more than half of my fish while trolling, and the fish that strike my fly were likely directly beneath my kayak just a few seconds earlier. The kayak doesn't bother them."

229. Florida Keys Kayak Fishing

At Big Pine Key in the Florida Keys, Stu Apte's base in his old guiding days, Captain Bill Keogh runs a flats-fishing, flats-touring, and kayak-rental operation of considerable note. You can arrange for four hours of fishing for $150 per person, two-person minimum. It's quite a bargain. Captain Keogh has just produced a new book, *The Florida Keys Paddling Guide*, and will send a signed copy for $22 after you call him at 877-595-2925 or 305-872-7474. The Web site for his Big Pine Kayak Adventures is www.keyskayaktours.com.

CHAPTER 5

Knots You'll Need: We Make Them Easy to Master

230. Easy Way to Learn Knot Tying

One of the best aids I've seen for learning to tie all the knots you need for fishing is the KNOT-CARD, available at www.KNOTCARDS.com. Costing $5.89 as of this writing, the cards fold into a 12-inch ruler and present superb step-by-step graphics on all the knots you need for fresh or salt water, including rope knots.

231. Fly Fishing Knots Made Easy

Here's one of the best sites I've come across on graphically presenting ways to tie the most useful knots in fly fishing: www.killroys.com/knots/knots.htm.

232. The Knot Book That Has Them All

Every knot you can imagine for fishing—both fresh and salt water—is shown in graphic, easy-to-follow steps in Lindsey Philpott's *The Complete Book of Fishing Knots, Leaders, and Lines*, Skyhorse (2009). Of all the knot instruction books I've ever seen—and I think I've seen them all—Philpott's is the most useful. Buy it at Amazon and other sites and practice the knots you need until you master them. If you're serious about your fishing, this is one book you want in your bookcase.

233. Orvis Makes Knot-Tying So Easy

Located in the fly-fishing section of the Orvis Web site, www.orvis.com, an animated knot-tying section lets you view, step-by-step, how to tie some of the most popular knots. This feature is aimed at fly fishers but will interest all anglers. Tune your computer to the Orvis Animated Knots Series in the Beginner's Corner of Fly Fishing Resources. You'll get the Tippet Knot, the Clinch Knot, the Blood Knot, the Non-slip Mono Knot, the Perfection Loop, the Surgeon's Knot, and the Orvis Knot.

234. The Alaskan Guides' Knot

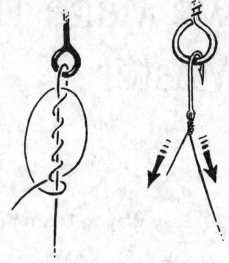

Guides in Alaska discuss knots all the time, and they positively hate knots that fail and lose big fish for their clients. The simple knot shown here is said to come from Alaska guide expertise. I first saw it in the book *Chalkstream Chronicles*, by the prominent English writer Neil Patterson (Lyons & Burford, 1995). Bringing the end of the tippet back on itself, Patterson would wind it over the line, then back through the loop in front of the eye, then back down and out the main loop. Instead of stopping there, he hooks the fly to the keeper ring on his rod, wets the knot, holds both ends of the line, and pulls the knot tight.

235. Knots for the Braided Superlines

The correct knots for using with the braided superlines—such as FireLine, SpiderWire, Tuf-Line, and others—have sometimes provided fuel for Internet discussions. In particular, there

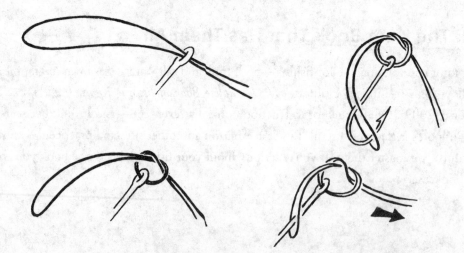

have been recommendations to use the Palomar knot for tying on your hook or lure, and to avoid the usually popular and widely used Improved Cinch Knot.

236. Tighten Down Those Fluorocarbon Leader Knots

Fluorocarbon lines and leaders are stronger and less visible (and cost more) than anything in traditional nylon. Fluorocarbon knots are stronger, but they do not absorb water as nylon does, tightening the knot by swelling. You, the angler, must pull the fluorocarbon knots as tight as possible.

237. Stu Apte's Blood Knot Special Trick

"When tying a Blood Knot using two different strengths of monofilament, make a couple of more turns with the lighter section of the leader then you do with a heavier section. As with all jam knots, pull with a firm motion so both ends come together simultaneously. Clip the tag ends off flush to the knot."

—Stu Apte

238. Twelve Knot Tips for Better Fishing

There's a lot of tackle and a lot of fishing know-how out there that can make every day on the water more fun. You might be able to get by without it, but knots are a different story. You simply cannot fish without them. Truth is, they're nothing to be afraid of. Follow these tips and you'll find yourself ready for most fishing situations. These are the basics. If you feel the need to get into the advanced stuff, like the Bimini Twist, you'll find plenty of classrooms on the Internet, in books, or by checking with your guides.

239. Tying on a Hook—the Improved Clinch Knot

Whether it's the best or not is arguable among experts and guides, but the Improved Clinch Knot is the most popular way of tying on a hook. Wet the knot before pulling it tight.

240. The Loop That Gives Your Lure Action

The Duncan Loop is a more advanced way of tying on a hook or lure than the Improved Clinch Knot. The Loop allows your lure to swing and dance, giving it enticing action.

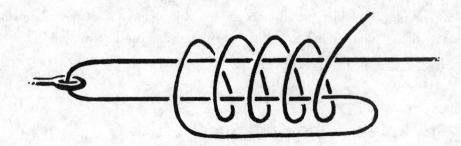

241. Looping a Fly Line to a Leader Loop

When both your leader and fly lines have loops, they should join together without tying problems. Some anglers still don't get it right, however. Here's how to join the two loops for better fishing.

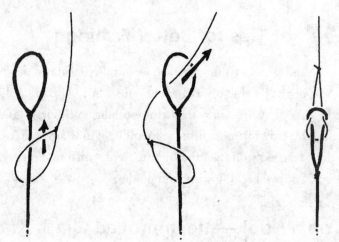

242. How to Join Leader Sections, Part One: The Blood Knot

Okay, your leader has been cut or broken so many times that it's too short for the kind of fishing you're doing. Now you need to add tippet material. The Blood Knot is the way to go for a smooth, powerful connection. Some anglers—like those with frozen fingers or arthritis in

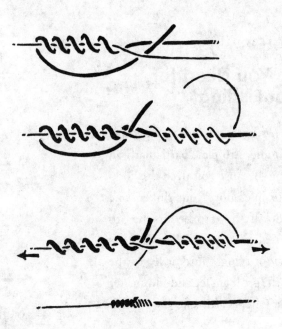

their fingers—find this one difficult to tie. In fact, there are gizmos you can buy to make the job easier. Here's how it's done. By the way, if you're trying to join line sections of mismatched sizes, you're in for a tough time unless you're very, very good at this.

243. How to Join Leader Sections, Part Two: The Surgeon's Knot

If you're not up to the Blood Knot for joining leader or line sections, the Surgeon's Knot will probably get the job done for you. Surgeon's Knot is a polite term for a good old Granny Knot.

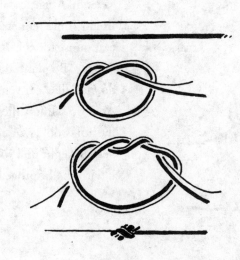

244. The Loop You Need for Drop Shot Fishing

The Perfection Loop has been around a long time, but today it's coming more into play, particularly in bass and walleye fishing, because you need this loop to attach a lure to your line above your sinker. The bottom of your line doesn't have to be attached to a sinker; it could be tied to a second jig. [Editor's Note: An alternate way of tying a lure or fly to the line was developed by the great angler and filmmaker Glenn Lau. See Homer Circle's article in the Panfish Section.]

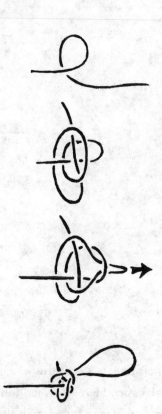

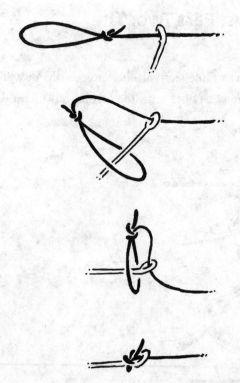

245. The Knot Atlantic Salmon Fishers Swear By

Veteran Atlantic salmon anglers like my friend Tom Hennessey, author, painter, and columnist for the *Bangor Daily News*, and Stanley Bogdan, the famous reel maker, do not like conventional knots for their Atlantic salmon flies. They insist that the fly not wobble or twist, but remain in a dead-straight pull with the leader. They get it with the Improved Turle Knot.

246. Add a Loop to Your Leader or Line

Your leader or line didn't come with a loop, but you want one. You can get it by tying the Surgeon's Loop.

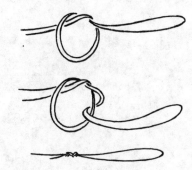

247. Connecting Fly Line to Leader Without Loops: Tube Nail Knot

If you're not connecting your fly line and leader by the loop-to-loop method, you're going to need the Nail Knot. It's not that hard to master if you take your time and practice.

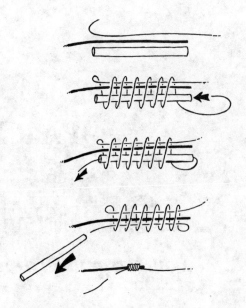

248. The No Tube Fly Line Connection: The Needle Nail Knot

"No tube," you say. Well, can you find a needle? This will work just fine and give you a strong, smooth, snag-proof connection.

PART TWO

ON THE WATER

For Largemouth and Smallmouth Bass

CHAPTER 6

Into the Strike Zone:
Tips to Stop You From Fishing Dead Water!

249. It's All About FINDING the Bass

"The great professional anglers are great because they find bass. Almost anyone can catch them if he or she knows where they're hiding. Finding them is the trick, not catching them."

—"Charley Hartley's Bass Wars," Feb. 9, 2009,
on the BASS site at www.sports.espn.go.com/outdoors/bassmaster/index

250. An Essential Truth About Bass Fishing

"When I'm casting toward the shoreline, I know 90 percent of the bass in the lake are behind me."

—Remark attributed to Bill Dance, legendary angler and luremaker

251. The Pattern Tells You What to Do

"Just go about experimenting in a systematic manner, and be aware of what you're trying at all times. When you catch a fish . . . you'll know the reasons . . . Then, most importantly, you can duplicate the technique and catch another."

—Grits Gresham, *Complete Book of Bass Fishing*, Outdoor Life/Harper & Row, 1966

252. My Most Important Bass Fishing Lesson

It took a lot of casts, and a lot of years, and a lot of wasted time before I finally grasped the most important lesson in largemouth bass fishing: You *must* fish weedless lures and baits. You will occasionally catch bass alongside cover with lures using exposed hooks, but the majority of your strikes will come when you fish your lure right among the stumps, limbs, lily pads, and weedy holes. Sure, open-water fishing is more visual and less work, but do you want to catch bass or do you just want to mess around?

253. Top-Water Patience Can Pay

You're probably familiar with the surface lure tactic of letting your lure lie motionless on the water after it splashes down—at least until the ripples spread out and die away. There's another method—requiring infinitely more patience—that sometimes pays big dividends: Let your lure lie still for about three minutes, then jiggle it every so slightly. Then jiggle it some more, and eventually start it moving very, very slowly. You might be surprised by what happens.

254. Where'd They Go?

People who tell you that bass don't school don't know what they're talking about, as Grits Gresham points out in his *Complete Book of Bass Fishing* (1966): "The truth is bass *do* school. It follows then that there must be a great part of every lake which is virtually devoid of bass."

255. Those Important Scatter Points

The areas along bass migration routes where the fish break away from their schools and begin fanning out individually along the shoreline are called scatter points. Think of them as exits off the turnpikes. Grits Gresham points out in his *Complete Book of Bass Fishing* (1966): "Big bass school in tighter groups than do the yearlings, and they are especially reluctant to move past the scatter point. They seldom do so, in fact, in any numbers." That's exactly why you seldom find the real lunkers along the shoreline, and why big catches can be made if the school can be located in deeper water.

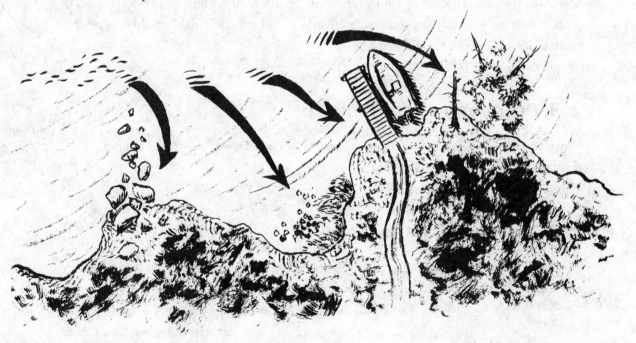

256. They're *Not Hitting* Because They're *Not There!*

As pointed out elsewhere in this book, when a stretch of shoreline that has been producing good fishing suddenly goes cold, the usual angling lament is, "They've stopped biting." Other stretches of shoreline are deemed to be poor because they seldom or never produce fish. The key thing to remember about the "good" stretches of shoreline is that when the fish "aren't biting," they probably have moved out along their migration routes to deeper water. Turning your back on the shoreline and exploring outside water, using charts, electronics, and local knowledge (if it is available), should lead to better catches when they're "not biting" along your favorite, dependable shorelines.

257. Here Today, Gone Tomorrow

The pros have a great way of describing a honey hole that suddenly goes dry. They lament, "I lost my fish!"

258. How to Fish Points

Points are favorite bass holding spots. Here's how the noted angler and luremaker, Tom Mann Jr., fished them, as related in the book *Structure Basics: A Complete Guide to Bass Hideouts*, B.A.S.S. Publications, (1999), by Wade L. Bourne: "Mann positions his boat off the end of a promising point. 'I think the jig works better coming downhill, and the important thing is to work it slow and keep bottom contact. Don't swim it.' Mann often makes multiple casts to a point to interest or tease sluggish fish."

259. Deep-Water Bass Bonanza

When you hook a deep-water bass, by trolling or casting, keep working the area and the same depths—hard!

260. Wolf Pack Bass

"The only way deep-water bass can effectively feed is in a pack, slashing into schools of baitfish together, so where there is one, there are usually more nearby."
—Rick Clunn's *World Championship Bass Fishing*, Cordovan (1978)
by Steve Price and Rick Clunn

261. A Bass Fishing Revolution Begins

It happened in the 1950s and '60s. Two great events came along that changed bass fishing forever. ("Ruined it!" some disenchanted stalwarts proclaim.) First, Carl Lowrance's "fish finder" underwater tracking device was invented, and then Buck Perry began preaching the gospel of bass following migration routes from shoreline shallows into deeper water away from the banks at varying distances.

262. When Bass Seem to Disappear

Bass migrate, just like ducks and geese, leaving for the winter. THERE ARE SELDOM ANY BASS ALONG THE BANKS WHERE YOU'VE BEEN FISHING. That was the amazing sermon preached by revolutionary luremaker Buck Perry back in the 1950s and 60s. " . . . might just as well have been fishing in your bathtub," Perry is reported as saying in Grits Gresham's classic *Complete Book of Bass Fishing* (1966). Perry believed (and was probably right) that bass were along the shorelines only during brief periods every day, mostly early and late. Anglers who thought the bass weren't hitting were mistaken, Perry believed. They weren't hitting because, in Perry's words, "they weren't there."

263. Finding Those Disappearing Bass

Fish finders, GPS units, and other devices, coupled with sophis-ticated boats and motors and a new knowledge of fishing honey holes in the vast waters of lakes and reservoirs, has lead not only to tournaments and halcyon days for cashing in on exploding tackle demands, but to the notion that would have made our grandfathers faint: "Turn you back on the shore . . . get out in the lake . . . that's where the fish are."

264. Buck Perry and His Magic Plug

A North Carolinian (1915-2006) and World War II veteran, Buck Perry is regarded as the father of structure fishing and a pioneer in pointing out bass migration routes and deep-water holding spots away from shorelines. He invented the Spoon-plug, which is still sold today, as well as the first diving and deep-running lures to exploit structure fishing. The Spoonplug burst into national headlines in 1957 when Tom McNally, writing in the *Chicago Tribune*, told of Perry catching enormous strings of bass in heavily fished local lakes. Perry published *Spoonplugging: Your Guide to Lunker Fishing*, in 1973. For more information click on www.BuckPerry.com.

265. Bass Travel Lanes: You've Got to Find Them!

Like it or not, the big reservoir and lake dilemma of bass moving away from the shoreline at various times of the day is very real. Buck Perry was perhaps the first—or certainly one of the first—anglers to focus on catching these wandering fish, but others soon followed. Grits Gresham, destined to become a television personality as well as top writer, discussed migrating bass in his *Complete Book of Bass Fishing* (1966), one of the first major books published on bass fishing in the modern era. Grits, a good friend, pointed out the discoveries of Buck Perry and went on to add, "Bass spend most of their time in deep water, in schools, and in a very restricted area—their sanctuary. That sanctuary is most often found in the deepest water of a lake or immediately adjacent to it."

266. Sanctuaries: Where Peak Action Awaits

In his *Complete Book of Bass Fishing* (1966), Grits Gresham said he looks for bass sanctuaries on bars, ridges, or reefs, or even clean spots in the lake bottom, and that bass would be moving along a regular underwater highway toward those spots twice a day. Expect to find the migration route along a ridge, with the sanctuary occurring at a break in the ridge—a fairly level spot somewhere along the ridge, "below 20 feet if the water is that deep."

267. Smart Bass Versus Naïve Bass

An incredible experiment on bass striking habits was reported by Grits Gresham in his *Complete Book of Bass Fishing* (1966). It seems that Missouri fisheries biologists placed tagged bass from heavily fished waters into a pond. They also placed tagged bass that came from waters that had never been fished into the same pond. They fished this pond with artificial lures in the spring and fall, and caught *twice as many* bass that had come from the unfished waters.

268. B.A.S.S. Pro Analyzes Moon Phases

Check out pro Richie White on the "Insider BASSlog Blog" at the B.A.S.S. site www.sports.espn.go.com/outdoors/bassmaster/index. White has done some amazing work on studies of the moon phases. The site also has many good articles on best lures and tactics.

269. A Creature of Habits

A bass caught in Texas or Georgia has virtually the same habits as one caught in Ohio or Pennsylvania. Their individual traits and preferences don't make a dime's bit of difference in terms of their needs in differing parts of the country. They all need food, cover, oxygen, and bottom cover they can relate to while feeding, moving, or hiding. The timing of their various activities may differ from place to place, but the way they go about their lives is virtually the same.

270. She—Not He—Is the Big One That Got Away

Anglers invariably call fish "He," but in the world of bass, the females are the biggest fish. When an angler says, "He got away!" he probably should have said, "*She* got away!"

271. For Dedicated Bass Anglers (And "Bassmaster" Wannabes)

Operated by the ESPN sports channel, the Internet's most intense and rewarding site for bass anglers is the B.A.S.S. organization site: www.sports.espn.go.com/outdoors/bassmaster/index. Here you can join B.A.S.S. and the B.A.S.S. INSIDER groups, for which you receive the *Bassmaster* magazine and all sorts of benefits. Tournament news and information, a vast array of how-to from the pros, blogs of the tournament pros, videos, the works—B.A.S.S. has it all. There are free trial memberships and introductory memberships.

272. Suspended Bass—They're Tough to Catch

When bass are holding, suspended at mid-water levels, with no baitfish near them, they sometimes can seem to be locked in those positions all day. You see them on your depth finder, but they seem to have little interest in your deep-running lures. As a last-ditch effort, try jigging for them, straight down.

273. Stay in the Strike Zone for Suspended Bass

On the www.lurenet.com site, a tip from bass expert Bill Dance dealt with the suspended bass dilemma: "Suspended bass can be some of the most difficult fish to catch—simply because when they're suspended they're usually in an inactive mood and don't want to chase a lure. But

if you can keep something appealing in the strike zone long enough, they're much more apt to bite. Two of the most effective lures I've found for this situation are the Smithwick 4 ½-inch Rogue and the Bomber Long A. [The Rogue indicated is the one that works below 4 feet.] The reasons these baits work so well is that they have the ability to deliver an enticing darting action and they suspend well in between twitches on or just above the bass's depth level."

274. If You're a Bass Fan . . .

The bass-fishing site www.bassfan.com is one of the best sites I've visited for tips, articles, news, and videos. It's a keeper.

275. Gimmicks and Gadgets

"An angler without the gadgets is *fishing* for bass, whereas one with all the modern equipment is *hunting* for bass. Indeed, some of the new breed of bassmen enjoy the hunt more than the catch. It's a separate sport, really."

—A.D. Livingston, *Fishing for Bass: Modern Tactics and Tackle*, Lippincott, 1974

276. Go Early for Spring Bass

"Bass stage sooner than many people realize as they typically can spawn in cooler water, often going through the spawn weeks before the big waves of smaller fish move up. It's also surprising to many anglers how active these early fish can be."

—Pro guide Troy Jens, Lake Guntersville,
Alabama, in the article "A Great Spot for Spring," on the Web site www.lurenet.com

277. Finding and Fishing Bass Highways

In his column in *Bassin'* magazine back in May/June 1992, veteran pro Hank Parker revealed a deadly system for finding bass after they've left shoreline cover once spring is over. Parker looks for points leading from shoreline areas where he usually finds and catches bass in the spring.

In particular, he searches for "a long tapering flat that eventually plunges into a channel." In summertime, he drops a buoy at the spot the point drops into the channel, then starts working along the point back toward the shore. He uses deep and shallow crankbaits and Carolina-rigged worm, and lizards. He also keeps a rod handy with a topwater plug.

278. Let Don Wirth Help You Catch More Bass

One of the most prolific, informative, and entertaining writers in the "Bassmaster" lineup is Don Wirth. His columns and articles are packed with the kind of information that really counts when it comes to finding and catching bass. Check him out at the Bassmaster site www .sports.espn.go.com/outdoors/bassmaster/.

279. A Pro's Favorite Wintertime Lures

Pro Richie White, who fishes 200-plus days a year at Lake Fork in Texas, writes from his "Insider BASSlog Blog" at the B.A.S,S. site www.sports.espn.go.com/outdoors/bassmaster/ index. White's articles on moon phases and lures and tactics offer solid advice on a variety of subjects. On wintertime bass fishing, White says he catches more bass with lipless crankbaits than any others. "As a guide on perhaps the best big bass lake in the country [Lake Fork, Texas], I've caught giants on quite a variety of baits. But I get more on the lipless crankbait than all other baits combined in the winter." White described how, in February, he caught a 10-pounder next to the ramp with the wind blowing about 30 mph. "She hit a ¾-ounce Xcalibur crankbait in the Rayburn red color." Almost every crankbait White uses in winter has red or orange in it.

280. Rigging Up for Winter Bass

Pro Richie White's complete rig for winter bass: "So be sure to have a lipless crankbait with some red or orange in it, a good casting reel, a long rod that has some flex, and the right line for long casts." He uses a 7-foot Kistler Helium rod, medium for lighter lures and medium-heavy for ½- to ¾-ounce lures. His reels are Citica by Shimano and Revo by Ambassadeur. His line is 15-pound Berkley Big Game.

281. Florida Bass with Larry Larsen

Veteran Florida outdoor writer Larry Larsen is an expert on many kinds of fishing, with books and magazine articles galore, but he is perhaps best known for his prowess on largemouth bass. In that regard—but with assorted side dishes of bluegills, redbreasts, and catfish—Larry serves up superb fishing guides to Florida bass-fishing lakes and streams in his books, *Larry Larsen's Guide to Florida Bass Waters*, Larsen's Outdoor Publishing, with separate books covering North Florida, Central Florida, and South Florida. Larry gives Florida rivers their full due, showing you where to put into and float classic black-water streams through swamps of cypress, moss-draped oaks, and tall pines on the hillsides. Available at www.amazon.com.

282. Florida's Beautiful, Natural Spring Creeks

Florida has so many good bass lakes that it's easy to overlook the great river fishing. Florida is blessed with twenty-seven spring creeks, with clear 72-degree water gushing up from the earth all day, all year—just like the famed spring creeks in Pennsylvania and out West, where trout thrive. Many of Florida's spring creeks are famous, like Silver Springs and Rainbow Springs, but there are others tucked away that you may not have heard of. Consider Alexander Springs Run, in the Ocala National Forest, a 1½-hour drive from Ocala. It has campgrounds and canoe rentals, but, of course, you can launch your own. This is a great river-fishing float, with scenic natural beauty that somehow seems even better than your dreams of Tarzan Country.

283. Let It Blow, Let It Blow!

"I actually like the wind! It does three things for me: 1) It moves the boat so I don't have to stay on that trolling motor all day; 2) It allows us to cover a LOT of water; and 3) It puts chop on the water to greatly reduce light penetration. That means the fish will stay shallow rather than hiding down deep in the grass to get away from the bright light."

—Jim Porter's *Guide to Bass Fishing*, at www.stickmarsh.com

284. Cracking the Code of Huge Impoundments

Impoundments with largemouth bass are mostly huge, and vast portions of the water on any impoundment hold no bass at all. Without a guide or insider information, how can we find the fish in all that water without spending weeks doing it? In his excellent book, *Rick Clunn's World Championship Bass Fishing* (1978), written with Steve Price, veteran tournament pro Rick Clunn describes the process as a systematic approach that eliminates alternatives, one by one, until a pattern is found. Random casting won't work. Going from spot to spot only eliminates spots, not water types. "At least when you eliminate types of water," says Clunn, "you can consider yourself getting closer each time to where the bass will be found. This is one of the hardest lessons to learn in big impoundment bass fishing."

285. Finding Those Early-Spring Bass

In the same book, *Rick Clunn's World Championship Bass Fishing* (1978), written with Steve Price, veteran tournament pro Rick Clunn describes a tournament at Tennessee's Percy Priest Lake, with all insider information forbidden. Arriving at the lake in early spring, he was given a topo map and immediately started studying the potential spawning areas to fish—points, flats, coves. On the morning of practice day, he fished many types of water before locating most of the fish he caught at the mouths of coves. There were no fish inside the coves. As the sun rose over Percy's clear water, the fish seemed to prefer brush piles, planted by crappie fishermen. Clunn spent the afternoon looking for brush piles at the mouths of coves. In the tournament he fished these with a buzzbait, backed up by a plastic worm. He won the tournament.

286. Why Bass Change Depths

"The various depths bass will descend to are never determined by existing water temperatures at those levels. Instead, the depths bass will go to are determined by a combination of other conditions such as existing light penetration, water stratification (when in evidence), and water oxygen."

—John Weiss, *Advanced Bass Fishing*, Stoeger Publishing, 1978

287. Oxygen Monitoring to Find Preferred Bass Depths

Early in 1974, when I was editing *Sports Afield* magazine, a young writer named John Weiss shook up the bass-fishing world with an article on the development of oxygen-monitoring equipment by Dr. Martin Venneman—the Sentry Oxygen Monitor. Dr. Venneman had discovered that an amazing 50 to 80 percent of the water in any lake does not contain enough oxygen to support fish life. Calling for the use of the Oxygen Monitor as just one more device to help find the fish, John Weiss pointed out that the monitors should always be kept in mind as the advanced angler commences his search for bass. "Oxygen monitoring equipment does not guarantee you will consistently be able to find or catch fish. It does guarantee you will not waste one minute of time fishing where no fish can possibly survive." In his book, *Advanced Bass Fishing* (1976), Weiss goes on to say, "It should also be mentioned that bass found in rivers and streams are not likely to be influenced by changing oxygen levels. . . . The greatest applications of oxygen evaluation are on the larger lakes and reservoirs." [Check out today's modern oxygen monitors at Bass Pro Shops and Cabela's.]

288. Best Oxygen Levels for Bass

"For the bass species, optimum oxygen levels are found in the range of 5 to 13 parts per million (PPM) though they highly prefer and will seek out the 9 to 12 PPM level."

—John Weiss, *Advanced Bass Strategies* (1976)

289. When River Bass Turn On

In an excellent article I published as editor in the 1972 *Sports Afield Fishing Annual*, Charles W. Edghill reminded our readers that smallmouth fly fishers often overlook using their trout dry flies and nymphs for river smallmouths in high summer. You won't catch the big bronzebacks, but you'll get plenty of action from the fish in the 10- to 15-inch class.

290. Smallmouth Floats on the Upper Delaware

If you're hankering for some great action with small smallmouths (a 14-incher is big up there), book a guided float on the Upper Delaware and be ready to use light spinning gear with jigs and soft-plastic grubs. You could easily get a fifty-fish day. If you insist on using your fly rod, you'll catch fish, but far fewer than you can spinning. These floats should be made in summer, not in the early season trout and mayfly times.

291. Summer's Smallmouth Dividends

Tired of getting skunked on your favorite trout waters during high summer? Then turn your fly and light spinning rods toward the smallmouth rivers. You'll find plenty of action from battling fish that are as strong and jump as much as any trout you ever saw.

292. Best in the West

In the western United States, among the blue-ribbon trout waters that get the attention of most anglers, are bass lakes and reservoirs that deliver solid, consistent action and lots of fish. If you're bored with the trout treadmill and live in the West, turn your attention to bass to put more fun back in your fishing.

293. Bass Fishing in the West

The site www.westernbass.com is loaded with information, tips, and observations of anglers from all over the western states. The site covers California, Washington, Oregon, Idaho, Montana, Wyoming, Arizona, Nevada, Utah, and New Mexico.

294. What to Expect on Post-Spawn Bass

"In some lakes the post-spawn bass do move off and suspend and an angler can't catch many of them for two months or so. Those waters during the post-spawn months are notoriously tough fishing."

—Larry Larsen, *Bass Fishing Facts* (1989)

295. Taking More Bass in Streams and Creeks

"Streams are typically not as wide, have swifter current and are clearer, so more natural colored baits work best. Rivers are usually deeper, wider and have more color, meaning brighter baits work best, but this isn't always true."

—Elite Series pro Brian Snowden, in a www.Bassmaster.com archive article by David Hunter Jones. Snowden grew up fishing small waters and continues to wade and float small streams near his Reeds Spring, Missouri, home.

296. Smallmouth Tackle: Heavy Vs. Light

In his blog for smallmouth bass lovers, Bassmaster smallmouth guru Stephen Headrick takes on critical, interesting subjects with no-nonsense advice, such as: "Heavy tackle is great when you can get away with it—like in dirty water or really heavy cover. But heavy tackle will adversely affect how you fish deep water for smallmouth bass. It takes longer for heavy lines to get pulled to the bottom. Heavy lines are more visible to the bass. Heavy lines dull the action of your lures. And by heavy I'm talking about anything over 10-pound test. I use a lot of 4-, 6-, and 8-pound line for my smallmouth fishing here at Dale Hollow Lake and elsewhere." Check out Hedrick's great articles at: www.sports.espn.go.com/outdoors/bassmaster/index.

297. Jump the Gun for Fall Smallmouths

Anglers waiting for hot weather to subside and fall action with smallmouths to kick in can miss the boat, literally, according to smallmouth Bassmaster guru Stephen Headrick, who writes a blog for the popular Bassmaster and Bass site, www.sports.espn .go.com/outdoors/bassmaster/index. Headrick says he starts checking on creeks in highland reservoirs before the heat breaks—just checking for lunkers, not spending the day there yet. "My favorite bait at this time is a $^3/_{16}$-ounce shaky head jig with a 4-inch Go To Bait Co. worm in pumpkin pepper. I throw it on a spinning outfit and 8-pound line. It's not a fast way of fishing, but it'll catch bass of all sizes, and I have a lot of confidence in it. If I'm out at night (and you can catch smallmouths at night all year long), I like to fish a ¾-ounce black and blue Punisher spinnerbait with a big blue blade."

298. Fishing Flooded Timber: Rule One

All flooded timber looks inviting to the bass angler. All that cover, all those shadows for bass to hide in and wait for prey. But when you're looking at hundreds—or thousands—of acres of flooded timber, you soon realize the fish aren't scattered throughout. They are not lying in wait behind every tree. Instead, as in other lakes, they relate to bottom contours. The timber near the right bottom contours and channels will be the timber that holds the fish. Think *bottom contours and conditions* first. *Timber*, second.

299. Targeting Docks and Bridge Pilings

Those shadowy docks and bridge pilings always look like great cover for fish. And they are! Bass, all kinds of panfish, pickerel, pike, even walleyes are probably lurking there. You'll catch more fish at docks or pilings by getting your boat into position and making your first casts parallel to the target. Cast in toward the bank and run your lure alongside the dock—as close to the boards as you can get it—back to the boat. Next, if there's room under the dock, try skipping side-arm casts to get your lure under the boards into the shadows.

300. Fish Rip-Raps for Early Spring Bass

Cold-water early spring bass can be tough to catch, but one way to cut the odds, says pro Timmy Horton, is to fish rip-raps—those rocky barriers supporting roads across lakes and reservoirs and dams along ponds. The rocks heat up with the warming spring sun, and the fish move into the adjacent waters. They can be on the rocks or as far as 30 feet outside. Especially good are the breaks in the rip-rap where boats can slide through. Horton likes jerkbaits for this fishing, and goes deep with the longer-bill models. Vary your retrieve from sudden jerks, to smooth pulls, to slow twitches. You'll catch bass, Horton says, on his "The Bass Pro" feature on the Versus Country Internet site.

301. How to Fish Early-Spring Bass

In another section of this book, I touched on the strategy of fishing river and creek inlets at the heads of lakes and reservoirs. These waters warm up first in early spring. Here's a tip on fishing them. It's from *Advanced Bass Strategies*, The Hunting and Fishing Library (1995), by Dick Sternberg: "In early spring, before spawning begins, look for clean Vs (shoreline breaks) in the back ends of creek arms. The weedlines of these Vs holds fish through the day, but the action is fastest in late afternoon because of the warming water." The Carolina rig is especially effective for fishing these spots.

302. How to Fish Jigs for Spring Bass on Points

Bass expert and luremaker, Tom Mann, Jr., explained his favorite way to fish points in early spring: "If I'm fishing 15 to 25 feet of water, I use a $6/7$-ounce lead-headed jig. If I'm fishing shallower than this, I use a $5/16$-ounce jig. In clear water I like a brown jig with a black twin-tail grub. In stained water, I reverse the colors, going with a black jig and a brown grub."

—Structure Basics: A Complete Guide to Bass Hideouts,
Wade L. Bourne, Publications, 1999

303. Where'd They Go? (Part One)

Ohio writer John Weiss was one of my regular contributors in the years I was editing *Sports Afield*. He was a reader favorite, and with good reason. His observations were backed up by real field experiences and research. In March 1973, John did a remarkable article on finding bass in big lakes. Called "Reading Substructure: The Pro Method of Fishing Big-Lake Bass," the article likened finding bass to finding coveys of quail on a big farm. The quail aren't everywhere; they are bunched up in certain locations. So are the bass. John's basic idea game plan calls for the following:

1. Fishing the midday hours, because that's when the bass have moved from scattering along the shorelines back to their sanctuaries, which are always on substructure.

2. Find the depth in the lake where the ideal temperature of 72 degrees shows consistently. (Be aware that 72 degrees is used as the optimum in John's Ohio area. Yours may be different. John uses the example of 72 degrees occurring mostly at 20 feet.)

3. Study your charts to find the areas where substructure is located in the 20-foot, 72-degree zone depths.

4. Eliminate poor habitat over muddy or murky bottoms. You want gravel, hard-packed sand, weeds, etc. In John's words: "Simply locating structure is not the key to success. You must locate substructure. If a treeline is considered structure, a gap in that treeline is considered substructure. If a creek channel is structure at the 20-foot level, substructure may be a sharp bend in the channel or a patch of brush along the edge of the channel. Bass will use the entire structure as a migration route to other places in the lake, but it is the substructure that will draw and hold the school for long periods of time. Locate the substructure and you've located a bass sanctuary."

304. Where'd They Go? (Part Two)

Continuing with the expertise John Weiss shared with readers of *Sports Afield* when I was editor there, he presented another landmark article in May 1973 called "The Best Bass Fishing Starts Where Light Stops." In it, John cited several scientific studies suggesting that light penetration—even more than desired temperatures—is what sends bass deeper in the water. Bass will go to whatever depth is necessary to escape light penetration. So how deep are the fish? Well, the answer is whatever depth it takes to get out of the light. For more of John Weiss' great bass-fishing tips, see his *Bass Angler's Almanac: More Than 650 Tips and Tactics*, The Lyons Press (2002), at www.amazon.com, www.finefishing.com, and other outlets.

CHAPTER 7

Super Strategies:
Start Catching More Bass Right Now!

305. *Field & Stream's* Largemouth "Ultimate Lure" Survey Winners

In what it called the "Ultimate Lure Survey," published in March, 2008, *Field & Stream* magazine asked 1,000 of its hard-core readers to name their favorite lures. The winners for the Largemouth Bass category were:

Soft-Plastic, 30%, Yamamoto Senko, with Zoom Finesse Worm second

Top Water, 16%, Arbogast Jitterbug, with Zara Spook second

In-Line Spinners, 16%, Mepps Aglia, with Worden's Rooster Tail second

Spinnerbaits, 11%, Generic Double Colorado Blades, with Booyah Pond Magic second

Crankbaits, 11%, Bomber A with Rapala Shad Rap second

Minnow-Type Lures, 8%, Original Rapala, with Rebel second

Jigs, 6%, Jig with Mister Twister, Strike King Skirted Jig and Trailer second

Spoons, 1%, Little Cleo, with Dardevle second

306. *Field & Stream's* Smallmouth "Ultimate Lure" Survey Winners

In what it called the "Ultimate Lure Survey," published in March, 2008, *Field & Stream* magazine asked 1,000 of its hard-core readers to name their favorite lures. The winners for the Smallmouth

Bass category were:

In-Line Spinners, 27%, Mepps Aglia
Soft-Plastics, 23%, Yamamoto Senko, with Zoom Finesse Worm second
Crankbaits, 13%, Bomber A
Minnow-Type Lures, 12%, Original Rapala
Jigs, 10%, Jig with Mister Twister
Top Water, 8%, Heddon Tiny Torpedo
Spinnerbaits, 6%, Booyah Pond Magic
Spoons, 2%, Dardevle

307. Bass Fishing's Super-Rig: It's Famous Because It Works

If you seriously want to catch bass—and not simply enjoy a nice day on the water—then sooner or later you're going to have to fish plastic worms or other soft-plastic baits. Yes, worm fishing makes some anglers yawn. Yes, it's tough to get the hang of, requiring patience and the development of all-important feel and touch. But the tactic catches bass, lots of them, big ones and little ones. Sometimes it catches them on days when nothing else works.

308. Rick Clunn's Most Deadly Lure Advice

Tournament bass pro Rick Clunn, writing with Steve Price in *Rick Clunn's World Championship Bass Fishing* (1978), says, "Plastic worms are probably the most deadly lures . . . but for many anglers they are the most disliked. The usual complaints include, 'It's too slow,' and 'I can't tell if I've got a bass or a stump.' The plain truth about worm fishing is that it takes practice, practice, and more practice to become efficient."

309. Smart and Easy Plastic Worm Fishing

In *Rick Clunn's World Championship Bass Fishing* (1978), pro Rick Clunn recommends fishing small ponds or slow-moving, clear creeks to get the hang of working plastic worms in the obvious holes and structure where bass are likely to be holding.

310. Plastic Worm Action: Are You Missing Out?

What pro Rick Clunn called the "most deadly" back in 1978 has not lost its appeal today. Plastic worms and soft-plastic baits are catching bass everywhere these fish swim, and if you want to snub the technique, you do so at the risk of having a lot of those slow, "nice days" on the water.

311. The Mother of All Plastic Worm Rigs

Today there are many, many methods and variations on fishing plastic worms and soft-plastic baits, but one stands alone as the mother of all plastic worm rigs. It's the famous Texas rig; once you learn to fish it, you'll catch more bass and bigger bass.

312. How to Set Up the Texas Rig

The rig starts with your favorite worm or soft-plastic bait, a worm hook, and a bullet-type sinker in a size to take you deep or shallow as you prefer for the location and conditions. First, pass the line through the slip sinker and tie on the hook. Second, push the point of the hook into the center of the end of the worm head and thread it about ½ inch into the center of the worm body. Next, bring the point of the hook out of the body. It should be about ½ inch back from the head. Now pull the eye and shank of the hook back through the worm body until the eye end of the hook disappears into the worm about ¼ inch. Lastly, push the point of the hook into the worm just past the barb. Now you have a straight worm that's virtually weedless.

313. Tweaking the Texas Worm Rig

Some experts refine this rig by pushing the hook point all the way back through the body so that the point lies just beneath the surface of the bait. Eventually, your worm fishing will lead to many different and exciting ways to fish worms and soft-plastic baits. But the good old Texas Rig will still be one you can count on. Two of the best places to learn all about worm fishing are the Bass Pro Shops and Cabela's Web sites.

314. The Deadly Carolina Rig

The ubiquitous Texas Rig is rivaled by the Carolina Rig for bass-catching effectiveness. Basically, the Carolina Rig differs by having the bullet sinker positioned up the line, instead of on the nose of the soft bait as in the Texas. This makes the soft-plastic lure or worm sink slower and float behind and above the bullet sinker. The lure or worm moves freely with an enticing action. The Carolina Rig is so effective that many top anglers never bother to use the Texas Rig at all. Many tournament anglers keep one rod loaded for action with a Carolina Rig all set up.

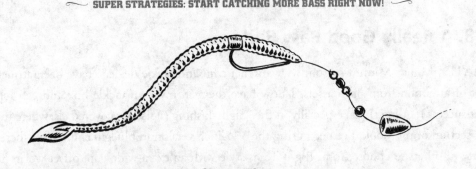

315. Setting Up the Carolina Rig

Here's how to set up the Carolina Rig as related in the book *Advanced Bass Fishing* (1995), by Dick Sternberg: "Make a Carolina Rig by sliding a 1-ounce bullet sinker and a glass bead onto 20-pound mono or 30-pound Spectra, tying on a Size 10 barrel swivel, then adding a 3-foot, 12-pound mono leader. Attach a 3/0 HP hook for a lizard, 2/0 for a French fry (small worm) or crawworm. The glass bead keeps the sinker from damaging the knot, and makes a clicking sound. The lighter leader prevents losing the entire rig should the hook get snagged." The preferred tackle for rigging the Carolina varies, and you can see a variety of ways to make the rig on Internet fishing sites. On Google, try "Carolina Worm Bass Rig."

316. Buy This Book and Catch More Bass!

The title says it all: "Advanced Bass Fishing: Tips and Techniques from the Country's Best Guides and Tournament Anglers." But what makes Dick Sternberg's book so useful is that the pages deliver on the promise of the title. The techniques are so well presented in detailed photographs and drawings that you will be able to put the best "insider" bass fishing techniques to work next time you go fishing. Published by The Hunting and Fishing Library (1995), the book listed on Amazon for $21.50 at this writing and less, used, at other Internet sites. Search the Internet, find it, buy it, use it. You'll start catching bass like never before.

317. Kevin VanDam's Early Season Tactics

At Strike King Lure Co. and on their Web site, No Tiger!, pro Kevin VanDam is held in the highest regard of professionalism. And with good reason: VanDam has won just about everything in tournaments and keeps on doing it. In an interview on his placing third in difficult conditions in the February, 2007, tournament at Lay Lake near Montgomery, Alabama, VanDam said, "My primary bait was the new Strike King Red-Eye Shad, a lipless crankbait. I was fishing a crawdad color with gold and white on the edge of the grass at Lay Lake. When the water's cold, as it was at Lay Lake, lipless baits like the Red-Eye Shad can really be effective . . . I fished the Red-Eye Shad because when you rip it out of the grass and it shimmies and shakes as it sinks, it actually swims down, instead of dropping like other lipless crankbaits do. . . . It's a killer bait." Available at www.strikeking.com/journal.

318. A Really Good Bass Bait

The YUM Money Minnows, from www.lurenet.com and tackle dealers, have been attracting a lot of attention from pro bassers. I now have them in my own tackle box and can report great success in using them, especially in the "Sight-Fishing" episodes covered elsewhere in the bass section of this book. I've been using the 3 ½-inch version in bluegill colors, but there are plenty of others to choose from. Rig it Texas style with an extra-wide-gap, offset worm hook or a shank-weighted swimbait hook—and make it weedless. The lure has a belly slot. I turn the hook up through it and out the top of the bait, then set the hook lightly into the back to make it weedless. Good instructions for using the weighted hook and getting the lure deeper are on the www.lurenet.com site. My personal use with this lure has me convinced that you'll catch more bass by using it.

319. Tie On a Strike King Zulu

The Strike King Zulu has become one of my favorite lures for fishing weedless in all kinds of bigmouth cover. It's soft plastic at its best, catching fish and holding up well after the tussles. I rig it with the hook coming out the top and turned to nestle just enough under the back to make it weedless. Buy it at www.basspro.com and many others.

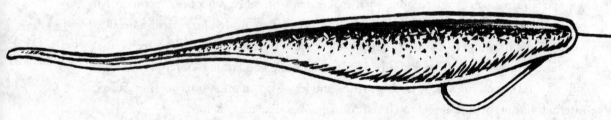

320. Locked-Down Sinkers on Texas Rigs

There are times, particularly when flipping, when you want the sinker tight against the worm or soft-plastic lure you're using, instead of having the sinker slide. You can do this by pegging a toothpick alongside the sinker to hold it against the lure. So many anglers are doing this now that bullet sinkers are available with locking devices to hold it to your plastic bait.

321. Try a Tricked-Up Dinger

The YUM Dinger worm, from www.lurenet.com, is a hot bass lure everywhere, but pro Tim Horton of Muscle Shoals, Alabama, has come up with a new tactic for using it, according to a report in *Field & Stream*, May, 2006. For flipping, getting the lure down through tangles and limbs, Horton rigs a 5-inch Dinger Texas-style with a 4/0 hook and no weight. He clips off the hook from a ¼- to 1/16-ounce ball-head jig with a keeper collar, and slips the jig's collar into the Dinger's tail. Now the Dinger is ready to dive tail-first down into the big-fish lairs.

322. When Schooling Fish Won't Hit

It's really frustrating when schooling bass are tearing the water apart, but they won't hit your lures. Perhaps the fry they're on is smaller than you've been accustomed to imitating. Drop down in lure size to see if they'll start hitting.

323. Try Clear Plastic for Schooling Fish

Clear plastic lures can be effective for schooling bass because the fish don't see them well enough to tell they're bogus. Working them fast helps also.

324. The Floating Worm: Fun and Good

Floating plastic worms, made to stay on top or sink far slower than normal plastic worms, have arrived in bass fishing with a big-bucks bang, winning tournaments here and there and catching bass for anglers who like topwater fishing. Bass Pro Shops, www.basspro.com, carries them in their own brand, the Gambler brand, and two types of floating worms by Berkley Gulp. You should check other sites as well, remembering that not all plastic worms are true floaters. Rig them Texas-style, with a 3/0 light wire hook, a small swivel, and 12 to 15 inches of leader.

325. Skipping Floating Worms

Do you know how to skip a floating worm? You should, it's fun—just like skipping rocks on the water when you were a kid—and you catch lots of bass to boot. Picture a deep, dark lair back under some overhanging trees, or under a dock. The only way you can get a worm in there is to skip it over the water like a flat rock. It's not hard to do with a floating worm. Practice it on open water until you get the touch. Then start skipping your floating worm back in there where the bass are waiting.

326. High-Tech Gear Can Be Loads of Fun

"He who finishes with the most toys *wins*," goes the old adage. In modern bass fishing, the toys are endless, from underwater devices to counters on reels to tell you exactly how much line you've got out. Throw in some awesome motors and boats strong and fast enough to master both speed and distance over any body of water, and you've got a lot of toys to play with on any day's fishing. Even if you don't catch a fish, you can have fun with your dials, gauges, and flashing lights.

327. When High-Tech Goes Wrong

Be careful not to become the type of bass fisherman who seldom makes good catches because he can't resist cranking the motor and heading for greener pastures—in other words, playing with his toys. After a few casts in any spot, he announces, "They're not here. Let's race on!" And he does.

328. Here He Comes! Now What?

When you see a fish following your lure as you retrieve, but not moving in for the strike, what do you do? Slow down your retrieve, speed it up? I once asked that question to popular TV fishing and sports personality Grits Gresham. Grits replied, "It doesn't make a bit of difference. Whichever one you do will be wrong." Well, there's a lot of truth in what Grits said, but with heart pounding, and even hands shaking, in anticipation, we've just got to do *something*. Here's my play: First try slowing down the retrieve. If that doesn't work, try speeding it up. That's about all you can do.

329. When Spring Bass Become Active

"One of the most frequently asked questions thrown my way during guiding is, 'When do bass first become active in the spring?' My standard answer for people in the northern states is that bass become active as soon as the water is soft enough for the bait to sink. In the South, It's as soon as the water temperatures become consistent in the mid to upper 40s."

—Pro guide Troy Jens, Lake Guntersville, Alabama, in the article
"A Great Spot for Spring," on the Web site www.lurenet.com.

330. Catching the Year's Earliest Bass

"Dragging jigs and bottom draggers at a snail's pace in deep water is not the answer to big cold-water spring bass. These bass are after shallow baitfish, and my favorite baitfish imitator for these springtime cold-water periods is the Cotton Cordell Super Spot."

—Pro guide Troy Jens, Lake Guntersville, Alabama, in the article
"A Great Spot for Spring," on the Web site www.lurenet.com

331. Working Early-Spring's Deadliest Lure

When bass are staging for the spawn on breaklines from 4 to 8 feet deep, close to deeper water, pro guide Troy Jens of Lake Guntersville, Alabama, likes to go after them with the Cotton Cordell Super Spot. He uses the ½-ounce Super Spot and works it just fast enough to stay above the bottom. One reason he likes the bait is because it can be fished from very slow to super fast. Writing for the Web site www.lurenet.com, Jens says he uses the Super Spot from ice-out through water temperatures in the 40s. "As the water warms into the 50s, I begin fishing the tops of the humps and ledges and I begin moving further back into the creeks."

332. Floating Worms: Make Sure They Can

Not all plastic worms are real floaters. The genuine floaters are chemically designed and made to resist sinking. They do sink, but very, very slowly, and they ride above the sinker when pulled along the bottom—even when attached to a hook. Make sure you're getting the real deal, real floating worms.

333. Hooking Up Your Floating Worms

If the hook you use on a floating worm is too heavy, you'll be defeating the reason you are using a floater. A 3/0 or 2/0 that's thin and wire-like should be just right. Drive the hook through the worm, then back it up to make it weedless.

334. The Deadly Jerkbait Pause

"The . . . technique for cold water is working a jerkbait over steeply sloping banks in very cold water and long points during a warming trend. Using a Smithwick Rogue or XCalibur Jerkbait or Twitch Bait, make long casts, crank the bait down, and begin a jerk-jerk-pause retrieve. Many pros say that it's the pause, not the jerks or twitches, that is the key to this technique. Do not get in a hurry. Vary the duration of your pauses from just a second or two to excruciatingly long waits of up to a minute."

—Lawrence Taylor, www.lurenet.com

335. The Lure That Got Away

Every March, in the first teasing springtime weather, when it was still too cold to catch bass in several places where I lived as a young man, one lure—a yellow Heddon Tadpolly—produced fish almost every afternoon I went out. Working very, very s-l-o-w-l-y in the shallows, the Tadpolly's enticing wobble brought up springtime lunkers in a way no other lure has ever matched. An old saying goes, "When you find something you really like, buy several, because they're sure to stop making it." So true. Today, the Heddon Tadpolly is gone—except on EBay, where it is a popular collector's item.

336. Lure Action, Not Color, Counts Most

". . . I am convinced that color is not as important as action."

—A.D. Livingston, *Fishing for Bass: Modern Tactics and Tackle*, Lippincott, 1974

337. Do Lure Colors Really Matter?

"So far I haven't been able to make rhyme or reason of why a bass will hit a certain color at a particular time. But that does sometimes seem to be the case. Yet, I wonder."

—A.D. Livingston, *Fishing for Bass: Modern Tactics and Tackle*, Lippincott, 1974

338. Bass Expert's Favorite Lure Colors

"There are exceptions, but I generally use black (or dark) lures in murky water and shiny lures in clear water. I also tend to use black early and late in the day . . . shiny when the sun is high and bright, black when fishing deep, and shiny when I am fishing shallow."

—A.D. Livingston, *Fishing for Bass: Modern Tactics and Tackle*, Lippincott, 1974

339. Smallmouths on the Rocks

In his wonderful autobiography, *My Life Was THIS BIG and Other True Fishing Tales*, Skyhorse Publishing (2008), by Lefty Kreh with Chris Millard, Lefty not only points out the importance of fishing the rocks to catch river smallmouths, he puts a great deal of emphasis on the angle of the cast. Presenting the fly from the wrong side of the rock will not result in strikes because of the unnatural drift of the fly (much the same as in "drag" in presenting trout flies). For instance, a rock with current on both sides will fish better when the cast and the drifting fly are on the same side as the current. A fly cast across the rock to reach the current on the other side usually will not work.

340. When Smallmouths Go Berserk!

Smallmouth bass have a tendency to sometimes follow a fish you're playing. When this happens in clear water, you'll see that you're on a honey hole and know it's the place to keep fishing.

341. When Smallmouths Tease *You*!

When smallmouth bass make some passes at your lure, but don't hit, drop down to a smaller size lure. You'll probably get a strike.

342. How to Fish Early Spring Bass

In another section of this book, we related the importance of the strategy of fishing river and creek inlets at the heads of lakes and reservoirs. These waters warm up first in early spring. Here's a tip on fishing them. It's from *Advanced Bass Strategies*, (1995) by Dick Sternberg: "In early spring, before spawning begins, look for clean Vs (shoreline breaks) in the back ends of creek arms. The weedline of these Vs holds fish through the day, but the action is fastest in late afternoon because of the warming water." By the way, the Carolina Rig is especially effective for fishing these spots.

343. Reaction Strikes: Take 'Em When You Can

When bass are on the feed, searching for food like predators on the prowl, they are, of course, striking out of hunger. But many strikes occur when the bass is just sitting there, finning easily, not feeding at all. A case in point might be a bass lying under a log, or in a stretch of lily pads. A crankbait or other lure that suddenly flashes past sometimes elicits a savage strike that comes out of pure instinct to attack available prey. It's as if your lure woke up a sleeping bass. It doesn't happen all the time, but when it does, count yourself as fortunate.

344. River Sloughs: Don't Miss Them

Those deep bends, elbows, and sloughs just off the main flow of a river cry out to be fished hard. As Ray Bergman reminds us in *Fresh-Water Bass*, Knopf (1946): " . . . these backwaters are inclined to be somewhat weedy and stumpy with fallen trees helping to foster the feeling of wildness. The situation is enticing . . . Alluring pockets, deep looking holes, and enchanting little caverns formed by stumps and logs . . . "

345. Surface Plunkers: The Sweet Feel of "Real"

Everybody wants to catch fish on surface lures when they are hitting. The trick is to make those plugs look like fish swimming and feeding on the surface. Working these baits is all a matter of feel. Only the feedback, the muscle memory, of your hands and arms can tell you how it's done. Here's Ray Bergman on the subject, from *Fresh-Water Bass* (1946): " . . . you can't just throw it out, reel it in and expect it to do its stuff. {*Chug, splash, bob, wiggle*, like live fish.} To do this you jerk hard but use a short movement. One make of lure requires more jerk than another."

346. Darter Plugs: The "Extra" Surface Baits

Not all surface plugs are in the plunker and popper variety. Darter plugs, for example, have a deadly up-and-down motion. They should be in your tacklebox right alongside the plunkers. As Ray Bergman says in *Fresh-Water Bass* (1946): "When this lure is handled correctly with a twitch and pause it acts very much like a crippled or badly injured minnow. That is, it darts slightly under the surface speedily and quickly, and then just as suddenly gives up and comes to rest on the surface."

347. When the Wind Blows

Fishing in the big wind can be very tough, not necessarily because the fish aren't biting, but because the waves and the wind slapping your line and lure make it very difficult to present the bait with the proper action and speed—not to mention getting it into the proper location to start with. Ray Bergman, in *Fresh-Water Bass* (1946), reminds us we can still catch fish: "I do believe that when you can handle your lure correctly in the wind the fish will take, other factors being equal, regardless of the direction of the wind."

348. Lucas on Bass

If you have a few years on you and love bass fishing, you may be familiar with the name Jason Lucas. He was angling editor of *Sports Afield* magazine from the late 1940s until right at the time when I came to *Sports Afield* in 1967 as an associate editor. Lucas was gone from the magazine before I had a chance to work with him or meet him, but I was very tuned in to his reputation and work. Ted Kesting, *Sports Afield's* editor-in-chief in the mid-1940s, when the magazine was headquartered in Minneapolis, became acquainted with a man who could catch bass consistently, in all seasons, even in hard-fished waters. And, most importantly, the man could write! Jason Lucas became Angling Editor soon after Kesting discovered him, and built an aura of bassing skill by fishing almost every day—in one case fishing for bass for an entire 365-day straight run. Lucas came along before bass boats and sophisticated electronics. He was a skilled angler, however, with the curiosity to experiment and learn everything about bass fishing he could. Today, the best of his words survive in the book *Lucas on Bass Fishing*, originally published in 1947 by Dodd, Mead, and Co., and available today at www.amazon .com and other sites in a paperback edition published in 2005. You can find copies of the used original hardcover on the Internet.

349. Think Brown for More Bass

"Nearly all of the bottom-feeding fish which bass eat are of a dirty-brown color, with dirty-white or dirty-yellowish bellies. So, as might be expected, a dirty-brown plug often seems to get them down here when nothing else will."

—Jason Lucas, *Lucas on Bass Fishing*, Dodd, Mead, and Co.,
1947, reprinted since

350. Looks *Are* Deceiving

"It is impossible to judge the merits of a lure from looking at it, or seeing its action in the water . . . There's but one good way to find out how well they'll take a certain lure—try it on them!"

—Jason Lucas, *Lucas on Bass Fishing*, Dodd, Mead, and Co.,
1947, reprinted since

351. Uncle Homer: My Bassing Hero

Among the many pleasures that came my way when I was editor of *Sports Afield* magazine in the 1970s, none were more intense than working and fishing with Homer Circle, my Angling Editor. "Uncle Homer," as we all fondly called him, is a man of extraordinary talent and immense kindness. In his 90s as this is being written, Homer has been elected to several angling Halls of Fame. Some of his best articles—and glimpses into his vast knowledge of bass fishing—can be found in the book *Bass Wisdom*, available in a Lyons Press paperback version from www.amazon.com.

352. Never Underestimate a Bass' Vision

"I watched the large yellow butterfly as it 'flitted' along the canal bulkhead 18 inches or so off the surface. I just happened to glance its way as it neared an old dock that emerged from the cement-walled shoreline. The water's surface erupted and a 3-pound largemouth shot toward the flapping morsel. The bass' aim was off and it crashed back into its environment, no fuller for its experience. The happening, however, further reinforced my belief that largemouth bass have very good vision. The presence of the air-born butterfly was not detected through the bass' sense of smell, sound (lateral line), or taste. It was seen . . ."

— Larry Larsen, *Bass Fishing Facts* (1989)

353. Inside the Private World of Bass

The DVD *Bigmouth 35* is the thirty-five-year anniversary celebration of the amazing film by Glen Lau from the 1960s. Narrated by no other than Rod Serling of *Twilight Zone* fame, the one-hour film takes you into the world of the bass as you have never seen it before—unless you're a diver. Lau is also a great angler, and a close buddy of Homer Circle, and you can count on their combined expertise for ideas that will definitely help you catch more bass. Available at www.amazon.com.

354. Sight Fishing for Largemouths—Step One

As the great Yogi Berra once proclaimed, "You can observe a lot just by watching." Truer words were never spoken when it comes to largemouth bass fishing. When the water is still and quiet—usually early in the morning or at dusk, especially in late spring or early fall—the sight and sound of minnows on the move mean bass are in attack mode. Those minnows aren't just playing around. They're about to be gulped into a bigmouth's gullet, and they're trying to leave Dodge. Sometimes you'll even hear or see the bass slash into the school, or see big swirls. Your tackle should be ready for the next step.

355. Sight Fishing for Largemouths—Step Two

Your electric motor has just ceased humming, or you've carefully laid down your canoe paddle. You're drifting into the area where you saw or heard minnows on the run, or a bass swirl or strike. Your chosen lure (which we'll cover in Step Three) is ready. Ahead of you are lily pads, half-sunken logs, or a brush-choked shoreline. Here, in this moment and position, is where most anglers fail. Either they move too aggressively and spook the fish, or they make casts that are too far out in the open water. They're thinking the bass will come roaring out of the cover and strike. While it's true that sometimes happens, don't count on it. The cast must go as close to the cover, or even into it with a weedless bait, as possible. Right here is where casting ability shines. Putting that bait right into every nook and cranny is the key to getting a strike.

356. Sight Fishing for Largemouths—Step Three

There are about a zillion lures that will catch fish in this situation, but I have a couple of favorites, and it's my book, so here we go: I'm positively in love with two soft-plastic baits in the swimbait or jerk bait category. (No, I do not get them for free. I buy them, like you.) The Mann Hardnose and the Strike King Zulu have been absolute killers for me and my buddies in sight-fishing situations. Actually, they're good baits all the time. You can swim them and jerk them and expect savage strikes. We fish them with the Texas Rig, minus the sinker for the sight-fishing situations. With the hook embedded properly, they're virtually weedless. As with other recommendations, check Bass Pro Shops and Cabela's.

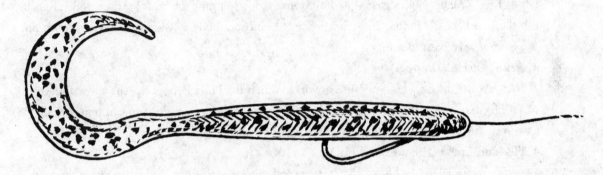

357. Time to Walk the Dog

Everybody wants to catch bass with topwater lures—and why not? When conditions are right, and bass are feeding on or near the surface, there's nothing like the explosive strike of an aggressive bass. You can fish topwater lures many ways, including the famous "Walk the Dog" technique of slowly working it over the surface. You can pause it, twitch it, or just let it lie there, waiting. Then slowly move it a foot or so, then pause, wait, and twitch once again. When the strike comes, you will know it!

358. Forget Top Water When the Time's Not Right

As stated elsewhere in this book, fishing top water is often a fruitless, fishless, exercise in futility. When the bass just aren't feeding on the surface, all you will get up there is casting practice.

359. Proven Topwater Lures

When the time and conditions are right for topwater fishing, the seven lures featured here are the ones you can absolutely count on to get strikes. Yes, there are others, endless numbers of them, and if you're willing to experiment, you'll probably find a new favorite or two among them. But these are my topwater best bets. I have seen them in action and witnessed them being used by many expert anglers. There are many topwater lures out there that are far less expensive than these. Quite frankly, in my opinion, they are not as good. These are the best. Fish them and have fun!

1. Rapala Skitter Pop

An absolute killer bait from the famous maker of wooden lures. This was Rapala's first-ever topwater lure, and it's a great one. The plastic cupped lip produces a "spitting" action. An assortment of color finishes, 2 to 2 ¾ inches, at $7.99 from Cabela's as this is written. The Skitter Pop will catch both largemouth and smallmouth bass wherever they swim. Available at www.cabelas.com.

2. Rebel Zell Rowland Pop-R

Moving down in price to $4.99 from Bass Pro Shops is this popular plastic bait, aka "The Pop-R King." Many good anglers who don't want to fork over the extra buck for the wooden Rapala fish the Rebel Pop-R. In four color finishes, at 2 ½ inches, the Pop-R is a lure you can count on. Available at www.basspro.com.

3. Arbogast Hula Popper

A favorite for decades—because it works. When the Hula Popper doesn't get strikes from surface feeders, you're probably in for a very slow day of surface action. You can pop it, walk it, let it rest, and tremble it. It comes in a variety of finishes. Costs $4.99 at Cabela's.

4. Heddon Lucky 13 and Baby Lucky 13

Created in 1920, the Lucky 13 has been catching bass ever since. Today's versions, the Lucky 13 (3 ¾ inches) and Baby Lucky 13 (2 ⁵/₈ inches), produce resonating sound and a weaving body action for a variety of gamefish, especially bass. Cabela's lists both at $4.99. Fish the Baby version for smallmouths.

5. Arbogast Jitterbug

This lure has been a mainstay in the tackleboxes of bass addicts for decades. The back-and-forth, plodding, popping action represents live prey struggling, and bass on the feed gobble it

with fury. It costs $4.69 to $4.99, and comes in 2- and 3-inch sizes, in a variety of colors. As with several other topwater baits, failure to get strikes with a Jitterbug does not bode well for your surface fishing that day.

6. Heddon Zara Spook, Super Spook, and Super Spook Jr.

Heddon's Zara Spook was one of the first—if not *the* first—topwater, Walk the Dog lures. It's still catching fish today, and costs $4.99 at Cabelas. The Super Spook is an upgraded version of the Zara, and at $4.99 is a solid choice for a variety of fish. The Spook Jr. is also $4.99 and is the choice for smallmouths and picky largemouths.

7. Lucky Craft Sammy

Ready to spend $10 for a single lure? If you're really hungry for topwater action, and nothing else seems to work, the Lucky Craft Sammy might save your day. At $9.99 (on sale) and $13.99 to $15.99 regularly priced (Cabela's), the Lucky Craft Sammy has a lot of new technology going for it and consistently gets strikes. If you can afford it, and are not afraid of losing it to a big fish or submerged log, give it a try. Comes in a variety of colors, 2 ½ to 4 inches.

360. What Hook Size?

"Always match your hook size to the head diameter of the soft-plastic bait you're using. Example: On an 8-inch plastic worm use either a size 4/0 or 5/0 hook; on a 4-inch worm, a size 1/0 to 2/0 hook."

—Bill Dance, *IGFA's 101 Freshwater Fishing Tips and Tricks*, Skyhorse Publishing, 2007

361. How Bill Dance Beats Windy Days

In his book *IGFA's 101 Freshwater Fishing Tips and Tricks*, Skyhorse (2007), bass guru Bill Dance described his favorite strategy for coping with windy days. He uses heavier jigs and lighter line. With the wind causing you to have poor control of your drifting boat, the faster your bait gets down, the better. "Seconds can make the difference in success or failure," Dance says.

362. Smallmouth Savvy: Go Deeper With Jigs When You Have To

J.B. Kasper's outdoor column in the *Trenton Times* (N.J.) is always excellent, but he hit a home run with readers in his piece on July 31, 2009. Kasper described his annual trip to New York's legendary Thousand Island area. Arriving at Caiger's Country Inn, in Rockport on the Canadian side, where he has always enjoyed great fishing, Kasper found high water and lower water temps (low 70s in shallow water) that made the fishing in shallow water very poor. "It became evident," Kasper says, "after about two hours that the bass simply were not there. A switch to fishing jig-plastic bait combination of 20- to 30-foot drop-offs off rocky points put us into fish." Kasper used jig-heads dressed with hellgrammites and Slugos. "Swimming plugs and crankbaits were ineffective, mainly because we could not get them down to where the fish were holding."

363. Fishing the Legendary Devil's Horse

In these pages, you hear so much about fishing soft-plastic lures directly in the cover that you may get tired of hearing about it. But it's the truth: Soft-plastics, rigged weedless, plunked into and fished directly in the weeds, sticks, and pads, catch the bass. You can, however, still catch bass on the old standby surface baits like Smithwick's Devil's Horse, with props fore and aft, by working it on the edges of cover at dawn's early light. Baitfish leave deep water to forage in the weeds and cover at night, returning to the deep after dawn. If you're going to fish the edges, dawn is the time to do it. And the Devil's Horse, or lures like it, should produce some action.

364. The 1 Million Tactic

That's what *Field & Stream* magazine in June 2008 called the tactic that won pro Scott Suggs the big prize in the 2007 Forrest Wood Cup at Lake Ouachita in Arkansas. As reported by Bill Heavey, Suggs yo-yoed spinnerbaits just above the thermocline. In summer, bass often drop down to the cooler layer of water just above the thermocline. The thermocline is where the water is much colder but lacks oxygen. Just above the thermocline, bass can suspend in water that's cooler than the surface areas and still have plenty of oxygen. To find the thermocline, you need to get a high-tech depth finder, call a local dive shop (if there is one), or note carefully the depths where you're finding fish. You won't make a million bucks, but you'll catch more bass.

365. A Bassing Blog You Shouldn't Miss

Of all the excellent articles and blogs available on the B.A.S.S. site at www.sports.espn. go.com/outdoors/bassmaster/index, "Charlie Hartley's Bass Wars"—found directly as this is written on www.sports.espn.go.com/outdoors/bassmaster/news/story?page=b_blog_Hartley _2009—has become one of my favorites. A successful businessman in Ohio with his Signcom, Inc., designing, manufacturing, and installing commercial signs, Hartley hits the tournament circuits hard and shares his experiences on the B.A.S.S. site. His articles are archived, so you can see them all, from 2008 on. He is sponsored by Venom Lures, www.venomlures. com. Hartley led the first day of the 2009 Bassmaster Classic and became something of an instant celebrity in bass fishing. Hartley knows bass, and he knows bass fishing tournament competition, and he shares what he knows brilliantly. You will not only enjoy reading Hartley, whether you are interested in tournaments or not, you will end up catching more and bigger bass.

366. Red Hooks, Bleeding Baits—Are They For Real?

In his excellent blog www.richlindgren.com, tournament angler Rich Lindgren shares both his skills and accounts of the competitions. He is an observant, serious angler with lots to say. In a report on the on-going trend toward using "bleeding" baits and red hooks, he said, "Granted some of these bleeding baits are a little overdone, but the adding of red coloring and bleeding spots is a trend that is not going away soon. In general I am a big fan of sprucing up my baits with touches of red. . . . I think the red hook gives the fish a target, so if you have a red hook on the front, you hook more fish on the front hook."

367. Add Red for More Strikes

Veteran tournament angler Rich Lindgren, in his blog, www.richlindgren.com, says he feels adding red hooks and touches of red on lures triggers strikes from bass that are only following and then turning away at the last instant. He adds red to not only crankbaits and topwater lures, but to spinnerbaits, buzzbaits, and jigs as well. You can add red hooks and colors to your favorite existing baits. "All in all," says Lindgren, "the color red is not going to make you an instant pro, but it can turn a good day into a great day and get you those extra bites . . . "

368. Fake Frogs: How Fine Are They?

One of my favorite titles from old issues of *Sports Afield*, was "Fake Frogs Are Fine." Like many another bass angler's, I have always been fascinated by frog imitations, spinning, bait-casting, and fly fishing. They look so real! How can any bass resist them? Well, in my own case, they resisted them with no problem. Most frog imitations just haven't paid off for me. I keep trying, though, and now, surfing the Web, I find that Bass Pro Shops—www.basspro. com—has a new entry in the race for the world's most realistic frog imitation. It's the Tru-Tungsten Mad Maxx Frog, so real it looks like it's about to jump through my computer screen. It costs a hefty $8.49 a pop. Will it catch bass? Well, if looks could kill . . .

369. Waders Not Required

Wading wet, doing without waders, makes a lot of sense in high summer on smallmouth rivers and creeks (and even some trout rivers). At first you might be a little cold, but you'll quickly adjust to the conditions and find a certain freedom of motion you lack with waders. You'll need good wading shoes, of course.

370. Casting to Bass Cover

A cast that lands more than a foot away from bass cover is a wasted cast.

371. When the Water's Falling Too Fast

When fishing rivers for bass, especially big rivers, the periods after heavy rains when the water is falling ultrafast will often cause the bass to move out into the depths and suspend. They'll stay there until the flow stabilizes.

372. Oxygen Content is Crucial

"Oxygen content is far more important than water temperature in locating fish during August and early September. Bass are willing to endure water temperatures in the high 80s providing there is ample oxygen."

—Mark Sosin, "How to Read Bass Water You've Never Fished,"
Sports Afield, April 1975

373. Find the Oxygen, You'll Find the Fish

"Certain banks will have ample oxygen, while others won't hold enough to support life. You can work down a bank and read three parts per million on an oxygen meter. Then, only a quarter mile away, the meter will show eight or ten parts per million on the same bank. That's where the fish will be and it may only last for 100 yards or so. Once you run out of oxygen, you must locate the next zone."

—Mark Sosin, "How to Read Bass Water You've Never Fished,"
Sports Afield, April 1975

374. Double Your Fun With Two Jigs

Deep-jigging for smallmouths is always a reliable tactic, but don't forget to take the trouble to add a second jig to your line. Fish a heavier jig on the end of your line, with a lighter jig of another color attached to a dropper about 18 inches up the line. A Perfection Loop Knot will

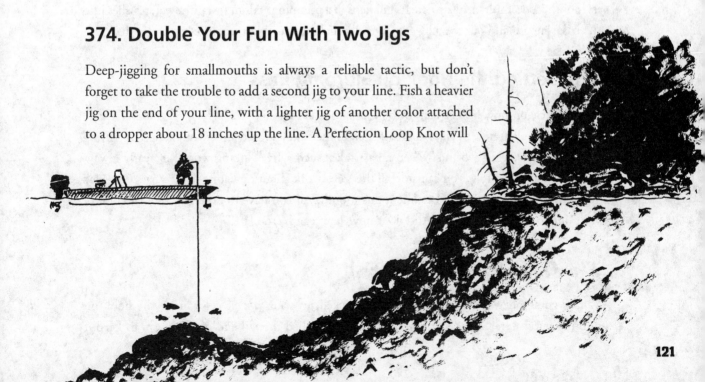

work nicely for the dropper, or some other type if you have a favorite. Don't be surprised to find yourself battling a pair of smallmouths at times. Sometimes a hooked bass creates a frenzy among its mates in a school.

375. Add Some Venom to Your Lures

The Ohio company Venom Lures (www.venomlures.com) offers an excellent array of largemouth and smallmouth lures and accessories. They also sponsor B.A.S.S. professional Charley Hartley, whose blog on the B.A.S.S. site at www.sports.espn.go.com/outdoors/bassmaster/index is one of the best around. I especially like Venom's Drop Shot Minnows. The 4-inch model is my favorite.

376. It's Not a Strike, It's a *Slurp*!

In a revealing article in *Sports Afield* in December 1971, Angling Editor Homer Circle went to great lengths to show readers that bass actually do not strike a lure, they suck it in, even when they're taking topwater baits. Armed with this knowledge, you should have better feel and touch fishing plastic worms.

377. How Bass Slurp Prey

Homer Circle continues on how bass strike: " . . . when a bass decides to take an object into its mouth, it does not have to seize it like a dog. Instead, it only has to get close to the object, open its mouth, and simultaneously flare its gill flaps in a pumping action. Instantly, water rushes into the bass's mouth and out the gill vents, literally sucking the object into the bass's mouth."

378. Setting the Hook on Slurping Bass

In his article on how bass strike, in the December 1971 issue of *Sports Afield*, Homer Circle went on to explain how the fact that bass suck in their prey should affect your action on setting the hook on a plastic worm: "When a bass takes such a free-sinking worm, it nearly always sucks it all in. Therefore, you can stop all this guesswork about how long to let a bass run. He's got worm, hook, and part of the line in his mouth. All you have to do is reel the slack out of your line so you can bust him. And do it now, later can be too late!"

379. Quick Pull, Then No Fish

What's going on when you feel a bass has picked up your worm, yet you set the hook on nothing but water? Chances are the bass simply grabbed the tail end of the worm to keep it from moving away, then dropped it as you tightened the line. The fish never sucked the worm into its mouth, because the angler kept it moving away too quickly.

380. Pre-Spawn Bass: More Strikes in the Afternoon

In the spring, as the water temps rise into the 50s at midday and during the afternoon, you should get more strikes from fish moving into warmer waters. On a cold morning when fishing is slow, if the water temps are slowly climbing, you can reasonably look forward to afternoon action. Don't go home at lunch.

381. Staging for the Spawn: Early Spring's Best Bassing

Reporting in his blog from Falcon Lake, Texas, in early February 2008, veteran pro Charley Hartley described the rewards of fishing bass as they are staging for the spawn. " . . . they're biting jigs thrown right into the bushes off the secondary points. The bass are staged on the last turn in front of the spawning bays. And when I mean staged, I mean they're everywhere. Like I said, they're hitting jigs today, but to tell you the truth they'd probably hit just about anything you throw in there. They're hungry and not at all shy."

—"Charley Hartley's Bass Wars," February 5, 2008 on the B.A.S.S. site at
www.sports.espn.go.com/outdoors/bassmaster/index

382. Why Live Bait Catches Giant Bass

Live bait—such as shiners, minnows, and even sunfish—are such a deadly attractor to bass for two important reasons. First, and obvious, is the fact that they are the real prey bass are accustomed to feeding on. But equally important, and often overlooked by anglers who use them in open water, these live baits swim into and underneath thick pads and cover where big bass lurk and lures never go.

383. Your Best Chance for a Monster Bass

If you are fortunate enough to locate a hole where a big bass resides, your surest way to get the lunker will be using a live sunfish. Not too big, not too small, a 4-incher is about right. Hook it up top, at the dorsal fin, with a Number 6. Feed out line to let the bait swim into the hole . . . then wait.

384. Picking the Right Hook for Plastic Worms

Picking the right hook size for the plastic worm you're using is simple. Basically, it's big worm, big hook; small worm, small hook. For a 7- to 8-inch worm, a 3/0 or 4/0 hook will be just right, while a 1/0 will be too small and a 6/0 too big. For a 5- to 6-inch worm, use a 2/0 hook. For finesse worms under 5 inches, use 1 and 1/0. Now all you have to do is to make sure they're sharp.

385. Rigging the Expensive Trout Lure

The thought of losing the expensive swim baits so popular with western bass anglers is downright scary. To make sure your Huddleston Deluxe Trout Lure is rigged properly go to www.bassresource.com and check out the detailed, step-by-step article and photos by "Fish Chris" Wolfgram, under the "Articles" and "Bass Lure Techniques" sections.

386. Those Super-Shallow Crankbaits

"Crankbait addicts can be so pleased with their big-lipped, deep-diving lures that they sometimes forget the effectiveness of lipless or super-shallow crankbaits," says Don Wirth in his basspro.com article, "The Inside Scoop on Super-Shallow Crankbaits." Baits like Mann's 1-Minus and the Bomber Square A are deadly swimming slowly through patches of water in or alongside tight cover.

387. Knocking on Wood

Lipless or super-shallow crankbaits are perfect for fishing tight cover, says Don Wirth in his basspro.com article, "The Inside Scoop on Super-Shallow Crankbaits." Wirth says, "You're probably thinking, 'Run a $6 crankbait through a brushpile? No way!' But a properly presented super-shallow diver is a deadly alternative to a jig or spinnerbait in this snaggy cover." He recommends using a short, under-handed pitch past the brushpile or other cover, then, " . . . reel s-l-o-w-l-y until you feel the bait contact the cover." Stop your retrieve the instant the bait touches something, and it will float upward, clearing the obstruction. Start retrieving again and hang on for action.

388. Crankbait Snagging Remedy

"Clip the leading hook from each set of the trebles on your crankbaits to reduce snagging in tight cover."

> —Don Wirth, "The Inside Scoop on Super-Shallow Crankbaits," www.basspro.com

389. Jim Porter's Guide to Bass Fishing

One of my favorite Web sites for bass articles and products has become Jim Porter's Guide to Bass Fishing, www.stickmarsh.com. The site has innovative lures for bass and panfish, and Porter's articles are solid with experience and usable information.

390. Bass Lures Don't Come Easy

Be aware that those pretty and expensive bass lures that tempt you in the shops and catalogs aren't overnight creations. The lure business is highly competitive, and much research and testing goes into every creation. Every curve and shape, every ounce of weight, affects the way the bait will swim.

391. How to Choose a Crankbait

There are so many crankbaits out there that choosing a winner can be a bit confusing. They may all look the same, but the bill makes the difference. Long bills dive deeper, wide bills give more side-to-side action, and rounded bills give a steady wiggle.

392. Crankbait Action: The Wrong Stuff

You can't expect a long-billed crankbait, designed to dive and fish deep, to perform well for you in a shallow-water patch of weeds. Every lure has a purpose, a job to do. Think about that before you tie one on and put it to work. What, *exactly*, do you want it to do in the existing conditions to catch fish?

393. Soft-Plastic: The Bass Won't Let Go!

In his excellent blog, Jim Porter's Guide to Bass Fishing, at www.stickmarsh.com, in an article on fishing soft-plastic jerkbaits, Porter debunks theories that bass spit out plastic baits: " . . . Unless you scare the bass with a sudden jerk on the line or letting him pull the line too tight, a bass normally WILL NOT drop that soft-plastic lure. It doesn't LOOK, SMELL, nor TASTE like real food to the bass. But if he thinks it is trying to get away in some manner, he just won't let go." Porter goes on to describe how to fish his company's soft jerkbait, the "RIPPIN' Stick."

394. Sea Anchors on Bass Boats

Saltwater anglers know all about sea anchors and drift socks to hold their boats better in the tides and currents. Savvy bass anglers know about them too—and use them to cut down on the drift in strong winds. Cabela's and Bass Pro Shops have them.

395. A Largemouth Angler Fishing for Smallmouths

There's one important thing to remember when you're an experienced largemouth angler heading out for smallmouth for the first time: Downsizing! With few exceptions, lures for smallmouths are smaller than your favorite largemouth baits.

396. Pass the Watermelon

In the BASSlog Blog, where he keeps tabs on things like moon phases and best lures of the pros, B.A.S.S. pro Richie White reports that favorite soft-plastic colors are green pumpkin, watermelon, and watermelon/red fleck. Other good choices are black/blue, junebug, black, red shad, and blue fleck. For diving crankbaits, the leaders are shad, baby bass, blue/chartreuse, white, firetiger, and green/orange. Shad is the best color for jerkbaits. Check out White's BASSlog at www.sports.espn.go.com/outdoors/bassmaster/index.

397. Bass Turned Off . . . Then Turned Right Back On

In his wonderful and now-mellow book, *Fresh-Water Bass*, Knopf (1946), the legendary Ray Bergman describes experiences when he learns that largemouth bass wise up to certain lures. He was using a white surface plug in a week's fishing, and each day his catch became smaller and smaller and finally stopped altogether. His companion suggested going to live bait. "But I didn't want to fish with live bait. I wanted to fish with plugs. I put on a green underwater one and used that, and I started to catch bass again. This seems to show clearly that these bass had become wise to the white plug."

398. It's Gobies for Lake Erie Smallmouths

"For Lake Erie smallmouths, there is one overwhelming choice: the goby. Gobies are nonnative fish that were introduced into the Great Lakes from the discharge of ballast water by ocean-going vessels. These fish are small but voracious feeders and are outcompeting many native species, such as perch, for food. On the positive side, the goby has created a tremendous forage base for smallmouth bass and the brown fish are bigger and badder because of it."

—Tony Hansen, "Drop-Shotting Smallmouth Bass," on the Bass Pro Shop Outdoor Library, www.basspro.com

399. The Single-Worm Trick for Bass

Bluegill and crappie anglers are sometimes surprised when the tug on their line turns out to be a hard-pulling, fighting largemouth bass in the 1- to 2-pound class. When bluegill fishing, you can make this unexpected treat happen more often by using a single earthworm hooked right through the middle. Set your float to let your worm dangle at various depths, and you'll catch a bass. I don't know why this single-worm trick works, but it does.

400. Destination: Lake Erie

Lake Erie is, without a doubt, one of the greatest smallmouth destinations in the world. Some say it's the absolute greatest. It's big water, so you have a lot of planning and preparation to do, but the resources for the fishing—guides, lodges, tackle shops—are all there.

401. Coping With Surface Lure Splash-Down

While bass will sometimes strike lures the instant they hit the surface—and even grab them right out of the air—most bass-fishing experts put their faith in letting their surface plug or bug rest on the water a few moments before starting the retrieve. The theory is that the bait splashing down will frighten fish in the immediate vicinity, even make them swim off some distance. Let the bait sit until well after the ripples spread away and die out completely, then give the bait a twitch. Then do some more twitching. Then, as you retrieve, try slow crawls with wiggles, violent jerks and pops, or whatever seems to be working.

402. Getting The Touch with Plastic Worms

"He [the plastic worm expert] knows by the delicate sense of feel that he has discovered which type of bottom cover his worm or eel is dragging over. That's right, he can tell by the feeble feel transmitted by his line what substances—hard, soft, tall, short, or snaggy—his lure is approaching, in, or coming off of."

—Homer Circle, *Sports Afield Fishing Annual*, 1972

403. Plastic Worms in the Strike Zone

" . . . all fishermen who crawl worms and eels over bottom cover will tell you their biggest bass, and most of their bass, grab the lure *immediately after* they feel it crawl over and drop off a branch, weed, log or other obstruction."

—Homer Circle,
Sports Afield Fishing Annual, 1972

404. Study-Time with the Bass Professor

Doug Hannon isn't called The Bass Professor for nothing. He has spent his life studying and catching largemouth bass in general, but specializing in big bass—really big bass, the 12- and 15-pounders. You see Doug on various TV fishing programs, but his headquarters is his Web site, www.bassprofessor.com. You can learn a heck of a lot about bass fishing by visiting with Doug there, including all the info on his Snake lures that catch monster bass and the new spinning reel he has developed that eliminates those troublesome loops that can mess up your fishing. Doug also has a terrific book, written with W. Horace Carter. It's called *Hannon's Big Bass Magic*, and you can get it from Doug's site and places like www.amazon.com. I bought the book and have devoured every page with great relish.

405. Doug Hannon on Making Bass Strike

The Bass Professor, Doug Hannon is a firm believer in the contradictory viewpoint that bass feed more in the day than they do after dark, but that the average angler will catch more and bigger bass by fishing late and at night. Behind Doug's belief is this logic explained in his book, *Hannon's Big Bass Magic*: "The darkness covers up an angler's presence and, most of all, his mistakes . . . I feel that bass have long since become conditioned to the fact that man spells danger. My studies show that only one in ten bass which sees a lure will strike it and that one makes a mistake . . . At night . . . close inspection is more difficult for a fish, and he may strike without any investigation."

406. Moon Up Early—Great Fishing

" . . . I am convinced that lunar influences have a big impact on bass and also that they will strike more frequently on those nights when the moon comes up in the evening before the sun goes down."

—Doug Hannon,
Hannon's Big Bass Magic

407. Doug Hannon's Moon Phase Choices

In his book *Hannon's Big Bass Magic*, Doug Hannon says that studies of world record catches in the 1970s revealed a definite correlation with his favorite moon phases to fish. Those are the three days on each side of a full moon and dark moon. It's interesting to note that these same moon phases are the favorite of legendary angler Stu Apte, who discusses them in another section of this book.

408. Good Bass Fishing Close to Home

Sometimes it's possible to ignore a lake that's close to your home, simply because it looks as if it's harboring too much activity. But when you really consider the people using the lake, and come to realize that they're mostly swimmers, kayakers, sailboaters, and float tubers—not fishermen—you may find you've got a good fishing spot all to yourself. Not on weekends, but during the week, especially at dawn.

409. Fishing Tidewater Bass

"The trick in fishing tidal waters is to fish the right spot at the right time. Mostly, the bass turn on when the tide first starts to move. It doesn't make any difference if the water's rising or falling, just so it's moving."

—"Charley Hartley's Bass Wars," March 28, 2009, on the B.A.S.S. site at
www.sports.espn.go.com/outdoors/bassmaster/index

410. Another Tidewater Tip

"The water will move first near the mouth of a creek or bay. Fish there for a few minutes and then, when the bite drops off, go back further into the tributary and fish another spot as the water starts to move. If you're quick you can fish several places that way every time the tide moves."

—"Charley Hartley's Bass Wars," March 28, 2009, on the B.A.S.S. site at
www.sports.espn.go.com/outdoors/bassmaster/index

411. The Carolina Rig as a Search Bait

Mark Hicks, in an article "Carolina Rigging," *Bass Times Tips and Tools*, November, 2008, reports that "Jared Lintner, an Elite Series pro from Arroyo Grande, California, regards the Carolina-style setup as a search bait." Lintner won several tournaments fishing California lakes to depths of 60 feet with a ¾-ounce Carolina Rig matched with a 6-inch PowerBait Lizard,

"Now," reports Hicks, "Lintner's favorite setup is 20-pound-test fluorocarbon line, a ¾-ounce tungsten sinker, two 8mm glass beads, and a 3/0 Gamakatsu hook knotted to the end of a 3- to 4-foot-long, 8- or 10-pound-test fluorocarbon leader."

412. Positively Swimbaits

The swimbait surge is one of the latest bass-fishing buzzwords, resounding from tackleshops to boats, coast to coast. These are realistic-looking, mostly soft-plastic designs made to swim in fresh or salt water. They are among the more expensive lures (some of them *very* expensive), and if they didn't catch bass and win tournaments you would not be hearing so much about them. Both Cabela's, www.cabelas.com and Bass Pro Shops, www.basspro.com offer good selections.

413. A Swim Bait Nation

The swimbait lure option has spread across the nation like wildfire, and the western-oriented site www.swimbaitnation.com makes the most of it with articles and reports from pros and amateurs on using swimbaits. In the clear waters of the West, a lot of bassers have caught onto the fact that bass love eating stocked trout. There are swimbait trout imitations that cost a bundle (how about $40 to $50 for the Huddleston Trout or the Baitsmith Magnum Trout?) but catch big bass and win tournaments. One of the sites mentioned for these swimbaits is www.basstackledept.com. The hunt is on to break George Perry's World Record (22 pounds, 4 ounces).

414. California, Here I Come

A lot of good fishing information and tips related to California fishing is available on the site www.calfishing.com.

415. A New Worm to Shake Up Your Bassing

Bassmaster Elite pro Jeff Kriet has earned a great reputation for his deep-water results in lakes like Kentucky, Oneida, and Clarks Hill. He fishes with quite an arsenal, but in particular likes drop-shot fishing and shakey-head worm fishing. Kriet has lately been cashing in (literally) on using his shakey-head techniques with the worm of his own development. It's the Jeff Kriet Squirrel Tail Worm, sold on www.bigbitebaits.com. What's unique about Kriet's worm is the thin, limber tail that literally dances every time the shakey head is pulled or bumps something. Kriet combines the worm with his Big Bite Shakey Head Jig, $1/8$-ounce 75 percent of the time and $1/16$ the rest. See the article "Shakey Details Matter," according to Kriet on www.bassfan.com.

© Pat Ford 2010

416. A Favorite Worm Rig

I have run the details of Col. Dave Harbour's favorite, shallow-water worm rig in several magazines, and I have fished the rig with great success in varying waters—from northern smallmouths to southern swamp bigmouths. Here's the rig, what Harbour called "The Super Rig:" Start with a soft 6-inch, straight-tail purple worm, with Crème's Wiggle Worm, Dave's worm of choice. Hook two No. 5 or 7 black snap swivels together, then add a leader of 14 inches the same test as your line. The worm is not hooked Texas-style; instead, thread the hook from the head deep into the body, then out, leaving the body pushed up over the eye of the hook. This gives the worm a humped position that really works.

417. If You're Not Drop-Shot Fishing . . .

If you haven't given drop-shot fishing a try yet, you're missing out on a great fishing technique. The variations on the technique are many, and you can have a lot of fun experimenting with them. Right here, however, I will keep it simple and explain a basic rig that will catch bass—not to mention walleyes and panfish—wherever you fish. Basically the rig is another wrinkle in the "Bottoms-Up" fishing trend. At the end of your line is a tungsten weight, say ¼ or ⅜ ounce, hooked to the line with a snap swivel so you can change the weight as the depth demands. Tied with a palamar knot 12 inches or so up the line is a No. 2 Wide Gap hook. Put your worm or jig on that hook, and you're in business. You can add a swivel above the hook if you wish. Hook your worm through the nose or through the body wacky-style. Drop it straight down and jig it, pull it along the bottom, experiment until you find what's working.

418. Bill Dance: *Pull* That Worm, Don't *Reel* It

Over the years, TV personality and celebrity angler Bill Dance has frequently recommended fishing a Texas-rigged plastic worm. He likes darker color worms early and late, and transparent worms in the middle of the day. He fishes the worm by letting it drop to the bottom, then pulling on the worm by raising the rod from a 45-degree angle to vertical. Then he reels up the slack. The worm is "pulled" with the rod, not reeled. Reeling is only for taking up slack.

419. The Spotted Bass Challenge

Also known as the Kentucky bass, the spotted bass and its subspecies, like the Alabama spotted bass, is lean and mean compared to the largemouth and smallmouth. A greenish bass with spots along the lateral line, spotted bass occur in clean, cold waters in lower midland America. They have also been transplanted in California. They are much coveted for their fighting qualities and as table fare.

420. The Toughest Bass of Them All?

Back in the 1970s when I was editing *Sports Afield*, I assigned writer Jerome Robinson to check out the spotted bass fishing down in Alabama's Lewis Smith Lake. [By the way, everything said about the lake back then still pertains today.] Robinson wrote in *Sports Afield*, January, 1972: "They [local anglers] also agreed on one point: that the Alabama spotted bass is the hardest to find, the hardest to catch, and the scrappiest bass species of the black bass family. Though he doesn't grow as large or as fast as the largemouth or smallmouth, the 'spot' is known by Alabama fishermen as the most challenging bass in their waters."

421. Alabama's Spotted Bass Headquarters

In the January, 1972, issue of *Sports Afield*, writer Jerome Robinson told readers about northwest Alabama's Lewis Smith Lake, a gem for bass fishing of all types but in particular the Alabama spotted bass. The lake is still fantastic today. Check into it on Google and other sites. Jerry said: "Lewis Smith Lake is a startlingly beautiful impoundment of 21,200 acres which was created in 1961 by damming the Sipsey Fork of the Warrior River where the clear green limestone waters flow out of the Bankhead National Forest. It is so deep (up to 300 feet) that the water on the bottom in the deepest sections remains at 39.5 degrees all year, the same as salmon rivers in Maine. Long and many-fingered, the lake has more than 500 miles of shoreline and even though it is heavily fished, it never appears crowded." Jerry went on to mention that water-skiers affect the lake's fishing in summer, making night fishing the best bet.

CHAPTER 8

The Tournament Trail: What to Expect, What to Know

422. How to Lose a Bass Tournament

In tournament fishing, catching lots of bass doesn't matter. It's the total weight of your five fish at weigh-in time that puts you in the money. For most of us anglers, a 2-pound bass is a nice fish. But in the vast majority of tournaments, catching five 2-pounders isn't going to be good enough. You've got to turn your back on those spots and find bigger fish most of the time. As in all fishing, there's no such thing in tournaments as "all the time."

423. Find the Other Boats, Find the Fish

Some tournament anglers, in the frenzy of competition, don't have the time to find bass on their own. Their strategy is to find where other boats are fishing and join the party. The next time you're on the water, keep an eye out for congregations of boats. If you're not catching fish where you are, then get over there!

424. Hitting the Pro Circuit, Part One: Dreams and Realities

Dreaming of becoming a professional bass angler, competing in tournaments for big bucks (and perhaps even making it to the Classic and winning a bundle)? Well, before you do something foolish like quitting

your job or taking out a second mortgage on your house, read the blog where one of the best professionals tells it like it is—costs, sponsors, the hard work, the "real" rewards. We're talking about "Charley Hartley's Bass Wars" blog, archived on the B.A.S.S. site at www.sports.espn. go.com/outdoors/bassmaster/index. In his reports of September 10, 18, and 28, 2008, and October 2, 2008, Hartley gives the clearest, no-nonsense look at the realities of turning pro than on any site we've seen. No matter whether he is writing advice on tournaments or simply giving you tips on lures and strategies, Hartley is worth reading every time he posts a new report.

425. Hitting the Pro Circuit, Part Two: Bring Money!

"Let me make something clear: I have never—not once in thirty years—tried to discourage anyone from turning professional and following their dream. I followed mine and wouldn't expect any less from anyone else. But there are financial consequences to the decisions we make."

—"Charley Hartley's Bass Wars," October 2, 2008 on the B.A.S.S. site at
www.sports.espn.go.com/outdoors/bassmaster/index

426. Hitting the Pro Circuit, Part Three: Assessing Your Chances

"So, when you analyze your skills realize that there are thousands of club champions and hundreds of anglers who have won big charity tournaments. Lots of guys can catch bass. That's not the test. The test is skill coupled with fanatical perseverance, a single-minded purpose, a love of the sport, and the marketing ability to make it all work financially."

—"Charley Hartley's Bass Wars," October 2, 2008 on the B.A.S.S. site at
www.sports.espn.go.com/outdoors/bassmaster/index

PART THREE

ON THE WATER
For Trout and Salmon

CHAPTER 9

Fly-Fishing Tactics:
How Top Guides and Experts Fish

427. The Biggest Key to Fly-Fishing Success

"Too many anglers spend too much time worrying about fly pattern and not enough thinking about presentation."

—Ted Trueblood, "Fish and Fishing" Department,
Field & Stream, May, 1947

428. Field & Stream's Trout "Ultimate Lure" Survey Winners

In what it called the "Ultimate Lure Survey," published in March, 2008, *Field & Stream* magazine asked 1,000 of its hard-core readers to name their favorite lures. The winners for the Trout category were:

In-Line Spinners, 65%, Mepps Aglia

Spoons, 15%, Little Cleo

Jigs, 9%, Marabou Jig

Soft-Plastics, 6%, Berkley Gulp! Worm

Plugs, 4%, Original Rapala

429. Learning from the Great Blue Heron

Beautiful to look at, the great blue herron is universally disliked by trout anglers who see the bird as a poacher on their favorite fish—especially after they have seen ugly holes in the backs of trout. Stop to consider the heron's fishing tactics, however, and you might see your own catches improve dramatically. Regard the heron as it lands in a likely spot, wades into position, than stands rock-still as the minutes go by—minute after minute, patiently waiting, for as long as it takes. Emulate this strategy on water holding trout that are either feeding or lying in the current. As you try to approach the trout and get into good casting position, they will spook. The trick is to get into position and, just like the heron, get your fly ready in your hand, get enough line out to cast, keeping it and your rod tip low and away from the fish, and wait . . . and wait . . . and wait. Sooner or later the fish will go back to feeding or lying in the current where they were before. Bingo.

430. Fastest Fly-Fishing Course Ever

In a Web site centered around fishing Pennsylvania's legendary spring creeks, such as the Letort, www.limestoner.com writer Gene Macri comes up with what he titles, "How to Get 10 Years Fly Fishing Experience Immediately." Macri's system is based on studying the surface of your favorite spring creek with binoculars. You will see the bugs, what they're doing and not doing, and the trout, what they're doing and not doing, in a way you've never imagined.

431. Meeting the Late Summer Challenge

"The big hatches are over, trout are well-fed and spooky. What's going to bring them to the surface? The answer may surprise you. . . . anglers bombard the water with hoppers when another insect is far more important. That insect is the beetle. Scientific studies reveal that terrestrial beetles are three to seven times more common in trout diets than grasshoppers . . . most anglers don't imitate them, so trout haven't seen a plethora of fake beetles."

—Jeff Morgan, in the article "Meeting the Late Summer Challenge," www.westfly.com. Get Morgan's new book *The Oddballs: Productive Trout Flies for Unorthodox Prey*, Amato Publications, 2010, at www.amazon.com. Also check out his previous book, *Small-Stream Fly Fishing*, Amato Publications, 2005.

432. Need More Convincing? It's Beetles for Trout

"I became a beetle addict after seeing how well they work on highly pressured summer trout water such as the Henry's Fork, the Yellowstone region, the Green River, and the many streams in the Missoula area. No other patterns brought the consistent success and confident rises that beetle imitations elicited."

—Jeff Morgan, in the article "Meeting the Late Summer Challenge," www.westfly.com. Get Morgan's new book *The Oddballs: Productive Trout Flies for Unorthodox Prey*, at www.amazon.com. Also check out his previous book, *Small-Stream Fly Fishing*.

433. How Expert Jeff Morgan Searches New Water for Trout

"Most anglers have little confidence in a pair of Size 20 nymphs in a 200-foot-wide trout stream. To overcome this reluctance, use tiny nymphs behind something a little meatier, such as a Pupatator. [The Pupatator is Jeff Morgan's buggy-looking nymph creation.] My standard 'starting' rig on new waters is a Size 8 Pupatator, a Size 16 rusty or olive beadhead Hares Ear, and a Size 20 Blue-Winged Olive nymph, Brassie, or scud. This allows me to cover an array of foods in a spectrum of colors and sizes. Once one fly outshines the others, I can then retool my approach with whatever the trout are keying on."

—Jeff Morgan, in one of the regular articles he writes for www.westfly.com

© Stu Apte 2010

434. Where Trout Are Always Hungry

Small streams that flow into some of the best wilderness streams don't have the amounts of food and insect life of the large rivers. The water is swift, and the trout will quickly grab prey floating into view. Some anglers mistakenly think these trout are stupid, but they're not. They're just hungry. Use floating flies like Royal Coachmen, Stimulators, and Humpies.

435. Make Your Dropper Fly Expendable

When tying a dropper leader to a dry fly or strike indicator, make the dropper in a lighter strength than your main leader. When you hit a snag, you're better off losing the dropper fly instead of your whole rig.

436. Dropper Fly Length for Dry Flies

When it's to be tied to a dry fly, most experts and top guides prefer dropper leaders in the 18-inch range. Much shorter, and you'll be fishing too shallow. Much longer, and you might as well be using a strike indicator instead of a dry fly.

437. Long Live the Long Rod

It's easy—and somewhat fashionable—to fall under the spell of trout anglers who preach the gospel of using the shortest rod possible. They point to its ease of casting under trees and brush, and to the sense of feel you get from a fighting fish. Long rod disciples are out there, however, arguing that short rods leave too much line on the water, more than you can handle with ease. One of the best of the Long Rod contingent was Leonard Wright, superb angler and writer, who once did an article in *Sports Aield* called, "Long Live the Long Rod." (February, 1974). In it, Wright said, "The most overrated piece of fishing equipment in America today is the short fly rod."

438. Tying on the Dropper Leader

Most trout guides tie the dropper leader to the bend of the dry fly hook. Some tie it directly to the eye of the dry fly hook. My personal choice is to use the bend.

439. The Dry Fly As a Striker Indicator

Whether your dry fly is one to search the water, or one to match a specific hatch, make sure it's large enough, and buoyant enough, to give your dropper leader and nymph a good floating platform, visible throughout its drift. If your dry fly is too small, or your nymph too large and heavy, you'll defeat your entire purpose.

440. Ted Trueblood's Dyed-Leader Experiment

Back in September 1951, Ted Trueblood wrote a remarkable, ground-breaking article for *Sports Afield*. In the story, called "A New Theory of Flies and Leaders," Trueblood described dyeing his leaders in the kitchen sink to imitate string moss, which did not seem to spook trout in his rivers. He experimented with green and brown dye with pinches of blue. A few days later he went to Silver Creek. He caught and released 21 trout on 2X. He went on with his experiments and found that, "In most waters I found I could hook fish on tippets a full size larger, and occasionally two sizes larger, than before." In the article, which has been reprinted in the book *Sports Afield Treasury of Trout Fishing*, The Lyons Press (1989), Trueblood also has some startling observations on flies trout take. "Except during the spawning season, all activity of trout is governed by two overwhelming stimuli: fear and hunger. They are hungry most of the time, the severe cold season excepted." Trueblood maintained that trout will take almost any fly, as long as it looks like something to eat and they aren't frightened by the leader.

441. The Spell of the Mayfly

"Mayfly adults provide a lesson in life. In no other insect is the adult stage so brief and with such singular purpose. We must appreciate its qualities as we might a sunset, for too quickly will it be gone. And we must appreciate, also, that a whole sport has grown up around it."

—Jay Cassell, "Mayfly Artistry," *Sports Afield,* May, 1982

442. Blue Ribbon Flies

Every year when I'm in the deep clutches of winter, I enjoy receiving the catalog from Craig Mathews Blue Ribbon Flies out in West Yellowstone, Montana (www.blueribbonflies.com.) They always come up with some new flies that snag my attention, and I particularly enjoy reading Mathews' rundown of his experiences in the previous season. Mathews and his associate, John Juracek, have some great books and DVDs, along with detailed maps for fishing the Yellowstone area.

443. Where Are the Hatches?

Among the lessons about trout fishing that have cost me considerable gobs of both time and money, one of the most important has been the realization that even on those rare days when hatches occur, they do not happen everywhere. Don't expect the entire surface of the river to burst with emerging caddis and mayflies. Hatches occur—*when* they occur—in scattered sections of the river, in varying water types. A riffle, a smooth glide, a deep pool—all might harbor hatches at different and varying times. You might have great fishing in hatches at one small section of the river at dusk, then meet your buddy at the truck later and learn that he saw nothing—no rises. Big rivers or small streams, that's the way it goes.

444. Upstream with Dries, Downstream Nymphs and Streamers

Stu Apte loves trout fishing almost as much as he does fishing for tarpon and bonefish. His favorite strategy is to fish part of a big river or small stream upstream with dry flies, then take a break and rig for nymphs and streamers and fish back downstream. This system can be particularly effective when you're fishing dries early in the morning, then switching to nymphs and heading back downstream as the sun gets overhead.

445. Big Sky Fishing Web site

The name rings with promise—Big Sky Fishing. And the Web site, www.bigskyfishing.com, delivers with superb information and coverage of high-country rivers and lakes.

446. Fish the Skwala Hatch for Openers

You would think that my years in magazine editing, particularly those at *Sports Afield* and *Outdoor Life,* would have seen me working with writers on the Skwala hatch out in the high country, but I missed it. Many top guides and anglers have not been missing out, however, and on rivers like Montana's Bitterroot this hatch of stoneflies in March (lasting into April) signals the beginning of some serious trout angling. The hatches are sparse, and localized, but the action is good in pockets when you find them. This is cold weather fishing, of course, so wear gloves, base layers, the works. Check outfitters and guides all over the high West to learn how you might cash in and kick off your season. Flies include Olive Stimulators and Skwala Stones and custom patterns like the Designated Hitter Skwala Stone from The Fly Shop, www .theflyshop.com.

447. Visiting The Fly Shop

Located in Redding, California, The Fly Shop is one of angling's premier spots to find everything you need, from flies to great destinations. Their catalog is second to none, and their Web site, www.theflyshop.com, has it all. I particularly like their flies—always some interesting new patterns there.

448. Trout Pellet Fly—The Real Thing

You may risk being scorned, laughed at, even cursed at, but at times you might be so fed up with your lousy luck fly fishing for trout that you feel like nuking them. That's when you long for a fly imitating trout food pellets. Now you can buy one—at The Fly Shop, www.theflyshop.com. Their Pellet Fly is listed under Stoneflies and Attractors, Size 10, $1.75 at this writing.

449. Trout Pellet Fly—The Reasonable Facsimile

A fly that you use all the time can actually be a pretty good imitation of a trout pellet. It's the Muddler Minnow, which, in its small sizes, has a predominate, bulbous head that looks very pellet-like. Whether you're thinking "Trout Pellet" or not, the Muddler in small sizes is a terrific fly to fish, dry or sinking.

450. How to Spot Nymph Takes

"The fish in the tail shallows were nymphing, and they hovered just under the surface, drifting forward restlessly in the current when they took something in the flow. Their mouths would open lazily, expelling water past their gills, and flashing white each time they intercepted a hatching nymph."

—Ernest Schwiebert, "The Mill at Longparish" in *Death of a Riverkeeper*, Dutton, 1980

451. Small Stream, Small Backpack, Big Day

Do everything you possibly can to find a small trout stream tucked away among the hills and mountains—the Appalachians, the Rocky Mountain high country, the New England ranges, the midwest forests, the northwest peaks. Once you find a stream that's just right, lots of clean water and trout (most of them won't be big, but so what?), completely isolated, enjoy it to the hilt as often as you can by strapping on a small backpack that has everything you need for a full day's fishing, pick up your light rod, and go. If you've never done this, I hope you give it a try. Someday you'll thank me!

452. Fish Streamers in Small Streams

Writer, fly tier and creator, and expert angler Jeff Morgan says in his book *Small-Stream Fly Fishing*, Frank Amato Publications (2005), that his favorite technique for fishing streamers in small streams is, "Sinfully easy." He crimps a split-shot near the eye of his fly and uses a floating line with 8 feet of 4X tippet. The fly is fished straight downstream. For other Jeff Morgan tips, see his archived articles at the WestFly Internet site, www.westfly.com, and see his newest book,

Productive Trout Flies for Unorthodox Prey: The Oddballs, Frank Amato Publications (2009). See Amazon for listings of Jeff's other books.

453. Traver Award Story Collection

Those who share my interest in great writing will be applauding *Fly Rod & Reel* magazine's first collection of stories that have been recognized over the years in the Robert Traver Award competition. Published by Fly Rod & Reel Books in 2009, the softcover book called *In Hemingway's Meadow* includes eighteen original tales of fly fishing. Since 1994, the award has gone to stories and essays in honor of the late John Voelker, who used the pen name Robert Traver on such trout classics as *Trout Madness,* St. Martin's Press (1960), and the best-selling novel *Anatomy of a Murder*, St. Martin's Press (1958). The title of this collection references the "meadow" where Hemingway's "Nick" camped in his immortal story, "Big Two-Hearted River," and is from the award-winning story by Jeff Day. The book was edited by Joe Healy. You can find it at places like the fly-fishing site, The Book Mailer, www.thebookmailer.com, Barnes & Nobel, and Amazon, or by going to www.flyrodreel.com.

454. Strike Indicator Flotation Help

You help your dry flies float with a little flotation spray or powder, so remember to do the same to flotation devices like strike indicators.

455. Fishing Small Streams Behind Other Anglers

It's frustrating, but there it is: Another angler is ahead of you on the stream. Unless you're going to leap frog far ahead of him (not just the next pool), you're better off doing two things: 1) Rest the water for a few minutes, if you can; and 2) Use different tactics than the angler ahead of you, provided you can see what he's doing. If he's fishing a dry fly, go to nymphs and streamers. If he's ripping streamers through the pools, try a dry fly with a nymph dropper.

456. Small Streams and Sink-Tip Lines

Handling awkward sink-tip and full-sink lines on small streams is unnecessary. Use tiny split-shot or beaded sinking flies to get down when you have to.

457. What's That on Your Dropper?

In his outstanding book *Small-Stream Fly Fishing*, Frank Amato Publications (2005), Jeff Morgan questions the wisdom of putting certain flies on your dropper attached to a dry fly.

Since your attached nymph will be riding 18 to 24 inches (the preferred length of the dropper leader) below the surface—not on the bottom—the nymph being used should represent a fly found in mid-currents, not on the bottom. The flies Jeff says he avoids for using on the dropper—because they're bottom-dwellers—are " . . . stonefly nymphs, caddis larvae, midge larvae, sowbugs, fish eggs, aquatic worms, crane fly larvae, and most scuds."

458. Give Small-Stream Trout Your Best Shot

Fish small trout streams slowly and carefully in an upstream direction. Keep your casts short, popping your fly into tiny pockets. Short, accurate casts are everything.

459. Finding and Fishing the Seams

Seams are places in the river current where a slight change-of-pace in the flow occurs between fast water and slow water. Imagine a rock in the stream. Think of the water rushing past on both sides as the fast lanes. The slow or still water behind the rock and directly in front are the slow lanes. Between the fast and slow lanes will be seams of intermediate flow, perfect for trout to ambush prey.

460. Don't Miss the Trout Bum

His book of essays called *Trout Bum* started the John Gierach surge in angling reading popularity some years ago (the book has been republished several times since), and by now the surge has turned into a tsunami of books, all of which should be on your list for reading pleasure. Gierach not only takes you fishing with him in his home Colorado waters, but everywhere else where the fishing is interesting, even when it's not always good. Gierach is the "everyman" trout writer, with engaging prose that makes you feel like you've met a friend for life. His books are everywhere, and likely some are in your local library.

461. On Sinking Lines: Drop Down One Size

Maine outdoorsman, writer, and painter Tom Hennessey gave me a tip on buying a full-sinking fly line—not a sinking tip or high density sinking, just a regular sinking line. Tom said he's had better luck with sinking lines by dropping down in size one weight. For example, if your rod's an 8, he'll buy a 7 sinking line. It will cast much, much better, says Tom.

462. Are the New Fluorocarbon Leaders Worth It?

The fluorocarbon leaders cost a lot more than the traditional nylon. Are they worth the extra dough? You get greater strength, far less visibility. They're perfect for the conditions when stealth counts for everything in your trout fishing—low, clear water and super-wary fish. There are a lot of anglers sneaking up on trout with fluorocarbon leaders these days.

463. Spring Creeks: Superb Trout Destinations

Flowing up clean and cold from aquifers and chalk beds inside Mother Earth, twenty-four hours a day, seven days a week, 365 days a year, spring creeks are worth every hour and every cent trout addicts spend to find and fish them. Here are trout you can *see,* prolific insect hatches, and easier wading than the rough-and-tumble freestone streams. They are tough to fish, but . . . so what? You can find plenty of them in Pennsylvania, scattered throughout the upper Midwest and far West, and in England the chalk streams are angling destinations to die for.

464. Why Spring Creeks Are Tough

Running smooth and clear with no breaks or riffles to cover the sound of your wading or awkward casts, spring creeks are a challenge for any angler, especially the novice. They're fun, yes, but challenging. Veteran angler and writer Ted Leeson describes the situation in his wonderful book, *Jerusalem Creek*, The Lyons Press (2002): "Nothing about a spring creek hides your presence or want of skill, or a faulty presentation or the inadequacies of tackle or miscalculations of method."

465. When You Can't Match the Hatch

One of the most frustrating experiences in trout fishing is to find yourself in the midst of a big hatch of insects, with trout taking them eagerly, and you just can't seem to get the right fly onto them. This happens all the time with hatches like the tiny Tricos. Instead of letting frustration overwhelm you, try putting on a fly that totally changes the pace of what's going on. Use a No. 16 Royal Wulff or Fan-Winged Royal Coachman, for instance, or a buggy terrestrial imitation. And there's always room for the Adams, the go-to fly when nothing else is working. The Stimulator ranks high with go-to flies also.

466. When Spring Creek Trout Turn On

"Spring creek trout have a reputation for being moody, which often means they are difficult, but when they're in the mood to feast, almost nothing—not sloppy wading, not poor casting, not a ridiculous choice of flies—will dissuade them."

—Ted Leeson, *Jerusalem Creek*, The Lyons Press, 2002

467. The Tuck Cast Takes More Trout

"I am nymphing a favorite run of broken water, using a weighted Perla Stonefly Nymph with a split-shot crimped to the leader 6 inches up to get it down quickly in the fast water. I use a tuck cast to further enhance the nymph's entry to the water. A cast developed by George Harvey and made famous by his friend, another local fishing fishing legend, Joe Humphrey."

—Chuck Robbins, writer and guide, in his Pennsylvania fishing days recalled in his first book, *Odyssey at Limestone Creek*, Tussey Mountain Publisher (1997). Chuck now guides and writes in Montana. See www.chuckngalerobbins.com

468. When Rain Is Your Friend

No one especially likes fishing in the rain—and thunderstorms are downright dangerous—but there are times when rain comes in just the right amounts at the right time to get trout moving and feeding. The rain washes all kinds of terrestrials and morsels into the stream, and the trout go after them with vigor. The only way you'll find out if it's a "good rain" or "bad rain" is to be out there. Chances are you'll have the stream to yourself. And, whatever you do, don't miss the spots where other streams or runs pour into the main river.

469. Fishing the Back Door to Yellowstone

The town of West Yellowstone—home of guides and tackleshops and the main entrance to Yellowstone National Park and its angling treasures—is not the only game in town. On the other side of Yellowstone, to the east, lies Cody, Wyoming, on the Shoshone River and entryway to the Shoshone National Forest and the eastern side of Yellowstone. Cody has the Buffalo Bill Museum and is home of Tim Wade's North Fork Anglers, headquarters for fishing the Shoshone rivers and the park. Their site is www.northforkanglers.com. They have everything you need to crack into the Yellowstone region's backside.

470. Where the Road Leaves the River

Some fishing tips seem so simple—like sharpening your hooks—that most people probably ignore them. A simple one that I hope you will not ignore is this: Fish where the road leaves the river. Walk to where the crowds don't go, and you will be rewarded with better trout fishing. Most people will not walk there. They just won't do it. At a health club I sometimes go to for workouts, I watch in fascination as people maneuver and jostle their cars into parking positions close to the front door. All that so they don't have to walk a couple hundred feet across a big parking lot. Walking . . . to do the very thing they came to the club for, getting exercise. It makes no sense. Neither does not walking into the woods to fish where you can't see the road. But that's what people do.

471. Sulphurs: The Year's Best Fly Hatch

In the West they have the glorious Pale Morning Dun hatches that fill the air with greenish-yellow bugs. In the East and upper Midwest, the highlight of the springtime hatches sees the arrival of a similar mayfly—the Sulphurs, most in the genus *Ephemerella* in various sizes with other Latin subtitles for those who take their fishing and fly-tying with textbook correctness. Where I fish, mostly in Pennsylvania and New Jersey, the hatches begin in mid-May, a week or so after the storied Hendricksons have played out. The party goes on until late in June, with the fishing getting tougher as it progresses.

472. Making the Most of the Sulphur Hatches

The Sulphur hatches bring out anglers by the droves on eastern and mid-western trout streams. Try to catch the earliest Sulphur hatches you can to beat the crowds. Look for cloudy and rainy days to be the best for Sulphurs. As the hatch goes on, look for the best action to occur from late afternoon into the evening, almost dark.

473. When the Sulphurs Have Competition

Sulphurs aren't the only mayflies you'll see in late May. They come at the same time that Green Drakes, Brown Drakes, and Gray Drakes can be on the water. A friend returning from Spruce Creek in Pennsylvania, where he had gone to fish the famous Green Drake hatch, told me he did not do well until he figured out that the trout were rising to the Sulphurs, not the few Green Drakes showing.

474. The High-Country's Forgotten Early Season Fishing

" . . . most destination anglers don't travel to the West during the off-season . . . I have recurrent dreams about the spring Baetis (Blue-Winged Olive) hatches along the upper Bighorn near Thermopolis, Wyoming, and the innocent, chubby rainbows and browns that rise freely to them. The pods of 18-inch trout that begin their first surface-feeding frenzies on the Missouri, alone and unmolested by boats and anglers, beckon. The newly restored Madison River with its reliable pre-runoff flows and its superb wading flats and reliable hatches are high on my list of destinations, as is the lower Henry's Fork around Ashton and other streams nearby. I have never hit a Mother's Day hatch on the Yellowstone, or a giant stonefly or *Skwala* hatch either. But they are on my list of sparkling experiences that lie ahead."

—John Randolph, Editor, *Fly Fisherman Magazine*, in the article "Spring Hatches," in May, 2004.

475. My Big Sulphur Hatch Mistake

I once wrote a story for *Sports Afield* called "Mid-Stream Crisis." It's about, among other things, being slap in the middle of a great Sulphur hatch coming off just at dusk. A big fish broke me off. I had no reading glasses, no penlight or even flashlight, and I simply could not see well enough to tie on another fly. How can you call yourself an experienced angler and be so unprepared? Fish were rising and taking all about me as I sloshed out of the stream, excited, but sad in defeat.

476. Fly Line Colors: They *Do* Matter

" . . . When Brian Clarke and I were engaged in writing *The Trout and the Fly*, we carried out many experiments with underwater cameras on fly lines . . . This proved, at least to us, that dull colors such as green or brown were far less fish scaring . . . "

—John Goddard, *John Goddard's Trout-Fishing Techniques*, Lyons and Burford, 1996

477. The Secret of Timing Trout Feeding Activity

In his wonderful book *The Ways of Trout*, The Lyons Press (1985), the noted angler and author Leonard M. Wright, Jr., culminated years of research by nailing down the period when you can expect maximum trout feeding activity. The secret: the time when the water temperature is rising faster toward the optimum of 63 degrees. At 63 degrees, feeding activity slows, the blitz is over. Reveals Wright, " . . . fish feed best when the temperature gradient toward the optimum is steepest." Wright found the reverse to also be true, fishing rising when the temperature is dropping back toward 63 after being much higher for hours.

478. Falling Barometer: Look Out Below

" . . . I have never recorded as 'active,' much less an 'aggressive,' rating for lights feeding during a low or falling barometer." ("Lights" being Wright's feeding pellets used on his home Neversink River to study trout feeding habits.)

—Leonard M. Wright, Jr., *The Ways of Trout*, The Lyons Press (1985)

479. Fly Rod Casting Techniques You May Never Master, But Should

In his book *John Goddard's Trout-Fishing Techniques* (1996), the noted British author John Goddard outlines why and how the following fly-casting techniques can help you catch fish. There are 13 very specific casts, ranging from "The Parachute Roll Cast," through such casts as "The Deep-Water Tuck Cast," "The Wet-Fly Swing Cast," "The Puddle, Pile, or Parachute Cast," "The Storm or Wind Cast," "The Bow and Arrow Cast," and "Curve Casts." As you can see, the skill of casting with a fly rod can be a never-ending learning and experience process.

480. Why Are All Those Trucks Parked Over There?

The surest sign a certain stretch of a trout stream or creek is a real hotspot for action is to see a few trucks or SUVs parked at a nearby opening in the woodlands. Such a visual tip means a lot more than the free advice you get in tackleshops.

481. Upstream Wading Made Easier

In a strong current, wading upstream is best done with sideways steps. Lean your whole body into the flow slightly.

482. Tests on Fluorocarbon Tippets

Noted Pennsylvania trout author Charles Meck did some serious testing on fluorocarbon leader tippets with his Patriot dry fly. What conclusions did he draw? "First, fluorocarbons appear to work. Second, use the finest fluorocarbon leader you can. Of course, there's a tradeoff: If you use 6X and 7X you're more likely to break off heavier trout."

—Charles Meck, *Fishing Limestone Streams*, The Lyons Press, 2005

483. More About Fluorocarbon Tippets

Continuing Charles Meck's fluorocarbon tippet tests: " . . . I did not catch any trout on the dry fly in that very clear water until I used a 5X fluorocarbon tippet. I caught even more trout on the Patriot dry fly when I used a 6X fluorocarbon. I feel confident that had I used a 7X fluorocarbon leader I would have done even better."

—Charles Meck, *Fishing Limestone Streams*, The Lyons Press, 2005

484. Buying Flies Before You Go

It's fun and easy to get into stocking up on trout flies just before you make a big, long-anticipated trip. If it's to be a guided trip, however, do the family exchequer a favor and hold up on the flies until you arrive on the scene. Chances are the guides will have plenty of the ones you'll really need.

485. You Can Bet on Beetles

To catch more trout on flies, concentrate on fishing beetle imitations, particularly June Bugs, not only in high summer, but throughout the season, from spring into winter. You can spend all the time (and money) you want trying to imitate the famous mayfly and caddis hatches, but beetles are what the trout are feeding on most of the time. Reporting in a fantastic article in *Field & Stream*, September, 1955, called "Mr. Botz and The Beetle," Angling Editor A. J. McClane discussed stomach contents taken from brown trout caught in New York's Catskill Mountain streams in April, May, June, and September. Beetles, far and away, were insects being digested. Make beetle imitations a mainstay of your trout fly offerings, and you'll catch more fish. And don't forget that many superstar flies like the Muddler Minnow may be mistaken for beetles by trout, along with other popular flies as well. McClane adds, "There's no doubt in my mind that some of our standard wet-fly patterns, such as the Silver Doctor, Leadwing Coachman, and Black Gnat are mistaken for beetles by the trout." McClane also puts the Royal Coachman in the same fish-taking category because of its appearance under certain light conditions.

486. Barbless Hooks Make More Sense

Required in many trout streams, barbless hooks have a lot going for them in every form of light-tackle fishing, fresh and salt water. First, they are easy to extract when the angler sinks one into his hand or body. Second, they are easier to extract from the fish, allowing your catch to be released and live to fight another day. Finally, they sink deeper than barbed hooks, making most hookups just as effective as barbed hooks.

487. Barbless Hooks: How to Know They're Legal

There are so many trout streams today that require barbless hooks, anglers need to be doubly on the alert to make sure the flies they are using in these waters are legal. Even after the barb has been mashed down with pliers, the hook may not pass the test. What tests? Fishermen in many states are confused over this issue and are asking for legal guideposts. One state, Arkansas, spells out its definition in the 2007 *Trout Guidebook* as, "Crimped completely, the hook is smooth and will not snag when passed through cloth." That sounds pretty clear. If it will not pass through cloth without snagging, it's not legal. Until a better uniform definition comes along, that one sounds reasonable.

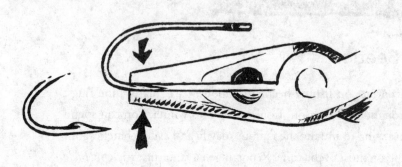

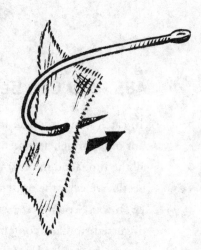

488. Making Your Hooks Barbless

For large bass lures, you're probably going to have to file the barbs down or replace the sets of hooks with new barbless ones (readily available, see separate sources). For trout flies, the procedure is simpler, but there are right and wrong ways to go about it. The correct way is to fit the point and barb of the fly straight into the head of the pliers. (Do not turn the hook crossways to the pliers.) Mash down carefully, working around the barb until it has been smoothed flush with the hook shaft. You might find it easier to use a special set of pliers for holding the fly, and another, more precise one for mashing the barb.

489. Where to Obtain Barbless Hooks

As this is being written, there are already several makers of barbless hooks for both fly fishing and fresh and salt water light-tackle fishing. By the time the book is in print, due to the rapidly growing interest in the subject, the list will no doubt be much longer. Check the Internet by Googling, "Barbless Fish Hooks." At present, for treble hooks one of the easiest ways to change hooks on your favorite bass baits is to go to the *Boundary Waters Journal* site, www.boundarywatersjournal.com. The magazine has been offering sets of treble hooks since barbless hooks became the law in the Quetico. Another site is www.QueticoFishing.com. Familiar hook manufacturers who have been active in the barbless area include Gamakatsu and Eagle Claw and Umpqua for barbless flies.

490. Wading Staffs Make Sense

Falling down while wading and fishing isn't fun—on any kind of water, small creeks or big rivers. You'll get hurt, break or lose some tackle, or at least get wet, possibly very wet. Small streams have rocks, slippery and rounded. Large rivers have powerful current, and sometimes, as a bonus, slippery and rounded rocks. If you're a geezer, you already know darn well you need a wading staff. If you're coming onto geezer age, you're probably thinking about using one. If you're young and strong, you probably think wading staffs are for geezers only. Wading staffs, clipped to your fly vest, whether homemade or store bought, make life so easy. If your legs are in the least unsteady, try using one. You'll never go wade fishing again without it.

491. A Common Mayfly Frustration

Perhaps nothing in fly fishing is so frustrating as to finally be on the water while a big mayfly hatch is coming off, and the trout just aren't interested. I personally have seen such inactivity on the Brodhead in Pennsylvania when the long-awaited Hendrickson hatch was underway and the trout were lying doggo—not interested in nymphs underwater or the duns that were floating on the surface like a fleet of galleons. The textbooks all say that when the trout aren't on the duns, they'll be taking the nymphs down below, or the emergers in the film. It wasn't happening. The day was cold and dull, and nobody was catching fish. What to do? You tell me!

492. Try Tailwater Trout at "High Tide"

In an interesting article in *North American Fisherman*, August/September, 1992, well-know outdoor writer Dr. Jim Casada says he's had better luck fishing tailwaters when they were running full. Most anglers don't fish then because of the high water and all the canoists and floaters. But Casada says he could always find some wadeable water, out of the main stream, and catch lots of trout there—alone.

493. You Can Count on the Griffith's Gnat

Ernie Schwiebert was either the first—or certainly one of the first—to write about the Griffith's Gnat in the original version of his book, *Nymphs*, Winchester Press (1973). Since then many famous anglers and writers, and countless legions of anglers, have gone on to embrace this remarkable fly, one of the best midge imitations ever. The fly imitates the midge characteristic of sitting on the water with only its hackle fibers touching, not the body. The imitation resembles a single midge or an entire cluster of tiny ones. Expert angler and author Gary Borger says he favors Size 16 generally, but has plenty of others ready. For picky fish, he sometimes trims the hackle and lets the body rest on the water.

494. The Key to Early Season Success

"It pays to add or subtract weight as necessary to keep the flies down near the bottom. Especially in cold water, trout are reluctant to move up in the water column."

—Writer and Montana guide Chuck Robbins,
www.chuckngalerobbins.com

495. Get Out of That Rut

"You've got to keep switching gears. The worst thing is to keep plugging away with something that isn't working in the first place."

—Writer and Montana guide Chuck Robbins, www.chuckngalerobbins.com

496. Fishing Cold, Early Season Water

"Streamers fished slow and deep, with or without a nymph trailer (18 inches or so is about right) often provide a wake-up call for spring trout. Vary the presentation pattern, add or subtract weight, until you find the right combination—then stick with it until the trout tell you otherwise. Many times just a subtle variation—size, color, add a shot or two—does it. Other times, it's more a presentation thing. For instance, start by casting down and across, let the fly(s) swing around; next cast bounce the rod tip a few times during the swing; then toss in a hand-twist retrieve. Next pick up, strip off a little more line and do it again, only this time use a short-pause, long-strip, pause, retrieve. No dice. Add a little more weight, change patterns, and repeat same. In a general sense, the colder the water, the slower the retrieve."

—Writer and Montana guide Chuck Robbins, www.chuckngalerobbins.com

497. Try Egg Patterns for Fall Trout

Trout egg patterns, especially in the fall, consistently take trout, if my experiences and those of my trout-fishing friends are any indicator. These flies need to be bounced right along the bottom, and it's very hard to tell if you have a bite or have ticked a rock. Sometimes the trout take the fly and spit it out so quickly that you can't react. In clear water it is sometimes possible to see the fish's mouth flash white as it takes the fly. Look for lots of strikes, a few hook-ups.

498. The Czech Express Has Arrived

When Czech fly-fishing teams started winning trout tournaments (yes, there *are* fly-fishing tournaments), American anglers began tuning into their techniques with intense vigor. Today Czech nymphing is so popular and taking fish so effectively that the flies are sold by many dealers (www.cabelas.com; www.theessentialfly.com), articles and videos are posted on popular sites, and entire books are available on the subject. (See *Czech Nymph and Other Related Flyfishing Methods*, by Karel Krivanec at www.amazon.com.) Basically, Czech nymphs are great-looking flies tied extra-heavy to sink fast. The rig to fish them consists of a strike indicator and a triple-dropper setup, each dropper about 10 cm. The heavy Czech nymph is tied to the middle dropper, then your favorite traditional nymphs to the other two. This is high-stick nymphing, with short casts and the high rod immediately following the indicator downstream.

499. When Brook Trout Ponds Come to Life

Those cold, black-water wilderness lakes—called ponds in Maine—hold brook trout in sizes and numbers to dream about. Yet, under the long days of bright sun in June, they can seem to be absolutely lifeless. There are no rises, and no matter how hard you fish with streamers, strikes are few—or none. Then, between sunset and dark, the big Green Drakes start emerging, and trout—big trout—start slashing the water everywhere. Here's how Arthur MacDougall, Jr., described the experience in his wonderful *The Trout Fisherman's Bedside Book*, Simon & Schuster (1963): "We had to wait all afternoon . . . When the sun set, and the wood thrushes began their ventriloquial harmonies, the trout began to rise. As if by summons, they were everywhere all over the pond. And these were brilliantly colored trout, fat, quick, and strenuous."

500. The Fly Hatch That Loves Bad Weather

"I have fished little Blue-Winged Olive hatches that have continued for hours on rainy days. Show me a cool, inclement, drizzly afternoon in April and May or September and October and I'll show you a heavy hatch of little Blue-Winged Olives."

—Charles Meck, *Fishing Limestone Streams,* The Lyons Press, 2005

501. Those Splashy, Leaping Rises

When trout are leaping clear of the water in splashy rises, they are probably chasing emerging caddis.

502. Casting to Rising Trout

Yellowstone area expert and outfitter Craig Mathews on his favorite way to cover fish rising to duns or emergers: "I like to use a short, set-length cast—never more than 15 feet. This allows me to pick up and recast after the fly has traveled just enough beyond the fish that I can do so without spooking him and can get back out to him without false casting or stripping in slack."

—Craig Mathews, *Western Fly-Fishing Strategies*, The Lyons Press, 1998

503. Trout on the Move

In his book *Western Fly-Fishing Strategies*, Lyons Press (1998), expert angler and outfitter Craig Mathews cites a biologist's report that cutthroat trout from Yellowstone Lake have been tracked migrating 6 to 8 miles between the lake and the Buffalo Ford area in a single day. Similar activity occurs on the Lamar River, Mathews adds, and other smooth-water rivers in the area. "An area that produces one day can be void of fish the next," Mathews says.

504. Random Casting: It Won't Work on Spring Creeks

"Generally, blind fishing a spring creek where there is no surface activity is unproductive and accomplishes little but spooking trout," says Yellowstone area expert author and outfitter Craig Mathews in his excellent book, *Western Fly-Fishing Strategies*, Lyons Press (1998). Mathews adds that an exception occurs when terrestrials or damselflies are active.

505. Try Joe Brooks' Broadside Float

The legendary angler and writer Joe Brooks did an article for *Field & Stream* in May, 1961, called "The Broadside Float." In it, he reported having great success holding his streamers broadside to the current as they drifted downstream. He manipulated the streamers into the broadside presentation using line mends. Brooks felt the broadside float gave the trout a better view of their prey.

506. Leave Those Stressed Fish Alone

In high summer, you may be lucky enough to fish trout water that still has fish around. But if you find them all schooled up in pods at spring holes, that's a sure sign the temperatures have them under great stress. If you catch and release one of these fish, it may not survive the ordeal. Leave them alone until cooling rains and lower temperatures bring the stream back to normal.

507. Casting with Either Hand

Like great baseball players who can bat from either side, trout anglers who can cast left- or right-handed have a tremendous advantage. Even if you're a righty, and your left hand feels like a foreign object, try to get out there and practice. It will pay off with far more fish caught.

508. Fish Nymphs and Emergers With Upstream Casts

Yellowstone author and guide Craig Mathews, in his book *Western Fly-Fishing Strategies*, Lyons Press (1998), on fishing nymphs and emergers: "An upstream dead drift is the most productive cast for larger trout." Mathews says that anglers who float their nymphs down and across, mending occasionally, take smaller trout. They do it because it's an easy way to fish.

509. Stream Wading Rule One

Take short steps when wading your trout stream, big or small waters. And don't step on rocks that might roll under your feet.

510. Netting Your Trout

Making wild swipes at the water with your net is a sure way to knock a trout—big or small—off the line. Jabbing at the fish tail-first is another bad move. The right way: Submerge your net, pull the fish over it headfirst, and lift. You've got him!

511. A Fly Fisher's Creed

"When fishing's fast, move slow! When the fishing's slow, move fast. Above all, keep moving."
—Chuck Robbins, author and fly-fishing guide. Check the Web site he maintains with his wife, Gale, for his blog, articles, and information on books, www.chuckngalerobbins.com

512. Fly Fishing Beyond the Basics

"Beyond mastering the basics—casting, wading, reading the water, fly selection, etc.—the hardest thing for beginners to grasp is to keep moving, making the first shot count, then move on."

—Chuck Robbins, author and fly-fishing guide.
Check the Web site he maintains with his wife Gale for his blog, articles, and information on books www.chuckngalerobbins.com

513. Fly Fishing Rule One

"Regardless the rig—streamer, nymph, dry—strive to make each cast different. Lengthen the cast, move a step or two, change the angle, change the retrieve, etc. The *only* exceptions are when casting to visible fish—rising, feeding, resting underneath cover, whatever."

—Chuck Robbins, author and fly-fishing guide.
Check the Web site he maintains with his wife Gale for his blog, articles, and information on books www.chuckngalerobbins.com

514. Get That Nymph Down

"Most urgent [in nymph fishing] is to add whatever weight necessary to keep the nymphs on the bottom. A wise man once observed, 'The difference between a great day nymphing and a skunking is often one measly split-shot.'"

—Chuck Robbins, author and fly-fishing guide.
Check the Web site he maintains with his wife Gale for his blog, articles, and information on books www.chuckngalerobbins.com

515. No Hatch to Match? It's Time for Nymphs

Advice for fishing western rivers from a top guide and author: "Lacking a hatch, it's tough to beat a pair of nymphs rigged 5 or 6 feet or so below a strike indicator. Limited to just two patterns, a No. 10 Pat's Rubber Legs and a similar-sized red San Juan Worm would be my picks though my nymph box contains a good selection of beadhead and standard nymph patterns—Prince Pheasant Tail, Hare's Ear, Micro-May, Bloody Mary, Copper John, etc., in a variety of sizes and variations."

—Chuck Robbins, author and fly-fishing guide.
Check the Web site he maintains with his wife Gale for his blog, articles, and information on books www.chuckngalerobbins.com

516. When Summer Trout Move Out

During extremely hot weather, the real dog days of summer, you may not find trout bunched at the mouths of spring creeks entering your river. Look for them up the creek itself. They'll be very spooky, but they'll be there. Realize that many trout anglers do not fish during times like this, when the fish are under stress.

517. Where Trout Hold and Where They Rise

When trout are in holding water, they fin slowly, suspended, facing into the current. When they rise to take a fly, the splash or tiny swirl you see will usually be a little downstream of their holding lie. They take the fly, then swim back into their holding position. Keep that in mind when targeting your cast.

518. Fish Big Boulders on Both Sides

As soon as most trout anglers take up the sport, they learn to expect trout to be lying in the pockets behind boulders. The front sides of boulders also contain pockets, and the trout love them.

519. John Merwin On Blue-Winged Olives

In an article called "An Olive Afternoon: Problems and Solutions in Autumn Trout Fishing," on the *Field & Stream* Web site, veteran writer and angler John Merwin relates dealing with the ubiquitous Blue-Winged Olive hatches which take place in autumn over much of America. And, as Merwin describes, the Olives are enticing trout at a time when most anglers have racked up their rods. Which Blue-Winged Olive imitation to use, however, can be perplexing. "Once I had special fly boxes filled with nothing but Olive imitations in dozens of different styles. Fishing a just-right imitation became an obsession. I've finally decided there isn't one. Just about anything will work sometimes. Nothing works all the time." Available at www.fieldandstream.com.

520. John Merwin's Blue-Winged Olive Fly Choices

John Merwin has reduced the sometimes-bewildering process of "Which Blue-Winged Olive should I use?" to easy choices that catch fish, especially in the autumn. "In the past couple of years I've settled on four fly patterns, one of which will almost always work during a hatch of little Blue-Winged Olives. Exactly which of the four will work seems to change not only from day to day but also during a single afternoon. These are a Pheasant-Tail Nymph, an RS2 Emerger, a CDC Olive Emerger, and an olive-bodied spinner—all in Sizes 18 through 24." Available at www.fieldandstream.com.

521. Why You Should Fish for Cutthroats

In angling literature and popularity, the cutthroat sometimes does not get the respect of the popular rainbows, browns, or even our native brook trout. A vast number of anglers, however, agree with some writers who pull out their best stuff in tribute of these beautiful, wild fish found in the high country of the West, from the Rocky Mountains to the Alaska coastlines. Here's Frank Dufresne at his best in a *Field & Stream* article, "Trout Trouble," May, 1955: "I've never known the right words to do justice to a cutthroat trout . . . It's not that they fight so savagely as some other gamefish . . . Could be it's that wild Alaska water they live in, the amber-tinted, foam-flecked stretches winding in the midday gloom of valley bottoms where

the logger's ax has never chopped a hole to sunlight. . . . Good chance it's the company they keep, because bear, deer, and timber wolves are their neighbors."

522. Give Trout Unlimited Your Support

Since July 1959, Trout Unlimited has grown to 450 chapters with 150,000 serious and avid anglers. Their work with stream restoration and trout conservation has been a national treasure. There are lots of benefits for joining. Check them out at www.tu.org.

523. Seeing Trout: Rule One

"Perhaps the most common factor that betrays the trout is its movement. So imprint this upon your mind: *movement equals fish.*"

—John Goddard and Brian Clarke, *Understanding Trout Behavior*,
The Lyons Press, 2001

524. Weeds: The Trout Stream Signpost

Weeds in trout streams are like signposts that say, "Fish Here!" Weeds not only provide cover for the trout, but for the food the trout needs to live.

525. Fishing Trout Stream Weeds

You'll find trout lying in the calmer water at the heads of weed patches, under the weed patches themselves, and downstream where the constant sweeping of the weed arms have eroded the streambed.

526. You Have to Be Sneaky to Catch Trout

Your approach to trout stream pools, and your very first casts, mean everything to your ultimate success. Careless approaches and careless casts will spook trout, sending them bolting from the pool, or—and this happens more often—alert trout that something is amiss. Once alerted, they may not strike for some time. You'll be thinking, "They're not biting today." But that's not the case at all.

527. When Your Fly Is Snagged

When your fly snags on the bottom or on a rock or limb in a trout stream, *do not* pull back hard in an attempt to free it. Instead, use a Roll Cast, which will pull the fly in the opposite direction and often free it.

528. The Roll Cast: A Fly-Fishing Must

Not only is the Roll Cast useful for freeing your fly from snags, in many situations you will not have room behind you or to the side for a backcast. That's where the Roll Cast will pay big dividends for every moment you've spent learning it.

529. The Upper Delaware: The Big East Trout Mecca

Its call is irresistible to the myriad of fly fishermen who live in the greater New York and Philadelphia areas—and beyond. The upper Delaware in the vicinity of Hancock, New York, about 300 miles from where it enters Delaware Bay, is the source of New York City's drinking water and about 80 miles of trout waters. The upper Delaware's three stems—the West Branch, the

East Branch, and the Main Stem—are often called the East's answer to the storied trout fishing in the American West. The Delaware is the longest undammed river east of the Mississippi. Fittingly, its upper reaches are the homes of myriad wild trout. But they are challenging to fish, as many anglers will attest.

530. How to Start Fishing the Upper Delaware

Articles are constantly appearing in popular fishing and outdoor magazines that focus on the difficulties of the wild trout fishing in the upper Delaware, in the vicinity of Hancock, New York. These tomes are fine in their own right, and I always read them eagerly. But, if you're really serious about fishing these waters, you absolutely must obtain your copy of the definitive book, the absolute must-have journal of fishing the upper Delaware. Paul Weamer's *Fly-Fishing Guide to the Upper Delaware River*, Stackpole Books (2007), has everything you need to know to start fishing this wonderful destination. He breaks the rivers down by sections, and tells it like it is on where, when, and how—including guides, tackle, *dos* and *don'ts*. This is one fantastic book!

531. The Upper Delaware's Dark Side

This truth about fishing the upper Delaware stands out as being an absolute fact: Fishing the water for opportunistic feeders during the day gets you nothing—most of the time. The fly hatches, and all the action, take place at the end of the day. Stretches where you would swear there are no trout during the day, come alive with rising fish.

532. When the Upper Delaware is Right

Bright, sunny days on the upper Delaware are tough to fish, with the action occurring at dusk only. The fish are super-sensitive to the light and the dangers that come from above, like the large numbers of eagles and ospreys that abound in the area. On a bright sunny day you may be in for a long boat ride, with splendid scenery but not the hatches and rising trout you came to find.

533. Which Upper Delaware Branch to Fish?

The realities on picking one of the three upper Delaware branches to fish can be summed up this way: The West Branch, the top water, is smaller than the Main Stem, and much more crowded in mayfly time than the lower waters. The Main Stem is larger, longer, has more places to fish, but considering its size the trout are more spread out than on the West Branch. The East Branch is smaller than the other two, packed with trout, but access is a major issue, and the fishing depends on the water being released from the Downsville impoundment. Of course, if you're booking a guide, he will know which branch is fishing the best.

534. Upper Delaware Guided Days

If the fish are really on, and the weather is cloudy and right for hatches, you may hit the upper Delaware exactly right with a guided float and have a day or two for the books. If these conditions do not exist, you probably have booked a long and expensive boat ride.

535. Blind Casting the Dry Fly

"Riffles [on New York's upper Delaware] break the surface and help disguise leaders and tippets in the chop. I have caught a lot of trout by blind casting dry flies upriver in the upper Delaware's riffles, but very few while casting upriver in the pools."

—Paul Weamer, *Fly-Fishing Guide to the Upper Delaware River*, Stackpole Books, 2007

536. Surface Feeders: Three Casts and Out

"Once I find a rising fish and slowly move into the proper casting position, I cast only three times for each time the fish rises. If the fish hasn't eaten my fly by the third cast, I stop casting and watch and wait until the fish rises again."

—Paul Weamer, *Fly-Fishing Guide to the Upper Delaware River*, Stackpole Books, 2007

537. The Dry Fly Fished Downstream on Big Rivers

Although upstream stalking and casting is the tradition for dry fly fishing, many shrewd anglers who fish big-water rivers like the Delaware in the East and the upper Missouri in the West favor a downstream cast. They get into position a good distance above the fish and slightly to the side. They cast quartering downstream to the rising fish, then mend the line upstream to get a straight downstream line-leader-fly float—without drag.

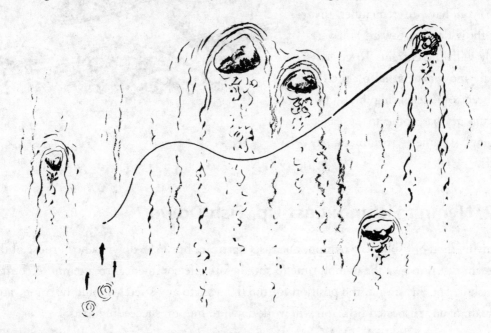

538. Streamers Need Speed

"Many anglers strip their streamers too slow. It is impossible to strip a streamer faster than a trout can catch it."

—Paul Weamer, *Fly-Fishing Guide to the Upper Delaware River*, Stackpole Books, 2007

539. Streamers: The "Go-To" Flies

"What kind of an artificial can be used at all times and anywhere, whether flies are hatching or not? The streamer or bucktail, of course, the development of which in the 1930s represented a major breakthrough in trout fishing."

—S.R. Slaymaker II, *Tie a Fly, Catch a Trout*, Harper & Row, 1976

540. Dry-Fly Purist Bunk

When you check out a dry fly "purist"—the flyfisher who says, "It's a dry fly, or nothing"— you'll often find he doesn't do any nymph fishing simply because he can't do it.

541. Ripping Streamers

Sometimes the only way to get into position to work streamers through likely looking water is from the downstream side, casting upstream. Then you have to remember that your fly is floating toward you very swiftly with the current. To get any realistic movement at all on the fly, you need to be retrieving line so fast that the act has come to be called "ripping streamers" by many fly fishers.

542. Nymph Fishing: Cast Up, Fish Down

"In my method of fishing the nymph, one casts upstream but *fishes* down. The purpose of the upstream cast is to give the nymph time to sink before one commences to attempt to control and fish it. For this reason, the position for the first cast to any stretch should be some yards upstream of any suspected fish. You will work down to him on succeeding casts."

—Charles E. Brooks, *Nymph Fishing for Larger Trout*, Crown Publishers, 1976

543. And Still Champion: The Muddler Minnow

The Muddler Minnow has probably made more "Best Fly" lists than any other. Why? Because it catches trout. You can find it in every fly shop and fly-fishing catalog, in many hook sizes. You can dress it and fish it dry on the surface; you can work it down and across like a streamer; and you can let it bounce along the bottom like a nymph. Like the Woolly Bugger, the Muddler Minnow belongs in your fly box.

544. Delaware Rainbows Are Special

"Delaware rainbows are genetically different, something special—a 14-incher can put you into backing. And because it's got plenty of space and food, every fish has the potential to be 20 inches."

—Famed Catskill and upper Delaware (New York) angler Ed Van Put, quoted in J.L. Merritt's *Trout Dreams: A Gallery of Fly-Fishing Profiles*, The Derrydale Press, 2000

545. Tactics of an Upper Delaware Legend

"I catch a lot of fish in the last thirty minutes of the evening. It's not exactly night fishing, because there's still a little light. I call it 'dark' fishing. You can't see the fly anymore, but you can see the rises. Cast ahead of them, and if the fish stop rising hold your cast until they start coming up again."

—Famed Catskill and upper Delaware (New York) angler Ed Van Put, quoted in J.L. Merritt's *Trout Dreams: A Gallery of Fly-Fishing Profiles*, The Derrydale Press, 2000

546. Don't Strike That Trout Too Soon

Upper Delaware rainbows take surface flies deliberately, and many anglers are spurred into a hair-trigger strike that misses the fish. "You've got to strike the rise, not the fly. Even if I can see the fly, I try not to look at it."

—Famed Catskill and upper Delaware (New York) angler Ed Van Put, quoted in J.L. Merritt's *Trout Dreams: A Gallery of Fly-Fishing Profiles*, The Derrydale Press, 2000

547. The Ed Van Put Fly Selections

"While Ed Van Put is reputed to fish the Adams exclusively, a glance through his fly box belies this. If no fish are rising, he said, he may search the water with a Chuck Caddis, a Henryville Special, or a Cream Variant. For nymphs he favors the Zug Bug, and he occasionally fishes downstream with traditional wet flies like the Royal Coachman and Cow Dung."

—J.L. Merritt on famed Catskill and upper Delaware (New York) angler Ed Van Put in
Trout Dreams: A Gallery of Fly-Fishing Profiles, The Derrydale Press, 2000

548. A Deadly Nymphing Technique

In his book *Trout Dreams: A Gallery of Fly-Fishing Profiles*, The Derrydale Press (2000), Jim Merritt describes fishing techniques of many legendary fly fishers. This excerpt on Chuck Fothergill, famed for his angling prowess in Colorado's Roaring Fork and Frying Pan rivers, describes Fothergill's deadly nymphing technique. What follows is an absolutely deadly way of fishing a nymph. You'll find it to be one of the most productive of the tips in this book: "Using a floating line with a leader weighted with several twisted-on lead strips, he quartered a short cast upstream. He held the rod high, his arm angled like the Statue of Liberty's, and kept it that way through most of the drift. As the line drew abreast of him and continued downstream, he followed it with the rod, which he lowered gently to maintain a drag-free float. At the end of the drift he lifted the rod, swinging the nymph toward the surface. Probing the run carefully, he was quickly into a fat rainbow which leaped explosively and stripped line off the reel as it charged downstream."

549. A Fly That Will Live Forever

Al Troth tied his original Elkhair Caddis from the hairs of a bull elk, then later switched to the cow elk, bleached for greater visibility. First tied in 1957, the Elkhair has joined the ranks of flies such as the Muddler Minnow, the Adams, and the Pheasant Tail nymphs as standard

fish-takers. Troth says that besides caddis, "It'll imitate stoneflies, little hoppers, any number of things. The trout ate it in 1957, they eat it now, and they'll eat it twenty years from now."

—Al Troth, in J.L. Merritt's *Trout Dreams: A Gallery of Fly-Fishing Profiles*, The Derrydale Press, 2000

550. Heads-Up Nymph Fishing

"Some 98 percent of mayfly nymphs come to the surface head up. For most imitations, therefore, it's not a bad idea to weight the upper third of the hook."

—Famed Pennsylvania angler Joe Humphreys, in J.L. Merritt's *Trout Dreams: A Gallery of Fly-Fishing Profiles*, The Derrydale Press, 2000

551. Hitting the Hatch at Prime Time

"The easiest time to catch rising fish is at the beginning and end of the hatch. Early in the hatch you'll find a lot of juvenile fish, but as the hatch gets heavier, the bigger fish appear, and a pecking order starts to prevail."

—Famed angler and author Al Caucci, in J.L. Merritt's *Trout Dreams: A Gallery of Fly-Fishing Profiles*, The Derrydale Press, 2000

552. Where Trout Are Feeding

"Consider the current as an underwater cafeteria line, only instead of the fish moving to the food, the food comes to the fish."

—Dick Galland, "Master Basic Nymphing," in *Fly Fisherman Magazine*'s "Nymphing for Trout" booklet

553. Current Seams: Where the Trout Are

"Then consider a trout's other requirements in moving water—relief from the current and shelter from danger—and you'll know where to begin. Target the edges of eddies, slower-water seams, and deep runs that are close to the main current. Trout swim out, take a food item, and return to cover."

—Dick Galland, "Master Basic Nymphing," in *Fly Fisherman Magazine*'s "Nymphing for Trout" booklet

554. Add Weight Before Changing Flies

"If you find yourself fishing a spot that looks ideal, but you are not getting strikes, add weight to make sure the fly is on the bottom before changing flies."

—Dick Galland, "Master Basic Nymphing," in *Fly Fisherman Magazine*'s "Nymphing for Trout" booklet

555. Saying No to Strike Indicators

"Today there is an implied presumption that if you fish a nymph, you must use a strike indicator . . . Though indicators are a necessity in certain situations, they are a handicap in other circumstances . . . On some heavily fished streams, the fish learn to associate the glowing orange ball with a threat and they become reluctant to feed."

—Jim McLennan, "Nymphing Without Indicators," in *Fly Fisherman Magazine*'s "Nymphing for Trout" booklet

556. Other Strike Indicator Negatives

Despite their popularity, strike indicators do have certain negatives: They splat down on the surface when cast . . . they drag on the surface, causing the fly to drift at an unnatural speed, usually too fast . . . they present the fly at a fixed depth, instead of getting it to the varying depths of the stream . . . they sometimes catch the wind on casts, making accuracy difficult.

557. Fly Stories: An Orvis Treasury

One of the many things I like about the Orvis site, www.orvis.com, is "Fly Stories" in the fly-fishing section. These are short tales told by anglers of various flies they have used—and the fly decisions were made and what happened. It's great stuff.

558. Gary LaFontaine: His Endless Legacy

Before losing a courageous battle with Lou Gehrig's disease (ALS) at the age of fifty-six, Gary LaFontaine became one of fly fishing's greatest anglers, authors, fly tyers, and ambassadors of sportsmanship. His books include *Caddisflies*, *Fly Fishing the Mountain Lakes*, *The Dry Fly: New Angles*, and *Trout Flies: Proven Patterns*. He is featured in several DVDs and co-authored many fishing guides in book form and pocket form. Living in the Montana high country, and fishing there and all over the world, Gary built a legacy that can be best experienced at the site dedicated to his name www.thebookmailer.com. Here you will find gear from the LaFontaine private label, plus books, DVDs, and fishing guides from scores of authors and sources. A newsletter is available. LaFontaine Private Label, PO Box 1273, Helena, MT 59624-1273; 800-874-4171.

559. Fishing the High-Country Lakes

If you're thinking about doing a pack trip into the high-country lakes of the great western mountains, you'll want to read a copy of the late Gary LaFontaine's *Fly Fishing the Mountain Lakes*, Greycliff Publishing (1998). The book is available from the site honoring Gary, www.thebookmailer.com. The book is packed with details on everything from planning and packing, to specific mountain lake fishing techniques. Gary loved this type of fishing so much that he became quite an expert on what to pack in—and how to do it—including his decision to always take a kick boat, no matter what packing challenges it created.

560. When An Entire Pod of Trout Are Rising Right in Front of You

Standing opposite a pod of rising trout, as can happen on the best rivers, will likely set your heart racing and your fingers trembling. Now's the time to be cool, however. A cast right into the bunch will probably scatter them in a frenzy. Try to get into position below the pod, downstream from it, and cast toward a fish on the outside. If he's hooked, and you can keep him from running into the pack, you may pick off a couple more doing the same thing.

561. Best Way to Fish Mountain Lakes from Shore

In his book *Fly Fishing the Mountain Lakes,* Greycliff Publishing (1998), available from the site www.thebookmailer.com, the late Gary LaFontaine describes his favorite technique for fishing from the shore in mountain lakes as "Multiple Roll Casts." He starts with three Roll casts *short* of the drop-off. Next three are *right on* the drop-off. Then five casts *beyond* the drop-off. The slowly advancing fly seems to excite trout lurking in the depths.

562. The Pack Boat for Mountain Lake Fishing

In his book *Fly Fishing the Mountain Lakes,* Greycliff Publishing (1998), available from the site www.thebookmailer.com, the late Gary LaFontaine describes in detail his favorite gear and techniques. An interesting aspect of his decision on what to pack in is revealed here: "A flotation device—for me it has to be an inflatable kick boat, not a float tube—gives the fly fisherman access to all the areas of a lake that the crowds don't fish." LaFontaine was willing to use whatever means possible—goats, alpacas, llamas, horses—to pack in everything he needed. If he couldn't manage a kick boat, he carried a lightweight backpacker's float tube.

563. Mountain Lakes: The Gifts From Above

"One of the secrets of mountain lakes is that the vertical winds, not horizontal ones, deposit most of the food on the water. The other secret is that trout in these lakes, given a choice, prefer to feed on the surface." This tip comes from the late Gary LaFontaine in his book *Fly Fishing the Mountain Lakes,* Greycliff Publishing (1998). He's referring to the anabatic winds that "rush up the mountain slopes like the air up a chimney." He continues, "Look for upslope winds on warm afternoons." With these tips, you can easily see why you would be foolish to plan a backpack adventure in the high Rocky Mountain lakes without reading Gary's book. You can obtain a copy at www.thebookmailer.com.

564. Pairing the Hatch

In his book *Fly Fishing the Mountain Lakes,* Greycliff Publishing (1998), the late Gary LaFontaine describes his technique of picking off a feeding fish when a multitude of bugs are on the water. He watches the direction the fish is feeding, picks up the next most-likely insect, then places his cast an inch or so in front of the natural. Focused on the natural, but with a sudden new opportunity in front of it, the trout usually takes Gary's fly. You can obtain Gary's books at www.thebookmailer.com.

565. Best Days to Fish a Mayfly Hatch

In his classic *A Summer on the Test* (1924, republished by Nick Lyons Books/Winchester Press in 1984), the English writer John Waller Hills takes dead aim at picking the best days to fish the big mayfly hatches of his beloved Test River and other waters. "My experience has been so unvarying, that if I were told I was to have only two days fishing during the period, I should choose my days with every confidence . . . By the fourth day (since the main fly hatch began) trout have acquired the taste of the newly hatched fly and are taking it confidently . . . the big fish are moving by then . . . This is the first great chance, the fourth day. And the next is the twelfth day, by which time the fly is going off and trout know it, and are making the most of the short time remaining."

566. Early Season Fly Hatches

Here's the legendary English writer John Waller Hills on early season hatches in his classic book *A Summer on the Test* (1924, republished in later editions): " . . . So I finished up with eight fish: a good day. . . . Now these two days were the opposite of each other; the first, fine and hot, produced hardly any fly and two fish, and the second, bitterly cold, showed an immense hatch and four brace of fine trout. Never, never believe that cold weather hinders fly. You will hear it, always and everywhere; but it is not only untrue but the reverse of truth. Except at the very beginning of April, you get more fly on a cold day than on a warm." Of course, Hills was speaking of his English hatches, but you can apply his wisdom to your own waters.

567. A Very Special Tip for Fly-Fishing Beginners

In this quote, the legendary English writer John Waller Hills in his classic book *A Summer on the Test* (1924, republished in later editions) is speaking of dry fly fishing in particular, but his intention to "clear the air" applies to all forms of fly fishing: " . . . what I want to impress on any reader who is not a dry fly fisherman is that dry fly fishing is much easier than it sounds. There is a conspiracy of anglers, started by Halford [the English expert and writer] and carried on with increasing momentum by later writers, to make out that the art is so dreadfully obscure that none but the gifted should attempt it. The perplexed beginner, poring over the great masters, reads of the accuracy and delicacy required . . . how a single mistake is fatal, how he must be able to recognize at a glance each of the hundred and one insects on which trout feed . . . He despairs of reaching this level . . . He is completely mislead. He believes what is egregious nonsense. The sport has its difficulties, and they are not small; but in the first place anyone with ordinary ability can surmount them, and in the second the price paid for failure is not nearly as great as writers would have us believe. You can make heaps of mistakes and yet kill plenty of fish on a difficult river and a difficult day. . . . believe me, it is not nearly as hard as it sounds."

568. Wade in Carefully, Stop Spooking Trout

I watched a guy wading into the Missouri River, his rod and fly ready. Clearly, he was looking out in the current, where several rainbows were rising in a nice pod. What he didn't realize, or take time to discover, was that there were many more fish holding in the current right by the shore. He waded into them, intent on the distant pod. The fish bolted away, taking the pod fish with them. It pays to not be in such a hurry. Look trout water over very carefully before wading ahead.

569. How an Expert Plays Big Trout

"Let a large trout get his head down and he will dictate the fight, but keep his head up and

he cannot run effectively. You will quickly realize how much easier it is to control a fish on the surface, and to bring the battle to a rapid conclusion."

—John Goddard, *A Fly Fisher's Reflections*, The Lyons Press, 2002

570. Big Trout in Weedy Water

"I learned early on—and painfully!—that when fishing for trout of 4-pound-plus in weedy water, it is a question of holding on as soon as you set the hook, or the fish is as good as lost."

—John Goddard, *A Fly Fisher's Reflections*, The Lyons Press, 2002

571. Stay Out of the Trout's Rear-Vision Mirror

In studies with English author Brian Clarke for the book *The Trout & the Fly*, noted angler and author John Goddard reached the conclusion that trout have superb 45-degree vision to the rear and recommends the following tactic to cope: " . . . try positioning yourself opposite or even slightly upstream of any trout rising very close to the surface and cast to him from this position as I think he will be less likely to see you, but do remember to avoid any sudden movements and where possible cast sideways with a wrist movement to avoid moving your arms."

—John Goddard, *A Fly Fisher's Reflections*, The Lyons Press, 2002

572. Nymph Fishing Made Easy

The greatest discovery in the history of fly fishing—as far as float-fishing guides in the high-country West have discovered—is nymph fishing. Not the classic nymph fishing of most American trout streams, spawned from English experts like Frank Sawyer and company, but using a couple of nymphs tied in tandem below a strike indicator that floats on the surface. That strike indicator—they come in all different shapes and sizes—is nothing more than an elaborate bobber. Picture this: You started out years and years ago fishing with a bobber. Now, you've got the money and time to book a top guide on one of Montana's top streams, like the

Big Horn or Beaverhead, and you're floating along in the raft chunking out a stretch of fly line (yes, "chunking" is the right word, not "casting") with a couple of weighted nymphs tied to a "bobber"—aka, "strike indicator"—riding the current. Okay, you're having fun, catching trout. I have no problem with that, so long as you see the irony.

573. How to See More Trout

"Trout are dim, uncertain and nearly invisible. You learn after a time where to look and what to look for. You must not expect to see a whole trout, outlined as solidly as though lying on a fishmonger's slab; any fool can see that: but what you have to train yourself to pick out is a flicker, a movement, a darkness, a luminosity which if you stare at it hard enough will resolve itself into a shadowy form."

—The legendary English writer John Waller Hills in his classic book *A Summer on the Test* (1924, republished by Nick Lyons Books/Winchester Press in 1984)

574. Play That Fish from the Reel?

You'll usually have some loose line in your hand when you hook a trout, and now the question becomes whether to pull the fish in by hand, or get the slack line onto the reel first? My own preference is to hold the line fast against the rod while reeling up the slack as quickly as possible, then playing the fish from the reel. I find that when I try to bring in the fish by pulling on the line itself, I lose a great deal of feel and break off more fish. On the other hand, when a big fish is on the line, fiddling around with the line and the reel during the first moments of the fight can be disastrous. I've had good results, and bad results, doing it both ways.

575. The Easy Way—and the Best Way

Fishing your spinning lure or fly downstream for trout seems a natural and easy way to fish. After all, the fish are lying facing into the current, where your bait or fly is headed directly to them. Fishing upstream, however, gives you the advantage of stealth, sneaking up on the fish.

576. The Right Times to Fish the Wrong Flies

There's an old trick that sometimes really does work when you're into rising trout and just can't seem to get them interested in your imitations. Switch to an easy-to-see fly like a No. 14 Royal Wulff or an Adams, and you might be surprised by the results.

577. A Trick for Fishing a Tough Hatch

In high summer in the East and on some Rocky Mountain rivers like the upper Missouri, the hatch of the tiny tricothrids (trico) is a landmark event, luring fly fishers who try to match the hatch. Despite the fish-rising activity, trying to get a fish interested in your tiny (No. 22) fly is quite a challenge. Some experienced anglers claim a change-of-pace is needed here. They go to a terrestrial, an ant, or a beetle. When the tricos come, trout have already been feeding on beetles a great deal, and your bogus beetle floated among the tricos may get customers.

578. You're Down Or You're Out!

Sometimes, the messages in magazine advertising copy are so well done that they simply cannot be ignored. This comes from the Cortland Line Company in an ad on page 22 of the February-March 2004 issue of *Gray's Sporting Journal*: "Get down. . . . Way down. . . Faster. . . . Way faster . . . In this type of fly fishing, you're either down or you're out." The ad was for Cortland's 555 Rocket QDs, made to get your fly into the strike zone faster. Available at www.cortlandline.com.

579. Rocks and Trout: Pinpointing the Lies

"The trout likes the upstream sides of rocks, logs, and . . . other solid objects . . . for exactly the same reasons that he likes the tops of hatches: because he has a splendid view of what the current is bringing him; and yet is cushioned from the weight of the water."
—John Goddard and Brian Clarke, *Understanding Trout Behavior*, 2001

580. Trout Under the Bridge

"Any fisherman with more than a morning's experience knows that the water beneath a bridge is a likely lie for a trout; and often, for a big trout. It is that rare phenomenon, the 'complete' lie . . . The narrower a section of the river is, the deeper it will be . . . "
—John Goddard and Brian Clarke, *Understanding Trout Behavior*, 2001

581. The Devilish Smutting Rises

In the United Kingdom, anglers call it a curse. The legendary "smutting rise" occurs plenty in America, too. It happens when trout are feeding in the surface film on tiny larvae and pupa of midges. Often only tiny rings show on the water as they suck in the flies. Reach for the smallest Griffith's Gnat you can tie on.

582. What Color Leader?

The question of whether or not your leader should be a certain color—or no color at all—has been around trout streams for a long time, even back when you had to dye your own leaders if you wanted them colored a certain way. Here are a few choice words from the legendary A. J. McClane, from his fishing column in *Field & Stream*, November, 1949: "I have made dozens of leaders dyed with methylene blue, potassium hydroxide, malachite green, Bismarck brown, tea, coffee, and iodine. Aside from messing up the sink, they left no other mark in fishing history. . . . I much prefer an opaque or nearly translucent material, the kind commonly labeled 'mist,' for all fishing above surface or below."

583. The Perfect Small-Stream Trout Rod

Opinions abound on the subject of the perfect rod for small-stream trout fishing. Here's one you can take to the bank: You want a short rod, 7 feet, to handle the overhanging limbs and close brush along the sides of the stream. You must have a fast, powerful tip. It will get your short line out fast and sure. You want all this in the lightest rod you can find, one that comes alive in your hand. You'll enjoy every cast, and the feel of a fighting fish will be your ultimate reward. The long-rod advocates will cry "Foul!" at this opinion, claiming to have more control with the longer stick. To each his own. In small streams, go with the short rod and keep your fly and line in the water instead of the trees and bushes.

584. Upstream Or Downstream?

You've got your favorite creek or stream all to yourself for a change. What's it to be: upstream or downstream? The usual method is to fish your floating flies in an upstream direction, while fishing nymphs and streamers downstream. There's not a thing wrong with that game plan.

585. The Most Important 10 Inches in Trout Fishing

"Scientists have found that most of the trout taken on nymphs are within 10 inches of the river bottom . . . That's where the food is, and because the food is there and the current runs more slowly, there'll be a lot of fish there."

—Lefty Kreh, with Chris Millard,
My Life Was THIS BIG and Other True Fishing Tales, Skyhorse Publishing, 2008

586. Midsummer, Low-Water Conditions: Go With a Dry Fly

Author and trout expert, Leonard M. Wright, Jr., was a writer I respected and felt privileged to publish when I was editor of *Sports Afield* magazine. In one, "Give Summer Trout a Moveable Feast," he went against tradition in urging anglers to use a dry fly fished with a twitch for midsummer trout. Wright reasoned that in midsummer, daylight hours, the nymphs and other bottom-dwellers were hiding under rocks, emerging only at dusk and night. "The main food supply most of the day is made up of insects that have flown or tumbled onto the surface and

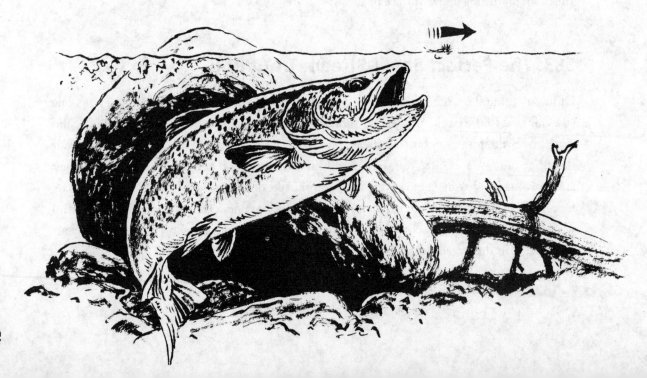

these, trapped in the rubbery surface film, are carried downstream on top of the water," Wright wrote in the article, republished in his book *Fly Fishing Heresies*, Winchester Press, (1975).

587. Twitch Your Midsummer Dry Fly

"To catch a loafing trout's attention (in midsummer) and to gain his confidence, your dry fly should move—and move as a living insect does. This means a small movement, not a great plowing wake. And it should move in an upstream direction. For all stream-bred flies, whether hatching out or returning for egg-laying, move in an upstream direction."

—Leonard M. Wright, Jr., *Fly Fishing Heresies*, Winchester Press, 1975

588. Leonard Wright's Summer Dry Fly Technique

" . . . you break with tradition and cast your fly in an across-and-downstream direction, when you give it a tiny twitch it will lurch upstream. Then let it float free again as long as it will."

—Leonard M. Wright, Jr., *Fly Fishing Heresies*, Winchester Press, 1975

589. Your Summer Trout Fishing Will Improve

"A fly twitched slightly on the surface will raise trout all day long on the much-neglected pools and long flats where the dead-drift nymph or dry fly would seem very dead, indeed."

—Leonard M. Wright, Jr., *Fly Fishing Heresies*, Winchester Press, 1975.

590. Finding Maryland's Best Trout Streams

For the outdoorsman, Maryland is a state truly blessed with opportunities—from the beaches of the Atlantic, the vast Chesapeake Bay and its environs, to the mountains and valleys in the western part of the state. There are trout streams galore here, of varying quality and stocking conditions, and the perfect guide to finding the stream that's right for you is the wonderful book, *Guide to Maryland Trout Fishing: The Catch-and-Release Streams*, by Larry Coburn and Charlie Gelso, Falling Star Publishing (2006, updated regularly). It's available from www.amazon.com and many tackle shops. This is an absolute "must-have" book for trout anglers looking for great fishing on Maryland streams.

591. A Trout Stream Where Legends Were Created

Maryland's Big Hunting Creek, not far from Frederick and a stone's throw from the famous Camp David, retreat of Presidents, is the stream where legendary angler Joe Brooks and others started the Brotherhood of the Jungle Cock group in the 1940s, teaching fly fishing to youngsters. There is a Joe Brooks Memorial in the upper section of the stream, which still ranks as one of Maryland's most interesting and beautiful to fish. See the book *Guide to Maryland Trout Fishing: The Catch-and-Release Streams*, by Larry Coburn and Charlie Gelso, Falling Star Publishing (2006, updated regularly).

592. The Drift of the Dry Fly

"The line of drift of the naturals is important to presentation too, and the fly must be placed to duplicate its route."

—Ernest Schwiebert, *Trout*, E.P. Dutton, 1978

593. Are Your Hands Poisoned?

"It is not fully known if trout and grayling are as sensitive to odor as salmon, but the old ghillie who taught me nymph fishing on the Lauterach in Bavaria believed that a particularly sensitive fish could probably smell his fingers on his flies. His secret was a leader soak box—thick felt pads saturated in trout slime—for his nymphs."

—Ernest Schwiebert, *Trout*, E.P. Dutton, 1978

594. Fishing the Spinner Rises

"Fully spent and exhausted spinners are virtually impossible to see on the water. Many seemingly unexplained rises of fish, particularly in late afternoon and evening, are triggered by large numbers of dead or dying spinners lying flush in the surface film. Often the only method of identifying such a spinner fall lies in identifying the mating swarm that precedes it, or observing the dwindling flight of male spinners that remain over the water."

—Ernest Schwiebert, *Trout*, E.P. Dutton, 1978

595. Stay On Watch for Sipping Rises

"Always pay particular attention to the fish which are sipping under the banks, and don't be deluded into the notion that because you see a fish make more break on the water than a minnow would, that he is a minnow, for he is quite likely to be a three-pounder."

—Francis Francis, *Book of Angling*, 1867, as referenced by Ernest Schwiebert in *Trout*, E.P. Dutton, 1978

596. Small Rise, Big Trout

"It is strange how quietly a big fish will often take fly after fly, close to a bank, with only just his upper lip pushed into the surface to suck in the victim."

—Francis Francis, *Book of Angling*, 1867, as referenced by Ernest Schwiebert in *Trout*, E.P. Dutton, 1978

597. Schwiebert's Fly Line Color Choices

In his magnum-opus, *Trout*, E.P. Dutton (1978), legendary angler and writer Ernest Schwiebert discusses the improved visibility of bright and white fly lines, saying they're great for photography and watching your line. But, for serious fishing: "Yet, I still use a dark mahogany-colored line for the difficult, hyperselective fish on my home waters in the eastern mountains, and I feel it has been more effective on the shy fish of our famous western spring creeks. Fishing deep I prefer darker colors . . . Pale colors are unwise in a sinking line that works deep among the fish and is viewed laterally against the adjacent colors of the bottom."

598. Eliminating Drag: The Key to Successful Dry Fly Fishing

From the moment anglers make their first cast with a dry fly, they start learning that drag is the great boogeyman of dry fly fishing. You'll see it often, and you'll hear about it everywhere fly fishers gather. Drag occurs when the current pulls the fly line and leader downstream from the fly, dragging the fly across the water, leaving a large, small, or even miniscule wake. It doesn't look natural, and the fish know it, and won't hit it. The late George Harvey, Penn State angling instructor, author, and an angler of legendary talent, made studies of drag with an intensity few have equaled and came up with some useful ideas on defeating it. He writes about it all in his book *Techniques of Trout Fishing and Fly Tying*, Lyons & Burford (1990): "I have seen anglers stand in one spot and change flies for over an hour and still never take a fish," Harvey says. "On many occasions, by moving just a step to the right or left the angler could, on the next cast, eliminate drag and take the trout on the original pattern."

599. Eliminating Drag: The George Harvey Solution

In a lifetime of studying drag and its deadly impact on dry fly fishing, the late, legendary Penn State Angling Professor George Harvey came up with some real answers. He decided that "perfect" casts were not the answer. The problem, he felt, lay in the leaders. When leaders straightened, a dragging fly was the result. He came up with a formula that would allow a leader to fall in S-curves, giving the fly a longer drag-free float. He started by going against the universal heavy-butt requirement of the times. He wrote about it in his classic, *Techniques of Trout Fishing and Fly Tying*, Lyons & Burford (1990): " . . . I do not use the heavy-butt leaders . . . I want the S curves in the leader to progressively get longer from the fly to the line. The heavy-butt leaders will not give you this progression . . . If you use this design for your dry-fly fishing, you will increase your catch by at least fifty percent." Here is the design Harvey recommended for a hard nylon 9.5-foot leader with 5X tippet: Starting with the nail knot, 10 inches of .017; 20 inches of .015; 20 inches of .013; 20 inches .011; 12 inches of .009; 12 inches of .008; 18 inches of .007; 22 to 30 inches of .006. Although not butt heavy, Harvey's leaders were constructed with stiff monofilament in the first four butt sections, then soft mono in the rest of the leader. Of course, there are many more details on constructing and using such leaders in George Harvey's book. Remember: We are talking dry fly leaders here, not leaders for nymphs and streamers, which need to straighten so you can follow the drift of the underwater fly by watching the end of the leader or the strike indicator.

600. Buying George Harvey S-Curve Leaders

No, you don't have to tie those George Harvey leaders to cut drag by 50 percent, like George Harvey promised—unless you want to. You can buy them from Frog Hair, the Gamma Technologies company that makes and sells leaders, tippets, and fly flotation dressings (excellent ones, I might add). Look for the Dry Fly Slack Line Leader with George Harvey's picture on the cover of the sleeve. Frog Hair offers 4X, 5X, and 6X tippet sizes in 11 ½ feet. I bought mine on www.amazon.com, but you can find other sites, including the excellent site www.feather-craft.com. Or Google Frog Hair Leaders or go directly to Frog Hair, www.froghairfishing.com. The leaders are knotless and are said to represent the requirements for the desirable S-curve that beats drag. Instructions for casting are on the back of the sleeve.

601. Gary Borger's S-Curve Drag-Free Ideas

Author and angler Gary Borger came up with a way to tie S-curve leaders with fewer sections (and fewer blood knots) than in the George Harvey method. He offered his ideas in his book *Presentation,* which is out of print and sells on Amazon and other sites for more than $225. In the book, Borger has optimum leaders for nymphing and other techniques as well. Perhaps someday an enterprising publisher will reissue the book.

602. Bottoms-Up Tactic for Finicky Feeders

When trout don't seem to be hitting and are probably hugging the bottom, particularly in lakes, try using a fast-sinking fly line, a short leader, 6 feet or so, and a floating fly like a

Muddler Minnow or a Woolly Bugger. Your line will go along the bottom, with the fly trailing behind and above.

603. Choke-Up for Short, Tough Casts

Baseball players choke up on their bats, golfers choke up on their clubs. Fly fishers ought to choke up on their fly rods when making short, difficult casts under or between branches of over-hanging bushes. Move your casting hand all the way up on the rod itself, several inches above the cork, for more control. Try it in practice. You'll be surprised at how effective this can be.

604. Make Dropper Rigs Your Wintertime Project

Why waste precious time on the stream tying the two-fly rigs that are so popular and effective today? Make it a wintertime project. Pick your floater dry fly, tie a leader 18 inches or so to the shank of the hook (some prefer to tie it into the eye of the dry fly hook), and tie a nymph to the leader. Store them in small plastic bags. When you're on the stream, all you have to do is tie the dry fly to your leader, dress it for better floating, and start catching fish.

605. Joe Humphrey's Best Nymph Tactic

In fishing upstream, to get a weighted nymph down and keep it down before the current drags the line and pulls the nymph back up, Joe Humphrey recommends what he calls the Tuck Cast. To make it, he stops the rod suddenly on the forward stroke at the 10:30 position by having the last two fingers of the casting hand pulling and the thumb pressing. Humphrey says, "It's a quick, squeezing action." The nymph is made to tuck back under the leader and drop to the bottom before drag sets in on the line. It's all in his book, *Joe Humphrey's Trout Tactics*, Stackpole (1981).

606. Joe Humphrey's Trout Tactics

The successor to George Harvey, the late legendary Penn State angling professor whose writing and influence has been widely felt in the world of fly fishing, particularly dry fly fishing, Joe Humphrey has emerged from the Penn State fly fishing classes as one of Pennsylvania's finest trout fly fishers ever. He holds the Pennsylvania record for the largest trout ever caught on a fly, a brown weighing 15.5 pounds, in 1977, and is a master angler who shares what he has learned. His book *Joe Humphrey's Trout Tactics*, Stackpole (1981), is a loaded with skills that will help any angler take more trout.

607. Taking the Temperature for Trout

The price of the gear mentioned may be out of date today, but the advice is not: " . . . a five-dollar thermometer can make more fishermen better fishermen than any other single piece of equipment."

—Joe Humphrey, *Joe Humphrey's Trout Tactics*, Stackpole, 1981

608. The Right Temperatures for Trout

The renowned flyfisher Joe Humphrey, in *Joe Humphrey's Trout Tactics*, Stackpole (1981), has read stream temperatures on thousands of trips, including many with the Penn State "trout professor," the late George Harvey. In his book, he cites the importance of temperature in trout fishing: "A trout's metabolism increases with the rise in water temperature. When its metabolism increases, the trout's demand for food is greater." Humphrey goes on to name 58, 59, 60, and up to 65 degrees as the "up-and-at-'em" temperatures for all trout species. He warns, however, " . . . these temperature ranges are *general* guidelines, and exceptions occur." See Joe's fantastic book for more details on the temperatures that will help you catch more trout.

609. Setting the Hook on Nymph Strikes

"There's an instant of tightness in the normal dance of a leader in current that indicates a trout has mouthed the fly—however briefly or gently—and you can tell, the way you can tell from the sound whether a guitar string has been struck by a musician or say, bumped by the tail of a passing dog."

—John Gierach, *Trout Bum*, Simon & Schuster, 1986

610. Trout on the Edge of Town

The Little Lehigh is one of Pennsylvania's treasured limestone creeks, with beautiful cool water pumped up by Mother Earth every day of the year. Located in Allentown, in a beautiful park, the Heritage section of the water is a mile or so of fly-fishing-only water from Hatchery Road off Route 309. Headquarters for anglers here is the Little Lehigh Fly Shop, www.littlelehigh-flyshop.com, 610-797-5599, located on Hatchery Road. The river is a treasure to behold, whether you are fishing or just having a picnic, as many Allentown folks and tourists do, with trout in plain sight all up and down the river. The trout are skittish as hawks, very difficult to approach and catch. You'll see lots of anglers here, few having hookups. Still, if you are longing to see some wild trout rising to flies right in front of you, give the Little Lehigh in Allentown a try.

611. Special Tactics for Giant Trout

When catching some of the biggest trout in the river is your objective (as opposed to my usual pursuit of just wanting to catch lots of representative fish and get lots of action), you've got to use big-fish tactics. That means focusing on the deepest, darkest pools with big nymphs and streamers and getting deep. Sure, lots of big trout are caught sipping tiny flies off the surface. If you're lucky enough to find them, tight lines! But in the main, you've got to fish down and dirty to lure out the big trout.

612. My Crazy Giant-Trout Morning

The theory of special tactics for giant trout came into play for me one June morning on a private stretch of Pennsylvania's Spruce Creek owned by friend Sylvia Bashline. Fishing with writer Nick Sisley, I studied a fine deep pool where the water pressed against a cut bank back in the shadows. I pulled out an olive land-locked salmon fly, about 4 inches long, tied it on, and cast. The instant I pulled the streamer into the shadows, several fish flashed in the pool, and I thought, "Oh, boy!" In the next instant, a pike-sized fish bolted up through the pool with the fly in its mouth. It was a brown trout, huge, powerful, the trout of my dreams. Somehow, I managed to land the fish. Nick took a picture or two, and we measured the beast at 25 inches and released it. As you can imagine, this encounter is one of my favorite trout memories.

613. Use a Glove to Fish the Tangles

When trying to wade the edge of a trout stream that's flowing through tangles of branches, vines, and assorted gremlins that stop your progress, you'll be better off if you have a work glove on one hand to help clear your way. It's crazy how a single branch will find your landing net if you let it.

614. Three High-Desert Trout Destinations

Mentioning the word "desert" doesn't exactly conjure up images of trout, but when you make it read "high desert" you've got a whole new ballgame. That's especially so in central Oregon's high desert country, where private lakes and river stretches offer trout-fishing opportrnities of the highest quality. Three of the best are the Grindstone Lakes at www.grindstonelakes.com; Lake In the Dunes at www.lakeinthedunes.com; and the Yamsi Ranch waters, which include the Williamson River, at www.yamsiflyfishing.com. If you're ready to book some really good fishing and lodging, check them out.

615. Snake River Triple Play

The words Snake River bring to mind mountain men, beautiful high country, and battling trout. Places like Idaho's legendary Henry's Fork of the Snake come to mind, as do remote sections of the South Branch of the Snake, which flow through wilderness beyond the roads. Three destinations in Idaho's Snake River area have linked together their Web sites so you can click onto the kind of fishing that interests you most. The three sources that inter-connect on guides and lodging in the area are the well-known Mike Lawson's Henry's Fork Anglers at www.henrysforkanglers.com; South Fork Outfitters at www.southforkoutfitters.com; and South Fork Lodge at www.southforklodge.com.

616. B.C. Wilderness Adventures Fishing

From Kim Sedrovic's Fernie Wilderness Adventures lodge, in the remote mountains at Fernie, British Columbia, trout anglers get top-notch action wading or floating rivers like the Elk. The scenery has been described as breathtaking in articles in sporting magazines such as *Sporting Classics*. And there are trout there to match the surroundings. Orvis endorsed. See www.fernieadventures.com.

617. Fishing the Housatonic

Fly-fishing the popular Housatonic River in Connecticut can be greatly enhanced by a visit to Housatonic River Outfitters at www.dryflies.com. They've got everything you need, and everything you need to know, to meet the hatches and catch trout here.

618. Fit for a King

"The flesh of the trout is a rare delicacy that comes from one of nature's most tender and perishable creatures. . . . by far the best time to enjoy your trout is beside the waters where they are caught. Take a fry pan along and some bacon or shortening, and a little cornmeal and salt, and have yourself a feast fit for a deposed king—or an ulcerated millionaire. But first take a trout. . . ."

—Robert Traver, *Trout Madness*, St. Martin's Press, 1960

619. Winter's Gift: The Secret Spring

"Two weeks ago, when it was thirty below, steam rose from the creek behind our home, from the riffle above the bridge. I'd never noticed it before . . . Then I realized there must be an underwater spring in that section of the creek. . . . and now I know where I can catch trout in extremes, whether in late August or the last week of November."

—John Barsness, *Montana Time*, Lyons & Burford, 1992

620. A Mistake-Proof Fly

"In western lakes a No. 8 olive Woolly Worm is never a mistake."

—John Barsness, *Montana Time*, Lyons & Burford, 1992

© Stu Apte 2010

621. Have You Got The Touch?

"There is no substitute for fishing sense, and if a man doesn't have it, verily, he may cast like an angel and still use his creel largely to transport sandwiches and beer."

—Robert Traver, *Trout Madness*, St. Martin's Press, 1960

622. The Upper Missouri: Fly Fishing's True Paradise

There are people who would say I should not be telling you about this particular angling destination. They lament that the place has received far too much publicity already, and that tattletales like Underwood should be thrown into irons for revealing secrets. I don't see it that way, but be warned that what you are about to learn can change your life, bend and skewer your schedules and priorities toward new directions. It's happened to many people before you, people who long to fly fish on spring creeks—the clear, cold slick reaches of water boiling out of Mother Earth 24/7 at the same temperature and filled with healthy, hungry trout. The Upper Missouri river is not a spring creek, but it might as well be. From its water release at Holter Dam near Wolf Creek, Montana, down past the fly fishing and lodging headquarters at Craig, eight miles downstream, and on down for scores of miles below that, the Missouri flows smooth and cold. It is filled with rainbow and brown trout and fly hatches to dream about. The Upper Missouri is the kind of water that makes people contemplate giving up their jobs and seeking employment in Helena, not far away. Those who can afford it, look to buy vacation homes and cabins there. Some of my friends in the eastern United States, where I live, treasure the Upper Missouri for fall "cast and blast" vacations, combining bird hunting with trout fishing there. There are books galore, maps, and information sites. We shall get to some of them here.

623. Fishing the Upper Missouri from Wolf Creek

The Fly Shop at Wolf Creek, Montana, is a great place for hitting the river along the eight miles from the Holter Dam release to the town of Craig. The Fly Shop, at www.wolfcreekoutfitters .com/flyshop, not only has guides but also rents drift boats and float tubes and is adjacent to motel facilities. Phone, toll free, is 866-688-7688.

624. Headhunters on the Missouri

The little town of Craig, Montana, is a larger village than its Wolf Creek counterpart, upstream, and hosts lodging, guides, and outfitters for fishing the Upper Missouri. Headhunters Fly Shop, www.headhuntersflyshop.com, is just a short cast from the river at Craig and is a full-bore operation for guides, boats, rentals, gear, lodging, and information. Craig is a colorful stop for the fly fisher, including a bridge over the river right in midtown, a railroad crossing, and ample watering holes to discuss trouting adventures.

625. The Upper Missouri's Trout Shop

Located among other fly-fishing operations in the thriving metropolis of Craig, Montana, on the Upper Missouri is The Trout Shop, a complete guiding and outfitting service where you'll find just about everything you need to enjoy fishing this fabulous river. Visit their superb Web site at www.thetroutshop.com to see what it's all about, then pay them a visit in person. You may never leave.

626. Flyway Ranch Missouri Access

For those who think the "city life" in Craig and Wolf Creek might be a little intimidating, there's the Flyway Ranch located between the two towns on the Craig River Road. The ranch features lodging right on the bank of the river. Visit their Web site at www.flywayranch.com or call them at 406-235-4116.

627. Schwiebert on Jackson Hole Cutthroats

"Bob Carmichael taught me about cutthroats in Jackson Hole [Wyoming] . . . *Young man*, he rumbled with failing patience, *When you know enough about this part of the country to have an opinion about the fishing—you'll know there's cutthroats and there's cutthroats. . . . These fish ain't no pantywaists—they're Jackson Hole cutthroats!*"

—Ernest Schwiebert, *Trout*, E.P. Dutton, 1978

628. Schwiebert on Jackson Hole Cutthroats, Part Two

"The fish worked steadily all along the current tongues, and when I finally hooked one it was a whitefish. *Forget your matching the hatch!* Carmichael always ragged me unmercifully. *Fish these big variants right in the rips—and you'll learn something about real cutthroat fishing!*"

—Ernest Schwiebert, *Trout*, E.P. Dutton, 1978

629. The Secret Weapon for Green Drake Hatches

"While the big news on Limestone Creek (a fictitious name for a Pennsylvania spring creek) is always the coming of the giant Green Drake, the best fishing is usually with one of the various sulfurs. It's no secret and a favorite saying of local veterans that the best Green Drake pattern is usually a Size 16 Sulfur."

—Chuck Robbins, *Odyssey at Limestone Creek,* Tussey Mountain Publishers, 1997

630. Alaska Tactics Come to New York

Ever see and hold one of the Mouse Flies recommended for the big rainbows in Alaska? Well, before the rainbows get totally focused on salmon eggs once the great salmon runs go into full swing, the Mouse Fly is considered a primary weapon, especially early and late in the day. At this time of year—dead winter—when I am inclined to dreaming of doing great things, I have decided to give the big Mouse Fly, complete with its curly tail, some quality time on New York's upper Delaware. I'll fish it just at dark, through a pool where I have reasonable expectations of raising a fish. Might work! Can't hurt!

631. That West Yellowstone Pose

"So we assume that recognizable West Yellowstone pose: modest, seasoned, and ever so slightly self-satisfied. The implication being, yes, I guess we do know a thing or two about fishing around here, and, no, we don't really care to go into it. If nothing else, we know how to fit in here. We understand that the less you say about fly fishing, the more people will assume you know."

—John Gierach, *Dances With Trout,* Simon & Schuster, 1994

632. The Trout Stream You Cherish Most

"Most of the fishermen I know—even those who think of themselves as Sportsmen with a capital S—have a creek like this somewhere in their lives. It's not big, it's not great, it's not famous, certainly it's not fashionable, and therein lies its charm. It's an ordinary, run-of-the mill trout stream where fly-fishing can be a casual affair rather than having to be a balls-to-the-wall adventure all the time."

—John Gierach, *Sex, Death, and Fly Fishing,* Simon & Schuster, 1990

633. Rookie Error: He Missed It!

When I first got into trout fishing, coming to the sport from a southern fishing background, I was quick to attribute missed hits as, "He missed it!" Or, "I snatched it away from him!" Of course, what I was seeing was a classic refusal rise. I just didn't know what it was.

634. The Approaching Cold Front: It's Hot Stuff

When a summer cold front is approaching, with thunderstorms threatening, your fishing can turn into a real frenzy of action for a while. You'll have to eventually take cover, however, or die!

635. The Cold Front Has Passed. What Next?

The first couple of days behind a real cold front, with the wind rising and temperature dropping, can challenge even the most experienced anglers. You can bail out for home, or hang in there and give it your best shot. If you do stick around, plan on fishing deep and slow.

636. The Catch-and-Release Code

"Game fish are too valuable to be caught only once."
—Lee Wulff, *Lee Wulff's Handbook of Freshwater Fishing,* J.B. Lippincott, 1939

CHAPTER 10

Spinning and Bait Tips: You'll Catch More Trout

637. Guaranteed: More Trout Spinning Small Streams

Dunking worms in deep holes for early-season trout in your favorite stream is relatively easy—as long as other anglers don't take over your hole. Spinning the entire stream, working your way carefully from pocket to pocket, is a lot more fun and will produce lots of trout, provided you are a skilled caster. The ability to cast light spinners and baits into pockets with accuracy separates the trout anglers who limit-out from the ones who come up empty. They just can't cast. We're talking about all kinds of delicate casts, underhand flips, sidearm throws under brush, things like that. It's not distance; it's accuracy that counts. The only way to obtain this skill is to practice, practice, practice. You'll catch lots of trout if you do.

638. The Strong Pull of Bait Fishing

"Bait is a connection with rivers that no other method of angling quite reaches. We are visual animals; although we use all our other senses to some extent . . . Bait fishing allows us to see through touch, like a coyote sees through his nose."

—John Barsness, *Montana Time,* Lyons & Burford, 1992

639. Best Bait for Early-Season Spinning

Hitting your favorite local trout stream when it's stocked with fish in early season is a coveted rite of spring. An absolutely deadly bait—even better than worms—is the mealworm, the larva form of the mealworm beetle. Find a baitshop that carries them, and you are in business. You can also order them live right off the internet at places like Cabelas, www.cabelas.com. (They'll keep in your frig.) Place a No. 6 or 8 bait hook about three-fourths of the length of the beetle. Notice that stuff will be oozing out of the beetle, creating a fantastic fish attractor. Use a single split-shot to get the bait down. Many anglers like a barrel swivel about 18 inches above the hook to prevent twists. Mealies stay on the hook fairly well. Cast them into pocket water, in front of boulders, around their sides, into deep holes, down through riffles. Using ultralight spinning gear, mealies, and a rig like this, you're going to catch lots of early-season trout.

640. Small Spinners for Small-Stream Trout

If you are a good caster, you can do very well on early season trout in small streams by using ultralight spinning tackle and the smallest, lightest in-line spinners your rig can handle. Mepps, Panther Martin, and Blue Fox are some favorites, but there are many others. The bigger and heavier the spinner, the bigger and deeper the water it takes to fish them without them hanging up constantly. You want the lightest spinners your stream can handle, working them into pockets and under overhanging cover. Casting and retrieving these spinners in a small stream is an art unto itself, as challenging as fly fishing—but a lot more productive most of the time.

641. The Downstream Swing: Your Spinner's Strike Zone

When your spinner is swinging on the downstream arc of your cast, just before it swings across the current and the line straightens out below you, don't be in a hurry. Far from it, realize that the next several seconds may bring the strike you've been waiting for. Alternate between little jerks and steady pulls as it swings across. When it's downstream directly below you, keep it still for a moment, then start a careful retrieve.

642. Small-Stream Spinning: The Real Art

The real magicians of small-stream spinning—the guys and gals who catch most of the trout—avoid snagging by careful manipulation of their line with a subtle sense of feel in their rod hand. They don't make long casts; you might even say they don't cast at all in the true sense of the word. Instead, they make little flips and tosses, putting the small spinner into the holes with backhand and sidearm moves. They also match the size and weight of the spinner to the conditions, and often hold their rod high on the retrieve to keep the lure from snagging the bottom. A good formula to remember: Flip the spinner out rod-low and retrieve it rod-high, watching the line carefully to make sure your little Mepps isn't about to snag up.

643. What Color Spinner Blades?

As in everything about fishing, there are no absolute rules regarding which color to choose for your spinner blades. However, a great many successful anglers like to use bright, silver-type blades on bright days. Use gold blades on dull or dark days.

644. Adding Weight to Your Spinner

When adding split-shot to your line to get your spinner deeper, place the shot several inches above the spinner, not on the spinner's nose. Placing it on the nose will interfere with the spinner's action.

645. Fish the Woolly Bugger with Spinning Tackle

Tie on an olive Woolly Bugger streamer, place enough split-shot to make the cast about 8 inches up the line, and fish it just as if you were using a fly rod. Whether or not to use a weighted bead-head fly, or the unweighted, depends on the current and depth you're trying to fish. Olive Woolly Buggers in various weights and sizes belong in your kit with your Mepps and other in-line spinners.

646. Fishing the Big, Slow Pools

When you're lucky enough to get a big slow pool all to yourself on your trout stream, don't make your first casts to the backside. Start by making a series of Fan Casts to the nearest part of the pool, gradually working your casts to the backside. You'll really be covering the water that way.

647. Keep it Simple and Fun

We talk elsewhere in this book about the importance of catching fish when you take kids fishing, making sure they get action. One of the best ways to do that on early season trout streams is to use a simple bait-keeper hook, like a Size 8, perhaps a split-shot and barrel swivel about 12 inches up the line, and a bobber. You can use a light spinning outfit, or even a plain long graphite pole or fly rod. Your bait will be one of the many Berkley Powerbaits, a glowing, scented trout tantalizer you carry in a small jar: www.cabelas.com. If you can find a good spot, the kid will see the bobber start dancing, then go under, and you'll have a fishing partner for life.

648. Try a Different Spinner Lure

If you feel that the trout in your local streams are being pounded too hard with traditional in-line spinners like Mepps and Panther Martins, consider going to an alternative. Two excellent choices are the Spin-A-Lure and Lil' Jake Lure, both wobblers with tantalizing action. Available at www.cabelas.com. Work them the same way you do in-line spinners.

649. Spinning with a B-17

We've mentioned B-17 products in the fly-fishing section of this book, but their unique baits deserve being pointed out here. B-17 makes fantastic lures in sizes and weights for both fly fishing and spinning for trout and bass, and just about everything that swims. They're expensive compared to your average spin-bait, but wait until you see and try them. Don't be put off by the unusual name of their Web site, www.b-17swimsuit.com.

650. Small Spinners Reveal Trout Locations

When using small spinners for trout, keep an alert eye on the lure as it swings through a pool or behind the rocks, especially on your first cast into a hole. Even when they do not hit, trout often respond to a spinner by a flashing movement.

651. The Deadliest Trout Spinner?

The Colorado spinner is thought to owe its origin to a man named John Hildebrant, who, in 1899, put a hole in a dime, attached it to a hairpin shaft, and started catching trout. In much-improved forms, it's been catching trout ever since. The late Ted Trueblood, angling editor and columnist for *Field & Stream*, in his *Angler's Handbook,* Thomas Crowell (1949), called it "The most deadly trout lure ever devised for fishing in the United States . . . " He added, "In various sizes it will catch all other kinds of gamefish." Fish the Colorado with line as light as possible, and with just enough weight on your line to make the cast. Although some experts do not like baiting the Colorado, I personally have had great success with trout using a Colorado spinner sweetened with a worm.

652. Spinning With Small Jigs Takes More Trout

If you want to catch lots of trout during early season when the water's cold and the streams are a little high and off-color, leave your fly rod in the truck and go with light spinning tackle. Use tiny jigs tipped with live bait or soft-plastics like Berkley's Power Nymphs. Small hair jigs work too.

653. Matukas and Spinners: A Deadly Combo

A Web site called Jerry's Flies, www.jerrysflies.com, is where I first started reading about Matuka spinner flies. Combining a Matuka streamer with a spinner creates a lure you can count on to get trout moving in whatever pool you work it in. Matukas, which I believe originally came from New Zealand, have been a favorite of trout fly fishers for years. Combined with a spinner, they are even more effective. Before Woolly Buggers came along, the Matuka was my go-to fly for searching the water. I like olive.

654. Sweeten Your Trout Spinnerbait

No need to send your Mepps or other spinner lure out there all by itself. Where legal, you can sweeten your trout fishing spinner lure by tipping it with a piece of earthworm. It spoils the action of the spinner a little, but you'll catch more trout. They love worms. The fly-fishing-only crowd hates all this, but what the heck . . . you're out to catch some trout. This will help you do it. Maybe someday you'll get into fly fishing. Right now, you'll be eating trout.

655. Spinning Tricks for Trout

You don't hear much about "spinning the bubble" these days, but it's still an effective way to catch trout on streams or lakes where all-tackle fishing is allowed. Tie your spinning line to the kind of ball float that you can get water into to add weight for casting with flies. Set your leader from the float to the depth you think will bring strikes, and tie on a nymph. Cast upstream, downstream, or across and let your rig float down through trout lairs. You'll catch fish.

CHAPTER 11

Steelhead, The Ultimate Trout Challenge:
Beating the Odds

656. Experts Only Need Apply

"These big rainbows are extremely secretive—almost never being seen before they're hooked. That makes it difficult even for expert anglers to puzzle out their habits, and almost impossible for the beginner."

—Clare Conley, "Tricks the Steelhead Experts Taught Me," *Field & Stream*, October, 1961

657. No Beginner's Luck Here

"Nine out of ten captured steelhead are taken by fishermen who have landed such fish before."

—Clare Conley, "Tricks the Steelhead Experts Taught Me," *Field & Stream*, October, 1961

658. Fishing Out the Swing

With your fly, lure, or bait swinging over a steelhead lie, then straightening out downstream, let the line hang for several moments before starting your retrieve. Sometimes, particularly in colder water, steelhead will follow the lure and not take until they have examined it thoroughly.

659. Find and Fish the Holding Water

You'll spot inexperienced steelhead anglers a mile away: They'll be fishing the entire river, every run and hole. The veterans have learned that the river can be divided between traveling water and holding water. That will cut the fishable areas down to about 15 or 25 percent of the river. Holding water will have the current, depth, and cover that are just right for resting and sticking around for a while. Traveling water is just that: water that you should travel through on your way to better spots. Learning to read the water takes time and experience. For outstanding advice on the subject, see the article "Reading Water: A Little Science and a Lot of Opinion," by Andy Batcho, on the Washington Council of Trout Unlimited site, www.troutunlimited-washington.org.

660. When You Can't Move That Fish

It's an enviable position to be in, but it can be frustrating: You've hooked a big salmon or steelhead, and he's into a pool he likes and you can't budge him—without breaking your leader or rod. Sometimes, as a trick of last resort, banging on the end of the rod butt with the palm of your hand will get the fish moving. This doesn't always work, but sometimes it does.

661. Where the Fish Are Lying

"The water was a tailout, the lower end of a pool at the top of a long rapid. Black [Dennis Black, Umpqua Feather Merchants] explained that steelhead usually move quickly through a rapid, then rest in the quieter holding lies above it. Once he pointed them out, I could see the shadowy forms of five steelhead hanging in the current."

— J.L. Merritt, *Trout Dreams: A Gallery of Fly-Fishing Profiles,*
The Derrydale Press, 2000

662. Pool Etiquette: It Makes Sense

There are violations all over the map, but *there is* a correct way to share the fishing in a steelhead or salmon pool where several anglers are gathered. Starting at the top of the pool, make a cast that allows your fly to swing down and across the hotspot or strike zone. Next take a step downstream and make another cast. Keep repeating the steps and casts until you reach the bottom of the pool, then go back to the top and start over. Of course, this assumes you are fishing with considerate sportsmen and women. You will on occasion run across a complete jerk and idiot who wants to camp on the best water and keep it for himself. When that happens, it's time for a diplomatic conversation.

663. Great Lakes Steelhead Fighting Qualities

"After catching 25-pound fish on the Kispiox, skating dry flies for surface-feeding steelhead on the Dean in British Columbia, and catching thousands of Great Lakes steelhead, I can tell you this: There is no difference between a hot Western fish and a hot Eastern fish."

—Kelly Galloup, "Spring-Run Steelhead," *Fly Fisherman*, May, 2002

664. Low and Slow for Winter Steelhead

Winter steelhead take slowly and deliberately. A fly whipping past over their heads isn't going to be chased. Nor will a lure or bait rig. Whatever method is used, you've got to get your bait on the bottom, where the fish are hugging, and move it slowly. The winter steelhead angler who isn't getting hung up probably isn't catching many fish.

CHAPTER 12

Salmon and Shad, Home from the Seas:
Be Ready for Them

665. The Truth About Atlantic Salmon Fishing

My friend Jim Merritt, one of the finest anglers I know and author of many articles on the subject, raises an interesting point about Atlantic salmon fishing: "With about a zillion books on trout fishing tactics, why are there only a few on Atlantic salmon fishing tactics? Is it not because fly fishing for salmon—both Atlantic and Pacific types—basically consists of making a cast quartering upstream and then letting your fly swing down and across? You might put a few mends in your line, straightening it out or getting a deeper drift and swing, but basically that's it. Cast after cast." Jim's dead right.

666. Those Mysterious Landlocks

Landlocked salmon, so coveted for ice-out fishing in Maine and Quebec, have backgrounds shrouded in certain mysteries. Were they descended from the Atlantic salmon, as some scientists believe, trapped in inland waters by geological upheavals long ago? Or is the Atlantic salmon simply a breed of landlock that wandered downstream long ago? Anglers looking for springtime's first pull from a battling fish probably could care less, but they do appreciate the gift of one of the gamest (and tastiest) fishes that swims.

667. Landlocked Salmon: The Source

Although they have been successfully planted in watersheds like Maine's Moosehead and Rangeley lakes, landlocked salmon were originally found only in the basins of the Presumpscot, Piscataquis, Penobscot, and St. Croix rivers of Maine and the upper reaches of the Saguenay River in Quebec, where they are known as *ouananiche*.

668. Best Landlock Salmon Flies?

"I have caught more salmon [landlocked salmon] with a Black Ghost streamer than any other fly. And the Gray Ghost comes next. . . . Because they are superior, as lures, or because I have spent more time fishing with them than with other patterns?"

—Arthur R. Macdougall, Jr., *The Trout Fisherman's Bedside Book,*
Simon & Schuster, 1963

669. A Good Day on Black Salmon

As has been shown elsewhere in this book, and as you will learn elsewhere in print and on the rivers, Atlantic salmon fishing is a big and expensive gamble, but well worth it in the minds and hearts of the faithful. For some, one idea that lessens the odds is to go for the so-called "black salmon" on New Brunswick's Miramichi River during the period April 15 through May. It is then that the spawned-out, fall-run fish which have stayed in the river all winter, still fasting under the ice in deep pools, start their run back to the sea. They are rather gaunt, compared to their condition when they made their run from the sea in the fall, and they are called, "black salmon" or "slinks" because they are rather dark and lean compared to summer fish. Many salmon anglers consider the practice of fishing for these fish to be a low-life practice, far beneath the dignity of the lofty Atlantic salmon gentry. Others say, "Hold on. This is great fishing, with fish much bigger and stronger than you might think. They jump, they run, they fight like Atlantic salmon should." These anglers catch lots of fish too, not the paltry numbers from regular salmon fishing. Rates at the Miramichi camps that offer this fishing are sensible, and the chances for success great. Check out some of the Miramichi salmon camps on the Web and make up your own mind if "black salmon" fishing is for you. A caveat: This is cold, bundled-up fishing with a full sinking line and big streamers worked deep and deeper.

670. The Truth About Grilse

I am fortunate to have fished at many Atlantic salmon camps, where the talk was always of grilse weighing an estimated "five or six pounds." In his book, *Fly Fishing Heresies* (1975), the late Leonard M. Wright, Jr., nails the subject once and for all: "Having weighed and measured

well over 100 grilse from several rivers, I can cite the following figures with confidence: Grilse average 33 inches long and weigh a shade under 4 pounds."

671. How to Get More Salmon Strikes

Leonard M. Wright, Jr., was a keen student of all forms of fly fishing for trout and salmon, with vast experience in fishing for both. From his Atlantic salmon experiences, he became convinced that most salmon casts resulted in the fly passing over and past the fish, too shallow and too fast. The speed and depth of the fly became critical issues to Wright, and he went to a method of fishing his salmon flies "low and slow." Wright says, "Many times I have heard salmon anglers claim that . . . the most killing part of any presentation occurs during the last part of the swing when the fly is straightening out below them." Wright became convinced that the catch success when the fly "is straightening out below them" was due to the speed having been too fast in the earlier parts of the presentation. Only in the last critical moments was the speed of the fly right for the salmon to take a look.

672. The Leonard Wright Salmon Cast

As described above, Leonard Wright liked to fish his salmon fly "low and slow." To do so, Wright cast out and across and began *mending his line upstream constantly* to get the end of his fly line and the fly in a straight, downstream drift. In his great book *Fly Fishing Heresies* (1975), Wright references legendary Miramichi River angler Ira Gruber, who reportedly said, " . . . if half the fishermen made their flies swing slower and fished them down deeper there'd be darned few big salmon left in this river."

673. The Hardest Fish to Predict

Everybody knows that in Atlantic salmon fishing, even after months of planning and dreaming, you might arrive at your river and find: 1) The fish aren't in yet. They're still holding offshore, waiting for the right water levels and temperature; 2) The fish have come and gone; 3) The water is high, and staying high, and the fish are running the river, not staying in pools; or 4) The water is low, hot, and the fish are dour, holding in some pools but taking absolutely nothing. In this instance, it may start to rain on your final day in camp, and when you return home you'll be subjected to the phone call that exalts, "Just after you left . . . "

674. Facing Atlantic Salmon Disappointment

Just back from my favorite Atlantic salmon river in New Brunswick, a 1,000-mile drive from my home in New Jersey, I am still nursing my utter disappointment in not getting a single strike in three days' fishing. Nor did my three companions. The river was high in continuous rain, stained, and the fish were running the river to the upstream pools. That's Atlantic salmon fishing. You drive 1,000 miles. The fish swims 5,000 miles, maybe more. Your visits to the river don't coincide. The only best-laid plans with worse odds is to try to change planes for a connecting flight in Chicago or Atlanta.

675. Why Salmon Hit Flies

It's an old, old argument, with opinions from all sides, so I might as well weigh in with my own. The question before the House is: "Since they are not feeding when they enter rivers to spawn, why do salmon hit flies?" Experts of every stripe have discussed the subject, in print, and I must side with Lee Wulff in believing that salmon take the fly due to a flash of memory from their years in the river as a parr. When certain conditions are absolutely right—the speed of the fly in the water, the slant of light on the fly's colors, the temperature—a salmon urged by some inner biological need to be "on the take" will hit a fly.

676. A Salmon Remembers

When Atlantic salmon fishing, one often hooks and reels in tiny parr that have eagerly attacked the fly. Years later, when the salmon returns from the ocean depths to its home river, memories of its years chasing flies will be strong enough to cause a response to your bogus fly if . . . and it's a big IF . . . the bite is on and conditions are right. A "taking fish" can be hard to find.

677. Check Out Newfoundland and Labrador

Two of the great destinations for brook trout and Atlantic salmon are Newfoundland and Labrador. Check out the Newfoundland and Labrador Guides Association at www.nloa.ca.

678. Hook a Salmon, Break a Rod

Alaskan guides have told me that they probably see more rods broken by chum salmon than any other types. The chums come in just before, and with, the silvers, and they can be big—topping 20 pounds. Add mint condition, fresh from the salt, and you've got a fish that will take you deep, deep into the backing. When trying to "horse" such a big fish in the final stages of the fight, many anglers over-stress the rod by pulling back hard just as the fish launches a final desperate run.

679. When the Bite Is On

When fishing for Atlantic or Pacific salmon there are certain times when the fish are in a taking mode, "on the bite," as anglers love to say. When this happens, for whatever reason—barometer, temperature, light, moon phases, whatever—have your line in the water and keep fishing hard. It won't last!

680. When Salmon Strike

The strike of the Atlantic salmon is one of fly fishing's most treasured moments. Alas, it can be a short-lived moment if you react too quickly and pull the fly away from the fish. If your

nerves are steady enough, the salmon will usually hook itself. Raise the rod slowly, feel the line tighten, and get set for a battle royal. Many salmon are hooked during idle moments when the angler is looking away or talking to a companion. A hair-trigger reaction to a strike is not the way to go.

681. Two Salmon Strikes

On the previous cast, a fish had swirled near the fly. Now, as my Green Highlander swung down through the pool, my senses were keyed on hair-trigger. A sudden flash, and I reacted as the water boiled then broke in a missed strike. "Rest him a bit," the guide suggested, and we did just that. When I got the fly back on the same float, a pair of black ducks banked overhead, suddenly and dramatically. I couldn't take my eyes off them and was so engrossed when the strike came. Even before I thought to raise the rod, the fish was on, the reel screaming, and we had a hookup. That's often the best way to handle a salmon strike: by doing nothing!

682. Ernie Schwiebert's Salmon-Fishing Advice

The late Ernie Schwiebert, a dear friend and one of the great angling authors, once told me that he believed that the strike of an Atlantic salmon on any particular cast stems from the *previous* cast. "That's the cast when you caught its attention," Ernie said.

683. Landlock Fever: A Springtime Malady

"Although spring fever is contracted easily by sportsmen up here in my home state of Maine, there are a variety of seasonal tonics that will at least arrest that annual affliction. For some, one dosage of dipping smelts will bring their temperatures down. For others, though, the sure-cure prescription of taking trout from big-feeling brooks may have to be refilled several times. There are, of course, those whose allergies and addictions require special medication. Not the least among them are the stalwarts whose worse fever begins to subside at the words, 'ice out,' but whose cure will not be complete until they are trolling streamer flies for landlocked salmon."

—Tom Hennessey, *Feathers 'n Fins,* The Amwell Press, 1989

684. The Perfect Landlocked Salmon Fly

"The streamer fly is to landlocked salmon fishing what the double-barreled shotgun is to bird hunting . . . Their names alone—Green King, Nine-Three, Gray Ghost, Pink Lady, Supervisor—are good for what ails you."

—Tom Hennessey, *Feathers 'n Fins,* The Amwell Press, 1989

685. Focusing on Landlocks

"With the exception of the Mickey Finn, Parmacheene Belle, and a few other patterns, the colorations of most streamer patterns are subdued—suggestive of smelts. Greens, grays, black and white barred with black predominate. As is the case with all fishing flies, streamers that are heavily dressed catch fishermen, those on the slender side catch fish. And you may know better than I that there are times which landlocked salmon lust for them."

—Tom Hennessey, *Feathers 'n Fins,* The Amwell Press, 1989

686. Buck Or Roe? You'll Feel the Difference

The male shad, the buck, leaps more and makes flashy runs. The roe, the female laden with eggs, the one you're after, makes your rod and line feel as if perhaps you've hooked the bottom. Then the "bottom" begins moving and pulling hard and steady, and you know you're in for a fight.

687. She's Quite a Lady!

"Years ago, the angler became enamored with Lady Amherst when she charmed his first Atlantic salmon . . . Her crowning accomplishment occurred on a mist-shrouded May 1 morning at the Bangor Salmon Pool when she lured the 'Presidential Salmon' off its lie. . . . Like all classic salmon flies, the Lady Amherst is a work of art. For that reason, it is seen most often nowadays in framed displays, where among Jock Scotts, Silver Wilkinsons, and Dusty Millers, to name a few, it represents what is considered to be the epitome of the fly tier's art."

—Tom Hennessey, *Feathers 'n Fins,* The Amwell Press, 1989

688. The Landlock Salmon Fly Retrieve

"Trolling streamers is an art mastered by few . . . the accepted rule is that the feathered lures should be fished fast and 'on the rocks.' In that regard, a saying attributed to old-school masters of the art is, "A streamer should be fished fast enough so's you'd seriously doubt that a salmon could catch it.'"

—Tom Hennessey, *Feathers 'n Fins,* The Amwell Press, 1989

689. Same Spot, Same Lures, Different Results

When you see two boats working on a shad holding pool or run, slinging shad darts, and one boat is taking fish while the other is getting casting practice, you can bet heavy money the losers are not fishing deep enough. If your dart is not heavy enough, you won't get down to the fish.

690. A "Must-Read" Shad Book

If you're a serious shad fisher and you've never read John McPhee's *The Founding Fish,* Farrar-Straus-Giroux (2002), do yourself a favor and grab a copy from Amazon, Barnes & Noble, or your library. The natural history of this great American fish, the angling techniques being practiced today—it's all there in some of the richest prose you'll ever engage.

691. Fluttering, Flashing Shad Lures

When I caught my first shad as a teenager on Georgia's Ogeechee River, experiencing for the first time in my life a fish's pull that actually made my wrist ache, we were trolling slowly upcurrent with Tony Acetate silver spoons. Today, fluttering, flashing spoons and lures seem to have been pushed aside by shad darts, but they are still effective choices, trolled slowly, upstream, just as we did years ago. Rig with swivels to prevent line twists.

692. A Clever Way to Troll for Shad

Here's a technique that can be particularly effective on a river like the Delaware in New Jersey, Pennsylvania, and New York. Troll with rods out on both sides of the boat, using bass crankbaits with the hooks removed. An 18-inch leader attached to the crankbait has a shad dart. By running various crankbaits at different depths, you can find the level where the shad are holding and keep your shad darts right in the strike zone.

PART FOUR

ON THE WATER

for Walleye

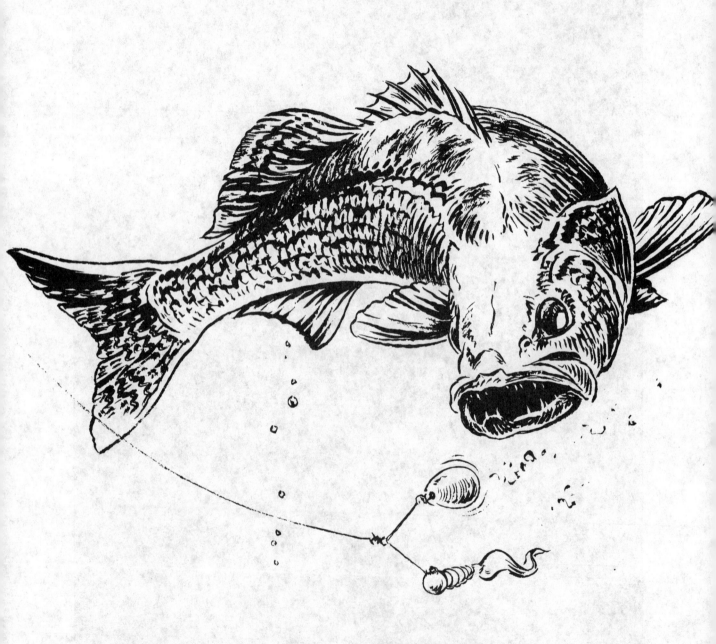

CHAPTER 13

Ultimate Walleye Tactics:
Tips to Master Heartland's Finest Fishing

693. White-Water Walleye Holes

In summer when walleyes go deep and may be tough to find in schools on the reefs, the current below the rapids on lake outlets can usually be counted on to give up some fish. They have everything they need here: plenty of oxygen, food coming their way, and cover to hide.

694. A Deadly Summer Walleye Lure

The jig-and-spinner combination lure has been catching walleyes—and other fish—a long time, but sometimes a new and successful wrinkle of tinkering with a jig-spinner comes along. Writing in the Spring 2009 issue of the *Boundary Waters Journal*, Darrel Brauer's article, "Walleyes for Dinner," reports on finding a winning combination for trolling for finicky summer walleyes in about 8 feet of water: "The precise specifications are: begin with a Betts Spin Size 3 gold spinner, add a 1/4-ounce Eagle Claw saltwater jig dressed with a pure-white 4-inch Berkeley PowerBait grub. Not only is this combination effective when trolled down to about 12 feet, it is absolutely deadly when fished in the current below rapids and falls."

695. Field & Stream's Walleye "Ultimate Lure" Survey Winners

In what it called the "Ultimate Lure Survey," published in March, 2008, *Field & Stream* magazine asked 1,000 of its hard-core readers to name their favorite lures. The winners for the Walleye category were:

Spinners, 54%, Erie Dearie
Jigs, 19%, Jig With Mister Twister
Minnow-Type Lures, 12%, Original Rapala with Smithwick Rogue secnd
Crankbaits, 9%, Rapala Shad Rap
Soft-Plastics, 3%, Berkley Gulp! Minnow
Spoons, 3%, Dardevle

696. The Rig That Worked Magic—And Still Does

The legendary Lindy Rig put today's Lindy Tackle Co. on the map. It's especially good for fall walleyes, reports Brian McClintock in the September 2007 issue of *Field & Stream*. Hook a 6-inch minnow or chub behind the dorsal fin with a No. 2 Octopus hook. The leader is 36- to 42-inch 10-pound test connected to a barrel swivel. Now comes a 1/8- to 1/4-ounce slip sinker that will slide and bounce along the bottom. For more fish-taking Lindy tips for walleyes and everything else, visit www.lindyfishingtackle.com.

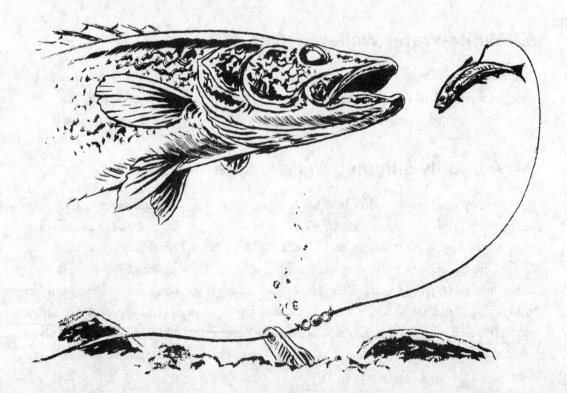

697. Northland Tackle Free Booklet

Northland Fishing Tackle, www.northlandtackle.com, is loaded with great walleye baits and information—as well as all other freshwater gamefish—and features a free 96-page catalog and fishing guide.

698. Walleyes for the Frying Pan: Beware the Cholesterol Police

You will not find many anglers who don't rank the walleye as No. 1 in the frying pan. For my taste, the fillets should be fried, even deep-fried. Yes, the docs will call this a heart-stopping meal, and that might keep you away. But . . . what the heck. How often do you do it? Some of the best meals I've ever had in my life have been shoreline lunches with walleye and pike fillets fried in a pan that the guides had first used to fry great slices of bacon as soon as they got the fire going. The Cholesterol Police were shouting in my ear, but I dug in with great gusto. Life's too short to miss this kind of culinary experience.

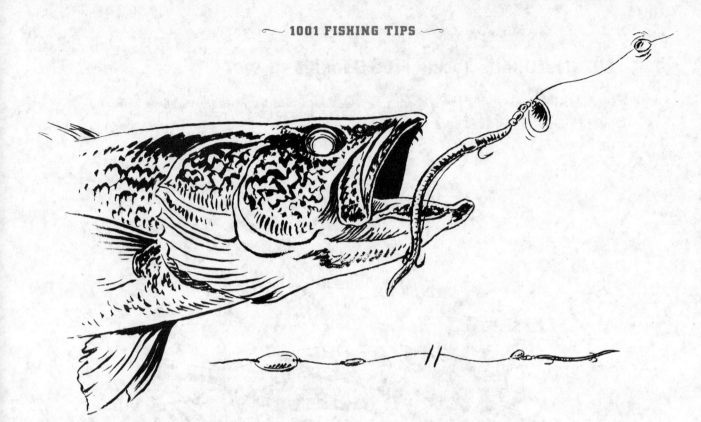

699. Putting Flasher Spoons to Work

On Lake Huron's Saginaw Bay, Mark Gwizdala was having a slow afternoon with his usual trolling lures and tactics. He started thinking of the ways other anglers use flashers for salmon and trout. He tied on a flashy spoon and in-line weight about 5 feet ahead of a spinner with a night crawler. Bingo! Mark's success that day has spread to anglers all over the Great Lakes trolling for suspended walleyes, and even into other techniques for bottom bouncing. The flasher spoon attracts the fish's attention, the lure and bait close the deal.

—Reported by Dave Scroppo in the article "Master Class for Walleyes," on the Outdoor Life Web site www.outdoorlife.com

700. A Trick for Cold-Water Fishing

Walleye expert Jeff Murray, writing in *North American Fisherman*, said that he favors fishing for cold-water walleyes with an inflated crawler hooked right in the nose so that it swims lazily through the water in a straight line.

701. Live-Bait Rig for Taking More Walleyes

A simple rig to catch more and bigger walleyes is to use a slip-sinker system, with a sliding egg or bullet sinker in front of a barrel swivel, with a leader that varies from 6 to 10 feet.

702. Try This Rig and Presentation

In an article on the Mustad Web site, www.mustad.no, Freshwater Fishing Hall of Fame angler Gary Parsons explains how a group of walleye fishermen in the 1990s started bending their hooks to get a unique presentation of their bait. Today, says Parsons, Mustad's Slow Death Hooks do the job for you in a deadly finesse presentation, a slow bottom-hugging enticing move that gets strikes. He uses a bottom-bouncer weight, 10-pound mono leader, and threads half a night crawler over the hook eye. There should be ¼ to ½ inch of worm hanging. See his article on the Mustad site.

703. Focusing on River Walleyes

"Walleyes will tolerate a slight current, but seldom will you find them in fast water, unless there is some type of cover to serve as a current break. When searching for walleyes in rivers, you can immediately eliminate a good share of the water because the current is too swift. Just how much current walleyes will tolerate depends on the season."

—Gander Mountain article, www.gandermountain.com

704. Overlooked Walleye River Hotspots

"You can find river walleyes in slack pools, in eddies, or downstream from some type of current break like an island, a bridge pier, or a large boulder. But many anglers make the mistake of fishing only the downstream side of obstructions. For instance, walleyes usually hold just upstream of a wingdam, a rocky structure intended to deflect current toward the middle of the river to keep the channel from silting in. Current deflecting off the face of a wingdam or other current break creates a slack pocket on the upstream side, providing an ideal spot for a walleye to grab drifting food."

—Gander Mountain article, www.gandermountain.com

705. Reading Walleye River Currents

"Current edges are to a river what structure is to a lake. Walleyes will hold along the margin between slack and moving water. This way, they can rest in the still water and occasionally dart into the current to get a meal."

—Gander Mountain article, www.gandermountain.com

PART FIVE

ON THE WATER
for Panfish, Catfish, and Carp

CHAPTER 14

Mixed Bag Panfishing: Tips for More Action Every Time You Fish!

706. Springtime Fun Guaranteed

For a mixed-bag springtime catch of crappies, bluegills, perch, walleyes, bass—you name it—fish a small jig, sweetened with a minnow hooked upwards through the lip, and use a sliding bobber at your preferred depth. Experiment to find the depth where you're getting strikes and enjoying the pulls and fun that make you feel like a kid again. Use ¼-, ⅛-, or

$^1/_{16}$-ounce jigheads, with white or yellow soft-plastic grubs, such as Kalin's Triple Threat (Bass Pro Shops). Your preferred float, stick, or bobber, should be on the small side to be sensitive to tentative cold-water hits.

707. Watch Those Spinner Blades

That spinners for panfish need to be small is fairly basic know-how, but often overlooked is the need for the spinner blades to be thin, therefore turning easily and quickly at the slightest and slowest pull.

708. When the Big Bluegills Spawn

"Regardless of where you live, bluegills generally start spawning just about when largemouth bass are finishing . . . If conditions are favorable they might even spawn several times a year."
—John Weiss, "Panfish Secrets the Bass Experts Won't Tell,"
Sports Afield, October, 1973

709. Look to Deep Water for Big Bluegills

Among the many landmark articles writer John Weiss did for *Sports Afield*, one of my favorites was his extraordinary "Panfish Secrets the Bass Experts Won't Tell," which appeared in the October, 1973, issue. As he often did, John Weiss gave serious panfish anglers lots to think about and tricks to try from what he learned fishing with expert Norm Saylor in a fully rigged bass boat at Lake Eufaula, Alabama. An experienced, deep-water, structure bass angler, Saylor used spinning-rod tactics exclusively in his search for big gills. Saylor's Strategy: If your favorite lake—or the one you're fishing—has any big bluegills, they're going to be in deep water most of the time. At different times, the big gills will move out of deep-water sanctuaries, using established migration routes, to reach their feeding areas. Then, back they go to deep water. To find them, you have to crack into their deep-water sanctuaries, just as in bass fishing.

710. Finding the Beds of Bull Bluegills

Continuing John Weiss' revealing look at the tactics of angler Norm Saylor: "Drifting along any shoreline, it's easy to spot the honeycomb appearance of several clusters of spawning beds," Norm explained. "But I look for mammoth concentrations where there might be as many as fifty beds in one small area. This first part is duck soup, and most anglers look no farther. They break out their fly rods and have a ball with 6-inch-long fish, not realizing there might be a group of 1½-pounders only 50 yards away." Working deep and deeper toward bars and a submerged island, Saylor and Weiss eventually locked on a concentration of bulls and took

eleven, with the smallest going 1 pound even and the largest exactly 2 pounds, a trophy bluegill anywhere.

711. Ever Hold a True Bull Bluegill?

"If you have never witnessed firsthand a bull bluegill in the 1 ½ or 2-pound category, it's quite an awesome sight . . . Usually, the bulls are much darker in color than their smaller counterparts, sometimes taking on an almost black color . . . The average length of these bulls is about 12 inches. Even the trophy bluegills seldom exceed this length . . . Now hold out your hand, palm-up. With a bull bluegill lying in your hand and his nose just covering your middle finger, your entire hand should be covered. His mammoth tail section will extend down your forearm, completely covering the band of your wristwatch."

—John Weiss, "Panfish Secrets the Bass Experts Won't Tell," *Sports Afield*, October, 1973

712. The Biggest Bluegill Ever!

"The world-record bluegill of 4-pounds-plus was only 15 inches long. As the bulls reach maturity, they gain practically all of their weight in girth and breadth, not length."

—John Weiss, "Panfish Secrets the Bass Experts Won't Tell," *Sports Afield*, October, 1973

713. A Deadly Sliver of Plastic Worm

In a February, 1972 article in *Sports Afield*, frequent contributor Col. Dave Harbour published the results of some really serious panfish lure experiments. He found he caught more panfish, and far bigger ones, by adding a tiny sliver of a white plastic worm. His No. 1 bait was a tiny lead-head black-and-white nymph with a No. 10 hook. He cut the sliver of worm the same length and size of the nymph and hooked it so most of the worm was off the hook, wiggling. "I don't pretend to know why the weighted black-and-white nymph tipped with white worm is such a lethal big bull bluegill magnet . . . but the worm sliver sure transformed the nymph into a dessert bottom-hugging bluegills couldn't resist."

714. A Super-Star Panfishing Tactic

Writing in the April, 1972 issue of *Sports Afield*, Angling Editor Homer Circle described one of the deadliest panfishing rigs he had ever seen. It simply consisted of a No. 1 Indiana spinner blade, super-polished and delicate to turn at the slightest movement, with a couple of beads up the line for weight and a No. 6 Eagle Claw hook baited with a sliver of flesh cut from the side of a panfish. The strip was 1 ¼ inches long and tapered like a minnow, from a starting width of ¼ inch. The angler who developed the method back then, Dave Goforth, said, "The spinner calls 'em, and the meat gets 'em."

715. *Field & Stream's* Panfish "Ultimate Lure" Survey Winners

In what it called the "Ultimate Lure Survey," published in March, 2008, *Field & Stream* magazine asked 1,000 of its hard-core readers to name their favorite lures. The winners for the Panfish category were:

Jigs, 40%, Jig with Mister Twister
Spinners, 33%, Beetle Spin
Soft-Plastics, 15%, Berkley Gulp! Earthworm with Berkley Power Grub second
Minnow-Type Lures, 8%, Original Rapala with Rebel second
Crankbaits, 2%, Rattlin' Rapala
Spoons, 2%, Dardevle

716. Which Crappie Is That?

Because the crappie is such a popular and widespread fish—famous for both the action and in the pan—much confusion exists over crappie identification. White crappie, black crappie, calico bass—three names, but, whoops, there are only two fish, two real crappies. The white crappie is the most common and widely distributed. The black crappie is the fish sometimes called "calico bass," although at times you will also hear the white crappie called "calico bass." It's very confusing, but throw out the "calico" label and you have the two fish everybody catches and loves to eat—white crappie and black crappie. The dorsal fins of both fish are different, but the easiest way to distinguish between the white and black crappie is by noting that the spots on the white crappie are arranged in neat vertical bars, while on the black crappie they are scattered randomly along the sides of the fish.

717. Fly-Fishing Bonus: Bluegills on the Bed

When bluegills are bedding—the time varies greatly from area to area—fly fishing for these hard-fighting panfish really comes into its own. After you spot the smoothed, rounded patches of the spawning beds, cast a nymph on a light leader into the spots and let it sink onto the beds. A bluegill will pick it up, take it off the bed, and then spit it out. The fish are not feeding, only housekeeping.

718. Don't Lose That Fish

They don't call crappies "papermouths" for nothing. Those lips with the wide section of thin membrane mean that you can never be sure of a fish until it's in the boat. Crappies, even big ones, are not powerful fighters, but what they lack in power they make up for in suspense, since

your hook can pull loose at any moment. I've seen some crappies-to-die-for lost right at the net or hand when the hook broke through the lips of the "paper mouth."

719. Catching Slab-Sided Bluegills in Midsummer

In the heat and blazing suns of high summer, you probably won't have much luck catching the really big bluegills by fishing your usual spots—shoreline cover, stumps, fallen trees. The occasional good fish might be taken early or late in the day, but mostly the pickings will be slim. Still, provided your lake has a healthy bluegill population, the slab-sided fish you covet can be found and taken. Instead of target casting to cover, fish for them deep with $1/16$- or $1/32$-ounce jigs, straight over the sides of the boat. Yes, straight down! Slowly work the jigs up and down at various depths and locations until you find the fish. Note the level where you've finally hit the schools of big fish, and you'll be in business of a close-up of the fish with the jig in the corner of its mouth.

720. Fishing the Deadly Lau Loop

Back in 1975, when I was editor of *Sports Afield*, Angling Editor Homer Circle came through with many articles on advanced skills, sometimes working with his friend, the legendary guide-turned-filmmaker Glenn Lau (producer of "Bigmouth" and others). One of the best presentations from this talented combo was an article on fishing deep for summer bluegills by using a method that is a virtual pioneer on today's drop-shot fishing. The irony is that the "pioneer" method is better than today's—because it used Glenn Lau's knot, which is a great improvement over the Surgeon's Knot or Palomar Knot used in today's drop-shot rigs (see separate articles). Homer and Glenn came up with a rig consisting of a weighted jig fly (or small jig) on the end of the line, then a dropper 8 inches above, and another 6 inches above that. Each dropper was 2 inches long, using very tiny mono. The dropper was attached to a ½-inch Lau Loop, which had a more-sensitive feel and presented the fly more enticingly. Homer and Glenn used very tiny 18-inch ice-fishing rods rigged with three guides and Ambassadeur reels. The flies were No. 12s to 16s and dropped straight down to the bottom. They were deadly when jigged and retrieved simultaneously. With a little imagination, you can put together a similar rig today and customize the tactics with various mini-jigs and flies. It's deadly on deep panfish.

721. Go Deep With Sponge-Rubber Spiders

Those sponge-rubber spiders that look and feel real enough to bite you will catch far, far bigger bluegills if you wrap some lead wire around their heads. They're made to be fished on top, but that's seldom where the big 'gills are hanging out. They're deep. You've got to find them, then get your spider down to them.

722. Catching Big, Summer Yellow Perch

Yellow perch are prime targets for anglers everywhere, but especially in the Great Lakes region where they grow big and fat. Veteran angler Steve Ryan explains how to cash in on the action in the article "Summer Perchin'" on the Lindy Tackle Web site, www.lindyfishingtackle.com: "Lake Michigan's fishery has changed considerably over the last several decades but the methods for catching these tasty fish remain the same. Crappie spreaders, Lindy rigs, jigs, and slip floats will catch you a limit of perch no matter where you fish. These rigs are nothing more than bait delivery systems designed to present live bait to fish in the most effective means possible." Ryan likes to set up his rigs with minnows when the water is cold, then night crawlers or softshell crawfish when the water temperatures top the mid-50s. See his article for more details.

723. Try Crankbaits for Summer Crappies

If you're not happy with the numbers of crappies you've been getting in summer, try using crankbaits. Especially on larger waters, where the crappie schools roam around a lot, and where they often go deep, crankbaits either cast or trolled can produce big crappies for you. Some favorite models of top guides include the 2-inch Bandits in sizes that dive to varying depths, and Rebel's 2-inch Deep Vee-R, which dives to 8 to 10 feet.

724. Turn a Bad Day Into a Great One

When your favorite fly rod and top-water floaters are producing absolutely no strikes, why spend the day flailing the water? Pick up a light spinning outfit, tie a ¼-ounce sinker to the end of your line with a dropper leader 1-foot long tied 18 inches to 2 feet above the sinker. Tie on a No. 8 floating bug and send your rig down where the fish are. Dancing the bug just off the bottom is especially effective when you're in an area where the bream are concentrated.

725. Tribute to a Very Special Panfish

To the eye, the redbreast sunfish is an explosion of color, shaped like a living sunrise portrait. At the end of a light rod or pole, whether cane or new-tech fibers, the redbreast's runs to escape are line-breaking, rod-bending displays of power, made effective by the deep, slab-sided body and the sweeps of the powerful tail. To the palate, the white, firm fillets of fried redbreast are delicious to a point that defies description. As a card-carrying Georgia boy from the heart of redbreast country, along the banks of the Ogeechee River, I have spent most of my life far from my beloved river, but its siren call has always pulled me back. I return to Georgia to find, catch, and eat redbreasts every chance I get—with corn dodgers on the side, thank you very much.

726. Redbreast vs. Brim

The ubiquitous bluegill—brim, if you will—completes the lure of black-water fishing with the redbreast, but does not quite provide the rewards of redbreast fishing. Bluegills vary in color from dark, shadowy blue to the sunburst colors of the redbreast, but they are not the same fish. The redbreast (*Lepomis auritus*) is better tasting and harder fighting.

727. Where to Find Redbreast

Redbreasts live and thrive in clean, dark, low-country currents of the southeastern United States that sweep over sandy bottoms, glaring white when the sun hits them, and through boggy swamplands of oaks, cypress, sweet gums, and magnolia. Towering pines loom on the higher ground along the serpentine courses of the rivers and creeks, where the never-ending cries of birds mark the flow.

728. Count on the Catalpa Worm

If you're fortunate enough to live in the South, treasure every catalpa tree you can find. For the catalpa caterpillar is the ultimate live bait for bluegills, redbreasts, and just about every other fish swimming in southern waters. Some of the old-timers used to recommend turning the catalpa insideout. Experiment if you wish, but I don't think you have to. Catalpa bonus: You can keep them in the fridge.

729. Cricket Know-How

Crickets are a mainstay of panfishing with live bait—and a mainstay of bait shops—but they come off the hook easily and you'll be plagued by minnows and tiny fish constantly stealing your bait. They're best used when you're after *big* panfish.

730. Hooks for Bream: When You Want Them to Straighten Out

One popular theory on choosing lines and leaders for panfish, especially bream, is to use very light leaders in still water so that the bait falls in a soft, lifelike manner, as if dropping from a tree. In current, or areas so filled with stumps and limbs that you're bound to hook into them, use a very strong leader and springy, light hook that will straighten out with a strong, steady pull. That way you won't keep losing your whole rig in the stumps.

731. Use Slip Bobbers for Crappies

We want to find crappies fast. Today! Now! One of the best ways to do it is to use two rods, with sinkers and baits for two different depths, and using slip bobbers. These bobbers allow every cast to return to its previous depth, saving time and putting you on the fish faster. Once you've found the depths the fish are taking on a particular day, you can set your bobber and forget it. The Betts "Mister Crappie" Slippers at www.basspro.com are good ones, as are the Cabelas "Easy-On Slip Bobbers," www.cabelas.com.

732. Bait-Keeper Hooks Do a Better Job

You may have fished for years with great success using regular hooks, but if you're a live bait angler you're going to do much better with today's bait-keeper hooks. They keep your bait on the hook much longer, thereby catching more fish.

733. Fry 'Em Up—Southern Style

Panfish fillets are great, but this old Georgia-raised boy likes the whole fish, deep-fried. Scale them, gut them, cut off the heads (being careful to save that big hunk of meat just behind the head), and slide them into the fat. I'm willing to put up with the bones to get every morsel of this delicious meat.

CHAPTER 15

How Catfish Experts Fish:
Follow the Masters to More Success

734. Giant Catfish: You Need Help

The biggest catfish—we're talking 20 to 30 pounds and higher—are caught on the bigger rivers, from deep holes. Fishing these waters, particularly where impoundment water is being released, can be treacherous. Think about hiring a guide before you tackle it on your own.

735. Finding and Catching More and Bigger Catfish

My friend John E. Phillips is a prolific and engaging writer whose prose has enhanced many magazine pages over the years. Not only are his articles excellent, but he is the author of several books, including "The Masters' Secrets of Catfishing," available from John's Night Hawk Publications Web site, www.nighthawkpublications.com. Click on "books," then go to "fishing books."

736. Chum Them Up With Dog Food

"Use an ice pick to punch two dozen holes in a can of inexpensive dog food. The day before you fish, sink the can of dog food on a rock, clay, or sandy bottom without mud . . . To chum cats in quicker, purchase the more expensive dog food packed in gravy . . . By the time you fish the next day, the dog food should have chummed the cats to the spot where you want to catch them."

—John Phillips, "John's Journal," Night Hawk Publications,
www.nighthawkpublications.com

737. Favorite Baits for Blue Cats

"For whopper blues, stick to fish. Big catfish almost exclusively eat other fish. Use whole fish, 4- to 6-inch-long strips or meaty chunks," reports John M. Felsher in "Big Game Sport on a Small Budget," on a www.cabelas.com Field Guide Story. Some of the largest blues hit "mere morsels," he says. Felsher notes that some guides prefer skipjack herring, cut into chunks or filleted. The fillet is hooked one time with the hook exposed and undulates in the current. Catfish can't resist it.

738. A Good Basic Catfish Rig

To fish your catfish bait right on the bottom, use an egg sinker, barrel swivel, 20-inch leader, and No. 6 hook.

739. Fish the Mussel Beds

Wherever you can find freshwater clams or river mussels, consider them to be catfish magnets. As these critters die and are washed off the shells, catfish will be on them. No clams? Then use spoiled shrimp or live worms.

740. Use Dog Food in Small Ponds

"When you fish small ponds or little lakes, use cheap, dry dog food to chum up catfish. Anchor your boat and every two to three minutes throw a handful of dog food out in the water . . . bream will show up first, allowing you to catch a mess of bluegills and shellcrackers. In a short while, the catfish will begin to come to the chum . . . "

—John Phillips, "John's Journal," Night Hawk Publications,
www.nighthawkpublications.com

741. Switch to Catfish for More Fun

"I used to specialize in fly fishing for smallmouth. But as I've gotten older, I've turned to catfishing. It doesn't take as much effort, and I can just about always count on getting a few." (Other southern anglers can do the same in the small creeks and rivers near their homes.)

—Buffalo River, Tennessee angler Joe B. Sweeney, in the Wade Bourne article "Lazy Days: Small Streams and Southern Catfish," Bass Pro Shops Outdoor Library

742. Best Water for Small-Stream Catfish

"Most people think catfish hang in deep, quiet holes. This may be true of the bigger ones, but smaller cats feed in shallow, swift areas. I'm talking about runs that are 2–3 feet deep and exposed to direct current. Also, a spot is better if it has a clean gravel or clay bottom instead of a mud bottom. Catfish hold around cover (logs, treetops, rocks, and so on) in these areas and move out into the current to find food. In fact, they feed a lot like a bass."

—Buffalo River, Tennessee angler Joe B. Sweeney, in the Wade Bourne article "Lazy Days: Small Streams and Southern Catfish," Bass Pro Shops Outdoor Library

743. Baiting Up for Small-Stream Catfish

Buffalo River, Tennessee angler Joe B. Sweeney says "catfishermen can bait with any range of cut-up fish pieces, crawfish tails, stink baits, worms, insects, etc. However, he has narrowed the bait choice to three top performers: red worms, chicken livers, and catalpa worms." Sweeney says the best way to keep chicken livers on the hook is to run it through a thumb-sized piece two or three times.

—Wade Bourne, in the article "Lazy Days: Small Streams and Southern Catfish," Bass Pro Shops Outdoor Library

744. The Deadliest Bait for TrotLine Catfish

John Phillips reports that "Mike Handley, a friend, had run out of catfish bait, but he used his creative ability and imagination to create a new one. He started with a pack of hot dogs. 'I cut the hot dogs into small pieces that would bait well on my hooks,' Handley explained. 'I put the hot dogs in a quart fruit jar, poured Fish Formula Catfish Lure into the jar to completely cover the hot dogs, and let the jar sit overnight.'" Phillips goes on to report that the next day Handley caught more catfish in two hours than he ever had before, and continuing his method for another night and a day, he caught more fish than anyone in his camp.

—John Phillips, "John's Journal,"Night Hawk Publications, www.nighthawkpublications.com

745. Technique of a World-Record Catfisher

In many years of writing about catfishing, including his very informative book, *The Masters'*
Secrets of Catfishing, John Phillips has interviewed many excellent anglers to learn their techniques. One of the best is Ralph Barbee, Jr., who pursued catfish at Clarks Hill Reservoir near
Augusta, Georgia, and caught a world-record 62-pound blue cat and a 55-pound channel
cat that almost broke the state record. According to Barbee, "I found a place where the state
had dumped concrete into the reservoir—making humps on the bottom. I'm convinced that
chumming is the key to catching big cats . . . I use a Humminbird Flasher to find the humps
in the river and chum . . . "

—John Phillips, "John's Journal," Night Hawk Publications,
www.nighthawkpublications.com

746. Baits of a World-Record Catfisher

World-record holder Ralph Barbee, Jr., on his favorite baits for big catfish: "I chum with Bob's Blood Bait, which is made in Texas, to call the cats to the humps. I also add cat mullet, a salt-water fish, to a mixture of blood bait and chicken blood and entrails in a long-gallon, plastic mayonnaise jar. I let this concoction sit in the sun in the jar for a day. The chum smells so bad I wear plastic surgeon gloves to dump the bloody mixture into a burlap bag. After I sink the bag, I fish close to it with large Louisiana pink worms, which are so big and thick they'll completely cover a large treble hook."

—John Phillips, "John's Journal," Night Hawk Publications,
www.nighthawkpublications.com

747. Best Time to Fish for Giant Catfish

World-record angler Ralph Barbee, Jr., (62-pound blue cat) says, "I've learned the most productive time to fish for big cats in my area on the Georgia/South Carolina border is between 10:00 PM and 10:00 AM when the moon is dark during August, September, and October. I caught my world-record catfish on a September 10 night."

—John Phillips, "John's Journal," Night Hawk Publications,
www.nighthawkpublications.com

CHAPTER 16

Carp Secrets:
The Mysterious Ways of a Great Gamefish

748. Don't Forget Carp Fishing

They're big and powerful, capable of making your reel sing and putting a bend in your rod that seems dangerously close to breaking. Although not one of the glamour girls and boys of fishing—and not good to eat (for most of us, anyway)—carp are a worthy gamefish that will pay you back in fun for every hour you put into learning how to catch them. In England, carp fishing has a fanatical army of devotees. We have our share of carp addicts here as well, and once you've tried the sport, you may find yourself hooked.

749. Fishing for Carp: Stop Missing Out!

"I submit carp are smarter, speedier, stronger, spookier, as selective and secretive and more durable than any trout, or any other freshwater fish for that matter."

—Chuck Robbins, noted author and fly-fishing guide.
Check the Web site he maintains with his wife, Gale, for his blog,
articles, and information on books: www.chuckngalerobbins.com.

750. Carp on a Fly: A Supreme Challenge

"For starters, carp, especially the river-dwelling variety, are stronger and fight harder than any freshwater fish, including trout and smallmouth bass. I honestly cannot recall hooking a single river carp on a fly that failed to run all the fly line out, and most went well into the backing. Lake-dwelling carp are tough customers too, but don't measure up to their moving-water cousins."

—Chuck Robbins, noted author and fly-fishing guide

751. To Catch Carp, Pass the Dough

You'll hear it from every side: Dough makes a wonderful bait to catch those bottom-feeding carp. Your first thought may be, "How the heck do I keep dough balls on a hook?" Major hook manufacturers such as Eagle Claw and Mustad have the specialized treble hooks carp anglers need to fish dough balls and other creative baits. A common rig is to use a sinker at the end of the line with two 12-inch dropper lines about a foot or two apart above. Carp have no teeth, so special leaders are not needed.

752. Essentials for Catching More Carp

Although they are not good on the table, carp are plentiful, powerful, and are best caught on lighter tackle than many other sportfish. You'll catch more carp by using a hook that is not too big—certainly no bigger than a 1/0 max—and a small split-shot sinker, or no sinker at

all. Carp will not pick up bait and take it if they feel any resistance. Dough balls, corn, and other homemade concoctions make the best baits. See Cabelas and others for special hooks and tackle.

753. Bubbles That Betray Carp

Carp like rooting around soft, silty bottoms with lots of vegetation and little current. While they are doing this, a line of bubbles rising to the surface will betray their movements. Try to get your bait on the bottom ahead of the direction they're moving.

754. Scent Sweeteners for Carp Baits

Most experienced carp anglers rely on scent-flavored baits in one concoction or another. The scent of the bait can be the clincher that convinces a carp it's time to dine.

755. Divide and Conquer Carp Tactics

"From watching the Redmire carp I learnt that certain groups of fish liked to follow a set routine while others lived a more individual independent life. It was these nonconformists that I usually

fished for . . . I preferred stalking the loners, especially as these solitary beings were often the largest in the pool."

—Chris Yates, *The Secret Carp,* Merlin Unwin Books, Great Britain, 2002

756. You Have to be Ready for Carp

"Over the last half-hour the carp have all dispersed in several different directions. Two of them—though not the largest pair—began to probe about near my bait, sending up clouds of bubbles, and there was a tense moment when I saw the line jag and tighten. Yet just as I was going to strike, it fell slack. There was a mighty swirl and both carp streaked away like meteors. That was my chance and I missed it."

—Chris Yates, *The Secret Carp,* Merlin Unwin Books, Great Britain, 2002

757. Fly-Fishing the Great Carp Unknown

"In *Carp in North America*, published by the American Fisheries Society, Ronald J. Spitler says, 'When it comes to fly-fishing [for carp] we are drifting a bit into the unknown . . . ' I don't know about you, but I kind of like the sound of that."

—John Gierach, *Another Lousy Day in Paradise,* Simon & Schuster, 1996

758. On the Hunt for Carp

"They're beautifully camouflaged against the silty bottom, but you can pick them out by the faint, lazy puffs of mud they blow through their gills as they suck in food, or by their tails waving slowly under the surface like big brown flowers. In deeper water you can sometimes locate them by the trails of tiny bubbles they leave while feeding."

—John Gierach, *Another Lousy Day in Paradise,* Simon & Schuster, 1996

759. The Carp as a Fighter

"No trout, except possibly a very old, very heavy, very wise trout, fights like a large carp."

—Steven J. Meyers, *San Juan River Chronicles,* Lyons & Burford, 1994

PART SIX

ON THE WATER

for Pickerel, Pike, and Muskie

CHAPTER 17

Pike Action Guaranteed: These Tips Won't Let You Down

760. On the Hunt for Pike

Northern pike, and their smaller cousins, chain pickerel, are masters of the art of ambush—fierce predators roaming the water in wolf packs. They're not always around, and sometimes they don't seem to be on the bite, but if you're fishing good pike or pickerel water, you should be in for prime action. Weedy, still-water bays with deeper "escape" water nearby are where you should find the fish.

761. When Pike Attack

"The greediness of pike knows no bounds," wrote Sergei Aksakov in *Notes on Fishing* back in 1847. Nothing has changed. As an example, note that when you're casting in good pike water, you might see a sudden swirl some distance from where your lure plunks down on a cast. "Spooked one," you think to yourself. No sir! You haven't spooked anything. That pike has just launched his attack. Get set for a strike!

762. A Fish of Wildness

Pike are similar to brook trout and lake trout in that their prime environment is the great north country. If you haven't been there, you owe it to yourself to do everything you can to plan such a trip. From Minnesota's Boundary Waters Area and the adjoining Quetico, up through all the vast reaches of the Canadian wilderness, wolf packs of pike patrol through the cold, clean waters. This is the land of spruce, white pine, and birch; of loons calling from across the lakes; of beavers, otters, and mink; of moose and black bear. If your heart cranks up a notch or two when you think about country like this, and the fish that swim there, you'll know you've just got to go.

763. Playing Those Pike

Despite their great size and fierce disposition, northern pike sometimes seem on the sluggish side when you're playing them. Then it happens: The pike sees the boat. It's a whole new ball-game now; time to hold on to your hat. The pike will pull the trigger, your rod will bow into a hoop, and you'll know you're in a fight.

764. Pike and Pickerel for the Frying Pan

Despite their vast number of bones, pike and pickerel make absolutely delicious fried meals. The trick is to slice off the fillets with surgical skill—and a sharp fill knife—and extract the long Y bones. Then pick through the remaining slab of clean meat for stray bones and get ready to fry 'em up.

765. Hang On to Your Hat

When fishing for pike and pickerel, watch for swirls in the water nearby just as you start your retrieve. No, you haven't spooked a fish. On the contrary, a pike or pickerel has his prey—your bait or lure—in his sights and is moving in for the kill. Get ready!

766. Northern Pike: Here, There, Everywhere!

Because they are found in so many northern latitudes, making them a Holarctic fish, northern pike can claim the distinction of being the most widely distributed freshwater fish in the world. (Now wait! Don't try to tell me you knew what Holarctic meant!)

767. Fly Rod Pike? Go Right Ahead

Because I have been fortunate to travel to fishing camps in both Canada and Alaska, I have been able to tangle with northern pike on a fly rod on several occasions, sometimes alternating between fly rod and spinning gear in the same boat. While pike aggressively hit big streamers under the right conditions, I feel the action is faster and sportier using light spinning tackle and lures. Some anglers go all *ga-ga* to say they caught a fish on a fly, and if that's your bag, go right ahead.

768. They Love Their Pike in Great Britain

As much as Americans and Canadians cherish their northern pike and its fishing, you have to hand it to the Brits for downright adoration of this fish. The excellent Web site of the Pike Anglers Club of Great Britain will show you what I mean: www.www.pacgb.co.uk/.

769. The Perfect Pike Spoon or Spinner

The perfect pike spoon or spinner is the one that will wobble, flash, and give the most action at the *slowest* retrieving speed.

770. Give the Devil a Chance

Like many another fishing "seniors," I caught my first northern pike—and a lot since—on the classic Eppinger Dardevle—red-and-white stripes on the front and flashing, silvery nickel on the back. Today's models, and all the assorted imitators, come in many different colors, but I always have the itch to tie on the red guy.

771. Sound Off for Northerns

Letting pike know there's prey in the water by splashing down lures and baits—and running spinnerbaits alongside weedy lairs—has been an excellent technique just about forever. However, a new twist worth trying comes along every now and then. On the site of the Twin Lakes Outfitters, Nakina, Ontario, www.twin-lakes-air.com, they're talking about doing The

DareDevil Slap. That's a name taken from the original Eppinger Dardevle, and the tactic is to cast the lure very high over your target zone, then jerk your line toward you when the bait's 2 or 3 feet above the water. The sound of the spoon slapping the surface triggers vicious pike attacks.

772. Team a Rapala with a Dardevle

In northern pike fishing techniques on the Web site of Twin Lakes Outfitters, Nakina, Ontario, www.twin-lakes-air.com, an idea that looks really good is to use a worn-out Rapala with a perfectly good Dardevle. Take the hooks off your broken Rapala, then attach it to a black steel leader. Attach another leader to the back of the Rapala with a spring-slip-ring, then attach your Dardevle (or whatever you want to use). The Rapala will get the pike's attention, and the Dardevle will complete the deal.

Cutting the Odds on Muskies:
Catching the Wolves of Fresh Water

773. The Fish of 10,000 Casts

The muskellunge, muskie, isn't called the "The Fish of 10,000 Casts" for nothing. That number may be exaggerated; nevertheless, the muskie is indeed a trophy fish and not easy to come by, especially on artificial lures. They can be caught, however, on both lures and live bait, but the top guides who know how to do it will never call it easy.

774. The Oldest Muskie Story Out There

To illustrate how difficult muskellunge fishing can be, this old anecdote has been around for a long time. Guy asks his friend, "How was your muskie trip?" His friend replies: "Oh, it was fantastic! In five days' fishing, we had three follows."

775. Why Those Big Mossback Muskies Are Different

Writing in his "Fresh-Water Fishing" column in the November 1945 issue of *Sports Afield*, Angling Editor Cal Johnson noted that the term "mossback" really fits the muskellunge—make that *big* muskellunge. When muskies go 30 to 60 pounds they have a coating of dark, slimy vegetation on their backs. Small or medium muskies don't have the "mossback" look simply because they do not spend the time lurking in the dense vegetation that the big fish do.

776. Muskies Prowling for Prey

Big muskies feed on big baitfish. In the November 1945 issue of *Sports Afield*, Angling Editor Cal Johnson reports on seeing a 6-pound walleye taken from the stomach of a 35-pound muskellunge. "The very large muskie is quite inactive and moves about very little," Johnson said. "He will go on a hunting expedition every so often and stalk and capture a large walleye pike, redhorse or big black sucker, swallowing them whole. Then he swims alongside some submerged log . . . or other piece of cover and lies perfectly still for several days until the food is digested." No wonder big muskies are so hard to catch.

PART SEVEN

ON THE WATER

for Saltwater Fish

CHAPTER 19

Special Section: Stu Apte's Best Fishing Tips

The legendary guide and angler shares the secrets of a lifetime of of tarpon, bonefish, fly fishing for sailfish, and playing and landing the most powerful saltwater gamefish.

In an exclusive interview with Editor Lamar Underwood, legendary angler Stu Apte discusses some of the most important tips he feels he can share with other anglers. A pioneer of the early days of flats fishing as a guide in the lower Florida Keys, a former Navy carrier fighter pilot, Captain of the giant 747 jets with Pan Am, and a dedicated angler who has pursued gamefish all over the world, Apte was elected a member of the International Game Fish Association Hall of Fame and is renowned for his fishing skills and experience. He lives in the Florida Keys and recently published his autobiography, *Of Wind and Tides*, available at many book shops and Internet sites.

777. Describe your basic fish-fighting technique.

No matter what the fish is or where you're fishing—it could be a bonefish on the flats or a trout in the mountains—you have to be smooth when applying pressure. I believe in fighting all the fish to the maximum of the tackle I'm fishing with and getting the fish in as fast as possible. This makes for a quick release and a healthier fish. It also lets you and/or your fishing companion get back to the fish while the bite is still on.

778. Is "being smooth" the key?

In all of the fish fighting that I do, there are some basic things, and it starts off with doing everything VERY SMOOTHLY. When I pump a fish, I do it very smoothly. I enjoy telling people that what breaks fish off is the *jerk at each end of the line!* When you want to break a line, you don't break it with a steady pull. You *jerk it!* You *pop it!* I have a lot of people say, "Man, I had a big one on yesterday, but that fish broke me off." And I say, "Now wait a minute. That fish didn't break you off. *You* broke that fish off! You did not do things smoothly, and there was a jerk on each end of the line."

779. What are some dos and don'ts for playing big fish with a fly rod?

When fighting big fish with a fly rod, do not hold a rod above the cork casting grip. While pumping the fish closer, keep the rod butt in the center of your stomach and rotate your body either to the left or to the right, depending upon the direction the fish is facing. Always try to pull directly opposite the direction the fish wants to go. When you get the fish close to the boat, continue the pumping motion by leaning back, arching your back, after winding your rod tip down close to the water. This should bring the fish to the surface ready to land.

780. Do you have any special tips on playing bonefish?

Remember that a 5- or 6- pound bonefish will almost always run off at least 100 yards of line on its first run and turn around, running right back at you faster then you can reel, especially if you're reeling with your left hand and you're right-handed. This is why many trout fly fisherman end up losing most of the big bonefish they hook on fly. I am a firm believer in winding line with your dominant hand. If you are right-handed you should wind with your right hand. You will also have more dexterity if and when the fish surges and you have to let go at the handle.

781. What about a leaping fish?

When big fish like tarpon, or even trout and salmon, make a mighty leap, it's time to literally "take a bow." To help keep from having that sudden jerk at the end of your line, it is important to thrust your rod toward the fish whenever it is surges or jumps.

782. When playing fish, do you hold the rod high or low?

On playing fish, when I've got a big fish on—say a tarpon or a billfish—and there's a lot of line out and the fish is more than 100 feet away from me, I fight it with a high rod in order to keep as much line out of the water as I can. That makes it easier for me to wind line fast, eliminating the additional drag of the line in the water, helping me get as close to that fish as quickly as I can. I can wind line quicker with most of it out of the water. I arch my back, pumping straight up, and wind like all get-out.

783. What happens when the fish is closer?

When I get close to the fish, around 30 or 40 feet, that's when I can really put the pressure on it. If it's facing away, or going away, and I can get the angle on the fish going away from me, either left or right or straight away, I get that low rod angle so that I can roll the fish down and under. It's actually the first time that fish can't arch its back and do what it wants to do . . . go about its business. It's the first time it's been stopped from swimming, because I'm really pulling down and toward its tail to back off its swimming ability. And that really panics it the first time or two, which is what you want. You want it to make a few screaming runs and exert the energy, rather than just giving you a dogg fight. So, when the fish is way out, I have a high rod. When I get him in close, I generally have a low rod.

784. So you've turned the fish. What next?

Well, more often than not, you're going to turn him down and under. If you have the rod low, and he's going away, say 30 feet to 50 feet away, and you stop that, he'll rotate down and under

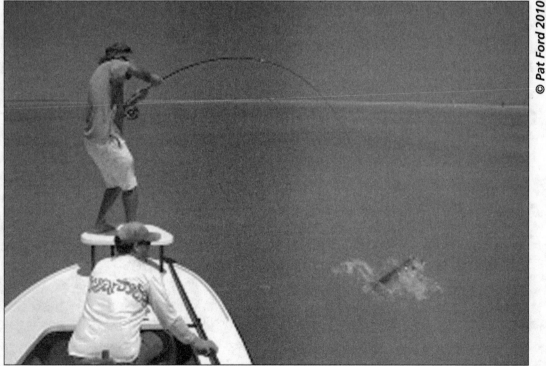

© Pat Ford 2010

and come back toward you. At that time, I have the rod tip higher and I'm winding line like a demon.

785. Describe the critical final stages of the fight.

The rod tip may not necessarily be kept high in the final stages. It may have to go low again . . . in order to stop the fish again. When you have a high rod on a fish, you're doing two things: You're using too much of the tip on the rod for fighting the fish, which doesn't put enough pressure on it; but the main thing is that the fish can just go about its business. It has a rigid spine, and it just sets its shoulders and does what it wants. So it's important to wind the rod tip down to within 2 feet of the fish's mouth and then lift with the back (butt) portion of the rod.

786. What are the best moon phases for flats fishing?

I personally prefer to do most of my shallow-water fishing, whether it's for bonefish, tarpon, permit, snook, or redfish, starting one or two days before the new (dark of the moon) or the full moon, right through three or four days after the full or new moon. Of course the weather (wind and water temperature) is the most decisive link in this chain in order to have good fishing.

787. The best flats-fishing weather is . . . ?

There are very little black and whites when it comes to fishing except in preparation. All your equipment should be in tip-top shape and you should have a number of alternative plans on where to fish, before and after you get on the water.

In flats fishing for tarpon and bonefish, I like light winds, proper water temperatures, which will of course vary with the time of year that you're fishing for these species. Obviously, the tides will vary from place to place, and the effects of the weather, the slant of the light on the water, the winds, the cloud cover—it's all part of the puzzle. That's why your alternative plans are so important. You can't be counting on just one place to fish on the flats.

788. For tarpon in winter, how do you cope with cold snaps?

In winter months, after we've had a cold snap in the Florida Keys, I generally look for an oceanside flat with an early morning high tide. But . . . I wait until the tide has been flowing off of this flat for at least three or four hours, giving the water a chance to warm up—creating

© Pat Ford 2010

a warmer flow of water from this flat toward the deeper water where the fish would be because of the cold. They will feel this warmer flow and move in toward that particular flat.

789. You've had a lot of success with early season tarpon. Is that your formula?

I seek a large flat on the Gulf side of the Florida Keys, on the down-current side where I know tarpon often congregate in the deeper water. They'll be moving onto the flat as it warms. This tactic has paid off for me repeatedly.

790. Why is your favorite flat down by Key West so good?

It's a good flat because it catches the sun and warms up and is adjacent to deep water. I still fish down there every April with a guide, and you'd be surprised that we never see another guide boat over there. Isn't that interesting? We go over there, and because my guide doesn't fish that flat either, I often say, "Why don't we go try over here, and we'll have fish." And he'll say, "Well, I haven't fished it in years . . . last time I was on it there wasn't anything there." Those things happen. It's a very big shallow flat. The tide coming in off the Gulf moves across that flat. Of course, it doesn't move all that fast, but it's a big flat, and the sun gets enough time to warm that water as it crosses the big flat, which is at least a mile wide, so when it comes across onto

the deep side where the tarpon are in the channel, it feels kind of good to them, and it sucks them right into it. That was exactly the scenario in April 1971 when I caught the 154-pound fly-rod world-record tarpon, which I described in my memoir, *Of Wind And Tides*.

It's the same thing with the bonefish in the wintertime. If we've had a cold snap down here, say tomorrow, I know exactly where I'd go. I'd look up the tides, and I'd be there exactly as I described. I'd want a high tide in the morning, so it gets a chance to warm up the shallow water before it gets a chance to go flowing off there, into the deeper water.

791. What makes saltwater casting so special?

One of the main differences between fishing in salt water and fresh water, for trout, or bass, or whatever, especially for trout in a river, is that these fish in fresh water cannot go anywhere. You make a bad cast, and it stops feeding. You can sit down, have a sandwich, admire the scenery, and if the hatch is still coming off, that fish will start feeding again in a very short time. If you make a bad cast to a bonefish on the flats, or a permit, or a tarpon, and spook 'em, you can go back to that same place every day for the rest of your life, and probably never get a chance at that fish again. That fish has gone into a different zip code area. It's changed addresses, without leaving a forwarding address, and there's a good chance it will not be back to that flat again anytime soon. The bonefish doesn't have to come back. The trout can't go anywhere else. In saltwater fly fishing, you have to be more accurate—and be able to do it with speed and accuracy, so that you can get the fly to the fish before the fish knows you're there or moves out of your range.

792. In tarpon fishing, the cast is critical, is it not?

The time that you take placing your fly in front of the fish can be the difference between a very successful fishing trip, or complete failure. The average cast is only 55 or 60 feet, though more big tarpon are probably caught within 40 feet of the boat. You might spend hours standing on the casting platform, holding your rod with one hand and the fly by the bend of the hook in the fingers of your other hand, waiting for that one cast, to that chance of a lifetime fish. All of a sudden the guide emphatically whispers, "There she is, 11 o'clock, 60 feet, hurry cast! Drop it right in front of her face. Now! NOW!" About that time your legs feel like jelly, your hands are shaking, and you feel like you're going to be sick to your stomach. You not only forget how to properly release the fly from your fingers with a Roll Cast, but you rush your cast, making the fly land only 15 feet from the boat. The guide may be one of the rare guides that would sympathize with your inability, or he might preface his choice words of wisdom with expressions that don't look good in print.

793. Is there anything special about your casting that could help a serious angler practice and learn to cast better?

Learn how to do the Fast Cast in order to get the fly to the fish with speed and accuracy. Whenever possible, it is always best to practice on the water, but a grassy area will also suffice. Start by having 8 or 10 feet of fly line plus your leader out of the rod tip. First practice a Roll Cast, pulling the fly from your fingers without the fly hitting the ground. As the fly reaches the end of the forward Roll Cast, start a sharp back cast with an abrupt stop of the rod near the vertical, creating a reasonably tight loop. At the proper moment let a small amount of line pull from your fingers. This is called shooting a little line on your back cast. What this does is help add a little weight, bending the rod which will in turn help you shoot enough line on your forward cast, to make that 50- or 60-foot presentation. If by chance it is necessary to make that rare 75-foot presentation, merely turn the first forward cast into a false cast. You would have approximately 45 feet of line in the air, which would ideally load the rod for a long cast.

794. What are your preferences in sunglasses for fishing the flats? In fresh water?

I prefer amber or tan polarized sunglass. I believe this gives a better color definition in shallow water, and that is what I am looking for, a hue of color, or anything that looks different from its surroundings. It helps to have side shields or even goggles to keep the glare out of your eyes.

795. In bonefishing, opportunities do exist for anglers to wade the flats alone. What flies do you recommend they carry? What would be your first fly tied on?

This depends on where you're wading, the depth of the water, the water temperature, and the tide. I would have a variety of flies, some weighted, most of them weedless in sizes from a 1/0 all the way down to a No. 8 to be able to cope with all the conditions. The patterns will depend on where I am wading. In the Bahamas, I would have many Charlie patterns and Gotchas. The colors will generally depend on the clarity of the water and the bottom: light-colored bottom, light-colored fly; dark-colored bottom, dark-colored fly.

796. When a bonefish seems to be near your fly, do you see anything special that makes the fish strike?

Most bonefish flies are too small to be able to see, making it important to watch the signals from the bonefish itself. Normally their body language will telegraph when they eat the fly. They generally telegraph eating your fly by some exciting wiggling of their fins and tails.

797. What's your "go-to" snook fly?

Once again this depends on the area, the time of year, and the water depth. I generally use one of my Apte Too or Apte Too-Plus patterns on a 1/0 hook or a Lefty's Deceiver pattern. Snook in shallow water are very aware and therefore spooky so it is important to make long, accurate presentations, generally, even more so than for bonefish. Unlike bonefish, they do have a very rough mouth and require a bite tippet.

798. What's your choice fly to get a permit to strike?

Any number of Merkin or crab patterns seem to do the job as long as your presentation is a good one under good permit conditions. The best days to get permit to eat a fly are on the windy days when they do not have the greatest visibility and have to make snap decisions. Often, putting it right in front of them or even behind them can work.

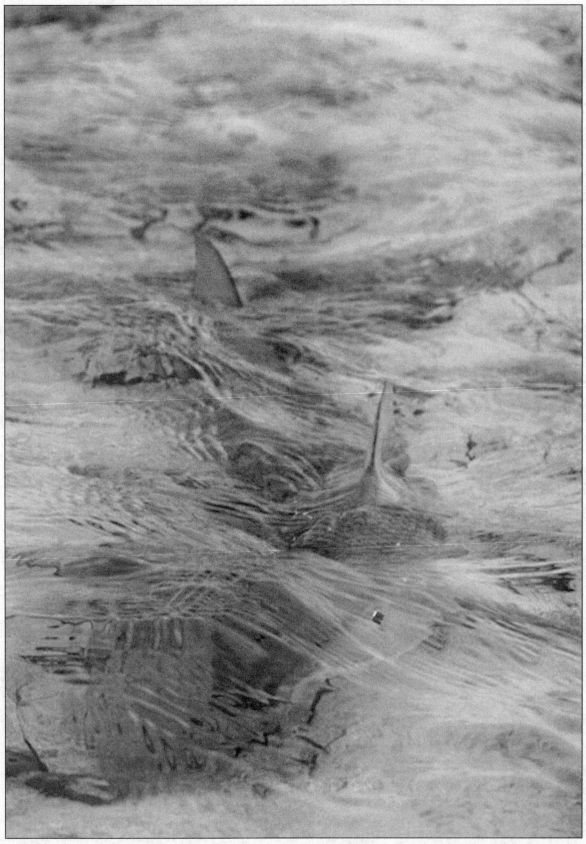

799. Describe the "Stu Apte Method" of presenting a fly or lure to a tarpon.

First, they should not see the fly hit the water. Next—and this is critical—the fly must be swimming *away* from them, not *toward* them. Now, in the old days (1950s and 1960s), these fish had not been run over by outboard boats with big engines or cast to every thirty or fourty minutes, and you could drop the fly on top of them, and they would turn around and eat it. It's not like that now. They have run the gauntlets of fly fishermen. And they know that something dropping out of the heavens is going to hurt, rather than be good. So they should not see your presentation hit the water. And it should be at the proper angle. They do not want anything coming *at* them, whether it be from the side or directly toward them. They'll spook from that, and I think that goes back to their youth when they were about an inch and a half long and looked like a pollywog before they started looking like a tarpon and started learning the difference between eating prey and being preyed upon. So you want your presentation to be *moving away* from the fish . . . directly away is the best, but on an angle will also work.

800. Do you keep stripping, or do you stop sometimes?

It depends on the reaction of the fish. I wrote a chapter for a book published for the University of Miami Marine Laboratory, and they wanted me to do a chapter on tarpon—the old days, the records, and so on. I described how I had a big tarpon come to the fly, and stop and turn away, and I stopped the fly, and I twitched it a couple of times, and the fish turned back and came to it and ate it. All of that is the angler's instinct that makes a difference. Probably, if I had kept stripping, he would have never turned back and just kept going away. I don't know. There is no black and white on what to do, how to strip each time, because you don't know where this fish has been and/or how many flies have been presented to it. Oh, yeah: Some of it *is* luck in doing the right thing.

I would much rather find one or two big tarpon in the backcountry during January or February than I would ten schools of ten fish each on the ocean side in May or June, because they'll be so skittish then.

801. What about a fly in front of the bonefish? What are the key things to remember for success?

Bonefish might not be as wary about a fly or bait coming *at* them as a tarpon, but you still want them to be the aggressor. You want it to be in front of them, and going kind of away from them. For the most part, the critters that they eat do not go very far with each movement. That's why I tell people to make a *1-inch strip*. You don't want it to go very far—it will be out of their line of action. But the things that bonefish feed on are small and don't cover 6 inches or a foot at a leap. You only want to twitch your fly each time.

802. What else do you do to get a bonefish strike?

Okay, here's an exact sequence of action I've used to catch lots and lots of bonefish: If I'm lucky enough to be within casting range of a bonefish that's slowly moving along hunting for something to eat, I'll often wait for it to tail, putting its snoot down to the bottom, before I drop the fly in front of where I think it's going next. Then, before I move the fly, I'll wait for the bonefish to stop tailing, rotating its body to a horizontal mode, hunting again. Then I start the 1-inch twitches. This will almost always get a take. In almost all conditions you will need a weedless fly.

803. You've now caught 200 or more sailfish on a fly. Any special tips on presenting the fly or playing them?

Most fly fisherman have become programmed to make their fly presentation directly in front of the fish. If you do that with a sailfish, it will more than likely hit your fly with its bill, whether it is a popping-bug or streamer. Their bills are so sensitive that they can tell it's not what they want, and will probably head for parts unknown. If a fish does crash your fly, the chance of getting a good hookup is only one in ten because your hook will be in the hard bone/bill portion of its mouth. Therefore it is best to either cast *directly behind the fish or off to the side of the sailfish.* It is important for the person handling the teaser rod to coordinate snatching the teaser completely out of the water before you start working your fly—especially if you cast behind the fish using a popping bug. When you start popping and gurgling your fly, the fish probably thinks it overran its prey and will often turn around, garbaging your fly with gusto, making for an easy hookup in the side of its jaw.

It took me many years to figure that out. And I figured it out by mistake one time, as you do most things. You have to have an analytical mind to figure out why it worked.

804. Is the presentation like that on any other fish?

No, only billfish.

805. Then, when he hits it, when do you make your strike?

You see it. Normally, it's happening no more than 30 or 40 feet away from you. You'll see him open his mouth and crash the popping bug, going away or off to the side. You just hit him right then. If you're using a streamer, you should wait until your line comes tight, because you can't see it like the popping bug.

806. Are streamers better than popping bugs?

No, I use popping bugs almost exclusively. The only time I use streamers is when we get out and the water's so calm that sailfish are balling the bait. We can drift down, and the sailfish will be circling this ball of bait. You can cast into this wad. What they do is go through the tightly packed school of sardines with their bills slashing like rapiers and bang them, as many as they can. Then they come back and pick up the wounded ones. It's quite a sight. You cast a streamer fly into it, twitch it a couple of times, then let it start to sink. You won't see it anymore, but you watch the end of your fly line, just like you're nymphing for trout, and when your line twitches a couple of times and then starts off, you set the hook.

807. What kind of popping bugs are those? They must be very special.

I have them made in Utah. Nobody has these popping bugs. You have to get them from me. People fishing my tournaments get the flies from me.

808. Do you sell them on the marketplace?

Not necessarily. But if somebody wanted some, I would. If sailfish anglers went to Bass Pro Shops, Worldwide Sportsman, and others, they would pay about twenty bucks a fly, because they have tandem hooks. I use special Owner hooks in them and I have them rigged in tandem. The hooks themselves cost almost $2 apiece, and I use two of them, done in tandem. The flies are made to my specifications. If anybody really wanted to get them, they would have to contact me and order a batch, at least ten flies. That's the only way I could get them made and sell them. My e-mail address is: stuwho@bellsouth.net.

809. In regard to the sailfish tips we discussed, do the lure presentations and other info apply to using spinning gear?

Using spinning or baitcasting tackle for billfish is probably the best way to catch your first or even your second one. It takes the edge off because it is considerably easier. Spinning and baitcasting reels have a gear ratio of between 4 to 1 and 7 to 1, whereas fly reels only have a 1 to 1 retrieve ratio, making it considerably more difficult and of course more interesting and rewarding.

To me, sight fishing is the most exciting way to fish for any species and that is exactly what you are doing when you tease up billfish and then present your bait to them. This is often called bait and switch.

810. What are some of the best destinations for sailfish on a fly?

My choices to fly fish for Pacific sailfish are Casa Vieja Lodge in Guatemala (December-March); Crocodile Bay Lodge in Costa Rica (January-March); Tropic Star Lodge in Panama (April-June); and any number of hotels in Mazatlan Mexico (June-July). I'm sure there are many other good places you might find by Googling sailfish. For Atlantic sailfish it would be difficult to beat Cozumel, Mexico during April and May.

811. Is it true tarpon live to be thirty or forty years old? If that's so, there are tarpon still swimming around now that you hooked back at Big Pine in your early guiding days. It's hard to imagine.

There is scientific proof they live to be sixty or seventy years old. I guarantee you there are tarpon that I have cast to every year down in the lower Florida Keys that I have fished over and cast to and maybe hooked, and maybe even caught, thirty or forty years ago. There are probably some tarpon out there swimming around that can say, "Hey, I heard Stu Apte's back." And the other tarpon would answer, "Yeah, he's back, but he's getting to be an old dude. We don't have to worry about *him* anymore." They are a very intelligent form of fish. I know they have to have some means of communication . . . I don't know what it is . . . You know, they actually date back to prehistoric days, back to the dinosaurs . . . and they've survived all those thousands of years because of what they have learned to do.

812. If I have the means (read, money) to fish anywhere I want, but had a problem with time, what would be the best time to go for big tarpon with a good guide?

That would be April in the Lower Keys, and preferably during the last moon phase in March and first moon phase in April. By moon phase, I mean full or new, with spring tides in April. That's when I have historically found the biggest fish down there.

813. You wouldn't go during the worm hatch in May?

Oh, Lord, no. That's a late May or early June thing, or July. It's definitely not the best big-tarpon time. I'll take April in the Lower Keys.

814. When would be the best time to go fish the back-country and get a mixed bag—snook, redfish, and small tarpon? And get a lot of action?

Mid to late October. November can be really good too. Let me tell you, here in November, until we got that cold snap at Thanksgiving time, the backcountry was covered with big tarpon. Most of the guides don't know about that. The reason they don't . . . well, I shouldn't say this . . . is that they're lazy. Many of them take the direction of least resistance. They're going to go bonefishing for the most part. People show up and say they want to go bonefishing, and it's easier for these guides to go out and find bonefish, especially this time of year, than it is tarpon. But to me, tarpon has always been the thing. I've always studied them, always wanted to know all I could about the *what, when, and where.*

815. So here at Thanksgiving, the big tarpon are in the backcountry?

Well, they were there, before this cold snap. That pushes them back into the Gulf. I guarantee you this . . . let me look at my book here . . . let's see, the full moon will be December 2. Okay, next Wednesday if the forecast is right, and it starts warming up . . . like it's starting to warm up here already . . . I guarantee you that next Wednesday there will be an influx of tarpon at certain places in the backcountry.

816. Can you tell us something about tarpon migration habits?

They really don't start doing the ocean side in a fishable way—down here in the Keys anyway—they start flowing down in late March from Miami Government Cut. April and May they're heading down . . . late May, June, and July they're heading back up . . . on the ocean side.

817. Is it a temperature thing?

I believe it is a combination of comfortable water temperature and following their food source. They do like a certain temperature, of course. For them, the primo would be 78 or 79 degrees

C. We've learned this through our Bonefish Tarpon Trust (BTT) organization's satellite tagging. Check them out at www.tarbone.org. A tarpon, I don't care if it's off Mexico or here in the Keys, or wherever, it will follow a temperature curve of around 78 or 79 degrees. I think a lot of that has to do with the food sources liking that temperature too.

818. Do the tarpon go from the Gulf side to the ocean side, back and forth?

They go back and forth through the various cuts under the numerous bridges in the Florida Keys. Depending on the time of year and their migration, many of the fish during the months of May and June will come from the backcountry (the Gulf of Mexico and Florida Bay). These are the fish that are heading *up*, or East as we say. On the way, they run into various shallow banks, which can be ideal places to fish for them. Oh yes—you do have to know which banks and when to be there. Because many of these banks are too shallow for them to cross they will parallel the bank until they can get around them to continue their easterly migration. They find a cut or channel, and they go into that channel, still heading east. BTT satellite tagged one at Flamingo here in the backcountry and three months later the tagged fish showed up in the waters off of Maine. Anyone interested should be a member of Bonefish Tarpon Trust and get all this information. They tagged some tarpon off Mexico, I'm not sure whether it was Vera Cruz or Tampico, a year ago, and these were big fish, 150-pound-plus fish, and the tag popped up after three or four months in Mobile Bay. Now that fish was heading for the Keys.

819. What if I can only go to the Keys in July and August? What are my chances for good fishing?

It depends again on the weather, which includes the temperatures and the moon phase. I did a TV show with my wife, Jeannine, on camera in August two years ago in the backcountry, and we had Dave Denkert as our on-camera guide. He is one of the better backcountry guides around. He'll periodically give me a call if he has a day off from guiding. This year snook season ended November 1 . . . and two days before that he called to ask if wanted to go "grocery shopping," he calls it. Catching a snook to eat. I will keep only two snook a year, and I catch many dozens of them that I release. On that August trip, with my wife filming a TV show, I think we caught twenty-nine snook, a number of Jewfish (which they now call Goliath Groupers), a couple of redfish—it was a mixed bag show using spinning tackle. Jeannine caught one of the biggest snook, and I also had a great big shark that came after a snook I had on. We also missed some great footage because the camera guy thought the shark was coming into the boat. It was a big lemon shark.

820. Are some sharks worse than others about getting after your fish?

Oh, yes. The lemons, the black-tips—they can all be bad, depending on how turned on they are to feeding.

821. What do you do when a shark is after your bonefish?

The best thing to do is get your fish in really quick. But if you can't do it, just back off the drag completely and free-spool the fish. If it's early in the fight, most bonefish can outrun a shark, but if the fish has already made a few runs, you would do best to horse it into the boat before the shark can get it. Put it in your livewell and either wait until the shark has left or go to another area before you release it.

© Stu Apte 2010

822. What was Joe Brooks like? In my magazine editing years, I never had the chance to meet him before he passed on. I've read everything he wrote and I've seen him in the video you guys did way back.

I would love to fish with Joe again. He was a one of a kind. He would go out of his way, under any circumstance, to help somebody, even somebody he didn't even know. He was more than a gentleman, he was a prince. He was a great angler as well, especially for that era. And Joe was truly my mentor. He was like a second father to me.

823. I wanted to talk about tipping. What do you tip flats guides these days?

Most of the guides in the Florida Keys and most other places in Florida charge between $500 and $600 per day with one or two anglers in the boat. The tip depends on the kind of day you've had. If you've had a good day—you really caught fish and you like the guide and you know you want to fish with him again—if he's charging $500, then maybe you give him a $100 tip. If you've had a pretty good day and he's charging $500, you give him $50. It's not a percentage per se, a fixed amount. As it is right now, I think they're getting a lot of money for their guiding. But now, a guide who takes you out . . . and doesn't run very far into the backcountry . . . and doesn't seem to be working very hard . . . and especially doesn't seem to be prepared, knowing where and when to expect the fish . . . he takes you out at 8 o'clock and brings you back in at 4:30 . . . chances are, from me, he wouldn't get any tip.

824. Can you describe a particularly good guide?

Take Steve Thomas as an example. You go out with Steve Thomas and chances are Steve will want you at the dock about twenty or thirty minutes before daylight, so he can be running to where the fishing is at the crack of dawn. He will burn all kinds of gas going from this place to that place, to find the fish. And even on the way coming back in, with the sun on the horizon, setting, you'll hear him say, "Hey, do you mind if we stop at one more place for a look?" Dave Denkert will do a similar thing. He may not stay out as long as Steve Thomas, but Dave will want you to be at the dock at daybreak.

825. When you go out at daybreak, do you come in earlier in the afternoon? Well before 5 o'clock?

No. The good guides will stay out there anyway. Steve Thomas and Dave Denkert will both want you on board their skiff at daybreak, and they generally won't be coming back in until the sun's on the horizon, and even then may want to make a stop.

826. Even in the long, long days of daylight in midsummer, you stay out all day?

When I hung up my spurs as a backcountry fishing guide I was sixty years old and no longer wanted to spend twelve hours a day on the water pushing the boat. Yet I did not want to cut my clients' days any shorter. Now that I will be eighty on my next birthday, an eight-hour day on the water is all I care to deal with. During my heyday in the early 1960s, I would take my clients out at daybreak during the months of July, August, and September, then come back to my air-conditioned house, getting out of the heat of the day, at around 11:00 AM. We would meet again at my house at around 3:30 PM and stay out until dark plus thirty.

827. Do the guides bring lunch?

No, they bring water and ice. In the Florida Keys—I don't know how it got started—the anglers furnish the lunch and snacks for themselves and the guide and all the assorted soft drinks they want. But the guide will have the bait, and he'll have all the tackle.

828. Are there any important differences between fishing the Keys and the Bahamas that you can point out?

The difference in the Bahamas is that you can make a bad cast to a bonefish and still catch him. You cannot do that in the Keys very often. You see a lot more fish in the Bahamas, but they don't run nearly as big. Bonefishing in the Keys, like around Islamorada, is much tougher than the Bahamas. But you can catch one bonefish here that will weigh as much as four that you catch in the Bahamas.

829. Where were you?

In Islamorada. The wind was blowing twenty-five knots that day. We were dunking shrimp on the bottom in an area where both the guide and I knew there were fish. Cast to them in that tide, and they were on the feed. We were using spinning tackle with shrimp and one split-shot, letting it go right to the bottom and then leaving it there. Put the rod in the rod holder so you're not moving it around. Watch the end of the line. The water's anywhere from a foot to 18 inches deep. You're fishing on a white sand bottom, because if you're on the grass, the pinfish are in the grass and they'll destroy your shrimp pretty quickly. Knowing where to stake out, knowing where the passes are—that's what it takes for a good day. That's why I think it's harder, much harder, to be a good backcountry guide than an offshore guide.

830. Where are the biggest bonefish in the Bahamas?

South Andros at Andros South Lodge has some of the big ones. There are also some big bonefish on the west side of Andros. And Abaco at Black Fly Lodge.

831. What's your favorite way to go after redfish?

There are many different ways of fishing for redfish. To show you what I mean, I'll tell you about some fishing I did in Savannah recently, on the twelfth of November, fishing the Red Trout Tournament for Cystic Fibrosis. We had some windy conditions, and I never picked up a fly rod. The reason I didn't was it would have been blind casting to the redfish and trout. And I really was more interested in seeing my angling partner catch the fish. Unfortunately, I aced him out, and I felt bad about that. Part of the time we were using live shrimp under a popping cork on a spinning rod; and part of the time just an artificial shrimp or jig under a popping cork; and part of the time just casting a jig or artificial shrimp without a popping cork. We caught redfish all three ways.

832. What happened with your partner to make you feel bad?

Well, my angling partner is the same one I've fished with for the past four years in this tournament. I broke him into fly fishing and he won the fly-fishing division of the tournament two different years. Neither one of us tried fly fishing this year. The conditions just weren't right, and we didn't run into a concentrated amount of fish anywhere. You'd just be blind casting a fly. You can catch more fish blind casting with a spinning rod. I actually caught the most redfish in the tournament, and I aced my partner out because the last one I caught was also the biggest one of the tournament. It was 32 ½ inches. My last fish made me the winner because we were tied with the amount of redfish and the rules state "the last fish caught first wins."

833. You've done a lot of redfishing through Louisiana and the Gulf States, haven't you?

That is the finest redfish sight fishing with the fly I've ever had. It's awesome. Those fish remind me of our Florida redfish fourty years ago. The two areas that I've fished out of are Port Sulphur and Venice. I have a friend down there, Bert Jones, the former quarterback of the Baltimore Colts, and he has a place in Venice, which is where we stay. It's a big area with lots of guides and opportunities to fish. I've fished those two places for two years and can tell you it's the best sight fishing for redfish I have ever experienced. We quit counting the first day after I caught forty-eight sight fishing on flies. I probably caught another fifteen, at least, over that. These fish averaged between 5 and 11 pounds.

834. Are fly lines so good today that you don't have to dress them anymore?

When fishing in lakes and rivers, or on the saltwater flats, your fly line *will* pick up scum or other forms of dirt. You'll first notice this when you start having to work harder to shoot your line through the guides. Wipe your line with a piece of paper towel or napkin, then apply line dressing in order to make your line once again shoot through the guides with ease. I may do this to it two or three times a day, if necessary.

835. How do you make sure your backing is up to the job?

When reeling line to be used as backing, it's important to pack the backing on firmly by holding extreme tension on the line. Failure to do so can result in losing a big fish that has run out all your fly line, into the backing, which will then bury itself into the remaining loose line on your reel. The additional tension loading backing will also enable you to wind more backing on your reel in case you do hook that big one.

836. What determines your fly rod and line choices?

Saltwater fly fishing is unique because of the large size and extreme fighting abilities of the fish. This designates the size of the rod you should use in order to have a weapon that will handle the fish. Then it's necessary to match the fly line to the rod in order to be able to cast. In retrospect, for most trout fishing scenarios, the area that is to be fished determines the size fly line to be used. For example, a rod for a small spring creek where short delicate presentations are needed will be a lot different than a rod for a big western river, like the Madison or Yellowstone.

The fly line, not the size of the fish, designates the size of the rod you need to fish trout water.

837. You've done quite a bit of light-tackle striper fishing in the Northeast. What were some of your impressions of the fish and the fishing?

I've probably done more than a half dozen television shows fishing for striped bass with flies, plugs, and live bait, both wading and from a boat. I can honestly say, I have enjoyed all of the ways to fish for them. I've sight fished with a fly along the coast of Maine and with a spinning rod and lures inside of the Kennebunk River. In Boston Harbor to the surface feeding fish—outside of Woods Hole, Massachusetts—a number of times fishing the flats around Martha's Vineyard, strictly sight fishing with the fly rod. And I did a couple of bang-up shows fishing from Block Island, off Rhode Island. The South Carolina and Georgia coastlines share an offshore area that is practically virgin. I have caught 15- to 20-pound striped bass in the river systems of both states while fishing in a Red Trout Tournament for Cystic Fibrosis during October and November. Talk about a surprise and a hard-hitting wild fight, using spinning tackle with 6-pound test line and a ¼-ounce bucktail jig, figuring on hooking a 1- or 2-pound trout or possibly a 3- or 4-pound redfish and almost getting spooled by an 18-pound striper.

838. Generally speaking, if we head for a tarpon pass where you expect prime action, and we stake out and not much happens, how long do you give it before we go to your first backup spot?

That is a difficult question, best answered with a point I continually make: There are very few black and whites when you're out fishing . . . it's almost always gray, and you have to have an analytical mind with numerous options.

How long to wait will probably depend on the time of the tide, such as whether it's early in the morning or later in the day, and the wind direction and velocity most certainly add or delete your options. I remember a day in the early 1960s when Capt. George Hommel and I were the only two boats on one of my favorite tarpon fishing banks in the lower Florida Keys. We were both there in the morning as it started getting light. The weather conditions were perfect and we had the last couple of hours of a full moon rising tide—the very best scenario possible. After a couple of hours of not having any tarpon come by, I watched George crank his engine and head northwest in a channel through one of the bridges that would take him into the backcountry side of the Keys. I could still see him before he went under the bridge about a mile away when the first big school of tarpon came meandering down the bank and my client had a gangbuster morning. So, here again, it's all gray and there is a lot of luck involved. I used to say given my choice between having the best angler in the whole world as a client or the luckiest one—I would always take the luckiest one.

839. Setting the drag is something many anglers wonder about getting right. What's your advice on setting drag for different fish?

It depends on whether you're using fly-fishing, spinfishing, baitcasting, or conventional trolling equipment. And of course this would depend on the type and quality of the reel. I will give you a couple of rules-of-thumb. With spinning tackle, you might set your drag at 20 percent of the line test you will be fishing with (with 10-pound test, the line coming off the reel could be set at 2 pounds). With baitcasting tackle, you might set your drag at 30 perecent of the actual line test (15-pound-test line could be set at roughly 4 ½ pounds). With fly-fishing tackle, you might set your drag at 20 percent of the leader tippet test (with 20-pound-test tippet, setting your drag at 4 pounds is more than sufficient).

840. In trout fishing, when you're out in the high country on rivers like the Missouri or Yellowstone, what's your favorite fly and rig when there are no rises to help you decide? And . . . do you ever use any of the nymph dropper lines, tied to a big dry fly or strike indicator?

If I am in an area where I have had success before and there are not any rises, I will go to a variety of nymphs, tying two of them in tandem. Depending on the time of year, I might use a hopper pattern as a strike indicator or even use an actual strike indicator. Again there are no black and whites and there are times I might use one or both with bead heads or even a split-shot on the leader. I tie a 16- or 18-inch dropper tippet to the shank of the floater, not to the eye. The flies are usually Copper Johns or Gold-Ribbed Hare's Ears.

841. What's your favorite forms of freshwater fishing?

Sight fishing is the most exciting type of fishing, and I would prefer dry fly fishing to rising trout.

842. Any special tips?

It is important to carefully approach the area you intend to wade fish and make a few presentations as close to the shoreline as feasible before stepping into the water. I have had numerous trout fishing friends from New England, New York, and New Jersey fish with me on Montana's Missouri, Yellowstone, Madison, Gallatin, and Bighorn rivers. And the first thing they would usually do is walk right over the top of the fish, thinking they had to make their cast out to the middle of the river. More often than not they would have missed their chance at catching the biggest trout of the day feeding on the nearby shoreline.

843. There are some big bonefish down there in the Keys. Just how big do you think they might go?

One day in 1963, after wearing out my anglers fighting big tarpon, I was able to get home much earlier than normal. I was pretty sure there would be some good-sized, feeding bonefish in an area close to my house. So I took my wife fishing with me during a late-afternoon prime bonefish rising tide. I quietly poled my skiff about three quarters of a mile just to get into the area that I wanted to fish.

Not too long after my wife caught a 7-pound bonefish using a live shrimp on a spinning rod, I saw a wake further down the bank, directly into the sun line, coming toward us. Being a hotshot guide I explained to my wife how I could tell the difference between the way a shark and a bonefish looks even that far away. I quickly pointed out that I could tell the fish coming toward us was a shark because of the way it seemed to swish its tail back and forth and that a shark would probably be showing its dorsal fin in that depth of water. Boy was I wrong! I had both hands on the push pole, instead of having a rod in my hand. In all fairness to me, though, I would have to say if it hadn't been for the glare of the sun line, I probably would have been able to recognize the biggest bonefish I have ever seen in my life in time and get a cast off.

© Pat Ford 2010

844. With a good guide, can a complete novice catch bonefish on spinning gear and baits, like shrimp?

Of course, I have produced literally hundreds of bonefish for lots of novice fishing people, mostly by dunking shrimp on the bottom in the areas that bonefish travel and occasionally after teaching them how to cast with a spinning outfit. I was recently fishing in the Islamorada Redbone Tournament, for Cystic Fibrosis Research, that was being filmed for a segment of the Saltwater Tournament series on ESPN. I always donate my time for these affairs and seldom know who will be the other angler in the boat. For this particular tournament Michael, my angler, was an enthusiastic eleven-year-old young man who had never fished for bonefish. I've probably said it more than 1,000 times, given my choice between having the best angler in the whole world fish with me or the luckiest, I would take the luckiest angler every time and teach him or her proper rudiments involved in fighting fish. This day was no exception to that rule. The wind was blowing fifteen to twenty knots, making it close to impossible to be able to spot the fish before casting to them, so the guide decided to anchor up on an ocean side white sandy area that bonefish normally travel on the portion of the tide we would have. You're not allowed to chum during this tournament and you're only allowed to fish one rod per angler, so Michael and I each had a spinning rod with 10-pound-test line, baited with a live shrimp. We each cast in the direction the guide suggested and put our rods in a vertical rod holder while waiting for the camera boat with José Wejibe, host of the Spanish Fly TV series, to get set up alongside for good filming. They barely had their anchor set when Michael's rod bounced once and went slack. I hollered for Michael to pick up his rod and start winding, telling him when the line comes tight to give it a little jab. This young man followed my directions explicitly and the fight was on. The first run was a screaming run of more than 200 yards and I was sure he was fast to a good bonefish. I gave him some instruction on lifting the rod tip and winding it down in a pumping motion whenever the fish was not taking line off the drag. I never had to repeat anything twice, and he did an outstanding job of landing his first bonefish ever, one that weighed 12 ¼ pounds on a registered Boga Grip scale before it was released. Of course Michael was pleased as we all were, especially getting it all on camera for the TV episode, but I wasn't sure that he truly understood that the feat he just accomplished was something many adult anglers had spent more than fifteen years fishing for bonefish and had never caught one that large. Michael ended the day by catching two more bonefish and three bonnet-head sharks and ended up with the biggest and the most bonefish that day in the tournament, with more than seventy anglers fishing.

845. Is it possible to catch bonefish without a guide in the Keys and the Bahamas?

Absolutely—for anglers who have done their homework and researched where the flats that can be waded are located. Obviously, you have to watch the tides. In the Bahamas, you'll be better off by wading the flats that are located close to the lodge where you're staying. Striking out on your own for any distance, with a boat or car or wading, without local knowledge, could get you in trouble, besides being a waste of time. Yes, you might get lucky. You also might have a very, very bad day if you don't know where you're going or anything about the depths, the currents, and tides you're up against. On tactics, with spinning gear or fly rod, it's possible to find and catch bonefish on your own if you've paid your dues and are an experienced angler. Keep in mind that the absolute best time to do this, if the tides are in your favor, is at the crack of dawn, when the wind will probably be down and you can see tailing or moving fish. Since most people can't stand to get up before dawn on their vacations, you'll probably have the water all to yourself. That said, be aware that having a guide in any new bonefishing destination will probably make your experience a more rewarding one.

846. In that regard, can you give me a *for-instance* place in the Keys where I could go bonefishing on my own?

Years ago I used to drive by a certain stretch of flats and see a lady out there, wading and casting alone. It was Mary Brooks, wife of my mentor, Joe Brooks. The place was lower Matecumbe Key, a half-mile stretch along the ocean side of U.S. 1, at around mile marker 76. There are others, of course, in the Keys and the Bahamas, and anglers who have a lot of curiosity and aren't afraid of research can find them and fish them.

847. If you went out with unlimited funds to find new, undiscovered waters for giant tarpon, where are the areas you would likely want to search?

If I had the time and finances, there are some areas along the north coast of South America I would like to explore for big tarpon.

848. As a kid, you went fishing with sewing thread and a pin. After many casts, many fish, and almost eighty years, does the idea of going fishing still excite you?

Yes, the idea of going fishing still excites me, but not with the same wild enthusiasm I had for the first sixty or seventy years of my life. There is no doubt I have slowed down, but I still do enjoy a multitude of different kinds of fishing in various places I'm fortunate enough to still be able to go to. Whether it be dry fly fishing or nymph fishing for trout in our western states or fly fishing for large Pacific sailfish, I do anticipate each of these trips with excitement. Of course, my favorite is in my backyard, fly fishing for big tarpon on the flats of my beloved Florida Keys. I'm home here, and God willing I will be after those great silver fish until the time comes for my last cast.

CHAPTER 20

Catching the Saltwater Superstars: Techniques for Striped Bass, Bluefish, Weakfish, Redfish, and Flounder

849. The Saltwater Challenge

The rivers that drain into the ocean, the bays that receive them, and the great seas beyond can be

heaven for anglers. However, their sheer size makes them a formidable challenge for anglers whose only experience has been in fresh water. When my father, brother, and I began fishing the Chesapeake Bay in the mid-1950s, we had a 19-foot Whirlwind boat, but virtually no knowledge of exactly how and where to use it from its dock in Annapolis. Thus began a learning process that took some years. Talking with other anglers, tackle and boat shop keepers, taking charter trips—all these activities were necessary parts of the famous School of Hard Knocks. I would not trade the experience for anything, and would do it all over again. But, unless you come from a family of saltwater anglers—or have been under the wing of a friendly neighbor who fishes the salt (and perhaps has a boat!)—be prepared to ask questions, read a lot, check the Internet a lot, take charter trips whenever you can, and experiment on your own to learn your way in fishing the big waters at the edge of the sea.

850. Head Boats Can Be Great Fun

Those fishing boats where you pay your way onto a boat right at the dock—they're called head boats—can be great fun, especially if it's your only way to get saltwater action or you're new and learning. Anywhere within a couple of hours driving distance to the salt, the Thursday and Friday newspapers will have ads and fishing reports for the popular boats leaving for blues, stripers, flounder, blackfish, porgies—whatever's running. Some trips are for the day, some half-days. Take your lunch and snacks in a small cool. The boats have the gear and the mates to show you how to use it. There are big-fish pools for fun and winning a few bucks if you're lucky. You can have a great day out there, and it's a great place to take kids.

851. Seasickness Can Hit Anybody

Be advised: People can and do get seasick on any size boat in salt water, particularly out of sight of land. If you're likely to get seasick, there's nothing you can do about it except take a dose of drugs recommended by your pharmacist or experienced friends. The prevention drug may make you feel a bit sleepy, but that's better than being seasick.

852. Saltwater Savage: The Bluefish

Their pictures should be in the dictionary beside the words "power" and "speed." Among fish, they are strong, far-ranging wanderers, along our coasts for weeks and months, then gone. When attacking schools of baitfish, they are so vicious they inspire prose like Ted Janes' great description from his article "Blue Lightning" in the December 1950 issue of *Field & Stream*: "They [bluefish] have an unlovely habit of slashing left and right through a school of fish nearly as large as themselves, biting their victims in two and passing on to a fresh kill." Janes reported that "Blood dyed the water over a wide area . . . and that even the gulls took great care to swoop and dive above the water and not plummet into it." Bluefish have even been known to bite swimmers.

853. The Bluefish Frenzy: You've Got to Be There

Whether you are out for the pan-sized blues called "snappers" in bays and coves, or the 15- to 20-plus pounders called "slammers" just offshore, you're in for rod-bending, tackle-busting action like few fishing trips can provide. And despite the complaints of those who don't like to eat them, many of us bluefish addicts think they're great on the table, especially when freshly caught. Even if you live in Kansas or Iowa, put bluefishing on your list of Things To Do Before You Die. By the way, if you're a trout fisherman and thinking of taking that small reel along, forget about it! A bluefish will blow it to pieces in one run.

854. Chumming: The Saltwater Action Creator

When you experience chumming for saltwater gamefish on charter trips or with friends who are showing you the way, you'll quickly learn to appreciate this fun and deadly way of fishing. Anchored in a likely spot for waves of moving fish or over a mother lode of suspended fish which are happy to not be going anywhere, you'll be grinding and chopping small baitfish, clams, and other delicacies and feeding the gump into the tides. Once a long "slick" is established, work your jigs or baited hooks into the "hot zone" and hang onto your hat. Chumming is saltwater's light-tackle heaven.

855. Keep It Quiet!

As related by distinguished writer John Hersey in his classic bluefishing book *Blues*, Knopf (1987), we have no less a sage than Aristotle to remind us that noise frightens fish. He related . . . "for they are observed to run away from any loud noises like the rowing of a galley." They will also "run away" from a variety of intrusions committed by anglers, such as banging tackleboxes and gear in the bottom of the boat and slapping the sides of a craft with oars or paddles.

856. You Know the Fishing's Really Lousy When . . .

You know the fishing's really lousy when the kids you've brought out start saying, "Can we go back and catch more bait? That was really fun."

857. If It Ain't Chartreuse . . .

In a *Sport Fishing* magazine poll of charter skippers by Doug Olander to find their favorite lure colors, in the all-important inshore fishing group, chartreuse was the strong winner—once again proving, "If it ain't chartreuse, it ain't no use!"

858. Great Easy-Chair Fishing

You can do a lot worse things with your time and money then spending them on *Sport Fishing* magazine and its Web site, www.sportfishingmag.com. The magazine is packed with articles on all types of saltwater fishing, from going for flounder in bays to taking on giant marlin offshore. There's information galore here, on techniques, gear, and destinations. The magazine can literally be the ticket to some of the greatest fishing of your life.

859. More Great Easy-Chair Fishing

Competition among magazines is good for readers. In the saltwater realm, *Sport Fishing* magazine is rivaled by *Salt Water Sportsman,* which has everything about fishing the briny one could possibly ask for. The magazine's Web site is www.saltwatersportsman.com and you will be rewarded by visiting it. You'll find how-to on everything, along with tons of videos and destination ideas. I've noticed that *Salt Water Sportsman* sometimes gets letters from readers in places like Kansas, who are fascinated by their magazine links to the strange and amazing world of fishing the salt. The pulling power of the oceans is strong.

860. Focus on Saltwater Fly Fishing

The magazine *Fly Fishing in Salt Waters,* with its Web site at www.flyfishinsalt.com, is one of my favorite sources for good ideas and information on fly fishing in the briny, from inshore tidewaters and flats, out to the deep waters where the big ones roam. The magazine will not only make you a better angler, it will send you to places where you'll find fly-fishing action to dream about.

861. Storing Leaders and Pre-Tied Fly Rigs

In a technique tip in *Sport Fishing* magazine's Web site, reader Bill Hallman explained his idea of storing leaders on plastic tubes wrapped on a plastic coat hanger, two tubes on the top arms, one on the long bottom. Secure the leaders to the plastic with toothpicks. Fly-fishing rigs with dropper nymphs tied to a dry fly can be kept this way as well.

862. Bluefish Seeing Red

Back in 1972, when I was editor of *Sports Afield,* Stephen Ferber, a friend in the process of building his own publishing company, wrote a tremendously informative article on bluefishing for the *Fishing Annual.* His top tip was one worth remembering today: " . . . the color that takes the most spring blues is red. . . . I won't come right out and say that Gene Hendrickson was the first to use the red plugs for bluefish, but it is possible. . . . He had rigged red plugs to each of the outriggers, a blue one to one stern rod and a yellow feather to the other. After two hours of trolling, he caught twenty-one blues—eighteen on the red lures. Now he carries a can of fluorescent-red spray paint on board for use when his plugs get too chewed up, or for changing, say, a silver non-producer into a bluefish killer."

863. When the Blues Are Running

"A school of blues can send panic hundreds of yards forward of their path as they wheel and turn en masse on feeding forays, making terror-stricken baitfish jump through the water's surface like a volley of arrows . . . He is a fierce predator, savagely running down and chewing up anything in his path—including other blues."

—Stephen Ferber, *Sports Afield Fishing Annual*, 1972

864. An Extra Bluefish Danger

When landing bluefish, "The one constant danger lies in the lure itself. Remember, there are nine hooks in each plug. The chopper jumps, twists, shakes, and thrashes after he's brought over the side. In many occasions, you'll have more than one hooked blue in the boat at the same time—so getting one of those barbs through the finger is a real possibility even for the most experienced of men."

—Stephen Ferber, *Sports Afield Fishing Annual*, 1972

865. Great Autumn Surf Fishing

In October and November along the Atlantic coast, reports J.B. Kasper in his *Trenton Times* outdoor column, storms push a lot of clams into the wash along the beaches, making them the bait of choice the first few days after a big blow. Kasper says to look for some of the best movements of stripers and blues, " . . . just after the new and full moon, especially when the top of the tide occurs around sundown and sunset."

866. When the Mackerel Run

When the mackerel tide flows north along the Atlantic coastline every spring, and anglers enjoy the year's first big run of fish, many of the mackerel-fishing faithful do not realize that these little torpedo-like speedsters are part of a great tribe of saltwater battlers, including tuna, marlin, and sailfish. The mackerel is also related to the albacores, bonitos, giant kingfish, wahoo, and the Spanish and cerro mackerels. The mackerel is the smallest of all his relatives, but anglers don't mind a bit when the action begins.

867. Surf Fishing's Scouting Report

Next to seeing fish breaking and knowing exactly where the action is (instead of guessing where it might eventually happen), try to get a look at your stretch of beach at extreme low tides.

Study where even the smallest cuts and channels show on the bottom. That's where you're likely to get strikes when the waves move in, bringing the fish with them on a rising tide.

868. Fish the Ebb-Tide at Night

"By and large, we found the early ebb the most fruitful time to fish . . . Many fishermen forget that bass are night feeders . . . If you wish to catch bass by daylight, fish when high water comes at morning and evening."

—Wyman Richardson, *The House on Nauset Marsh,*
W.W. Norton, 1947

869. Two Critical Rules for Stripers in the Surf

"He used to catch a lot of bass, and may well have taken more fish off that beach than anyone else. However, we chose to attribute this rather more to his observance of . . . Rule 1: Be there when the fish are biting. Rule 2: He catches the most fish who does the most fishing."

—Wyman Richardson, *The House on Nauset Marsh,*
W.W. Norton, 1947

870. The Joys of Full-Moon Fishing

When you're on the beach for stripers and blues when the moon is full, or nearly full, and the skies are reasonably clear of clouds, you'll enjoy night fishing with almost-daylight visibility.

871. Heed the Call of the Surf

If the call of the surf—the breaking waves, the flowing tides, the onshore and offshore birds with their flights and cries, the great vastness of sky and salt-scented air—means anything at all to you, I'd like to give you a shove, not a nudge, toward getting into surf fishing. In autumn, in particular, when the crowds have mostly gone and the fish are at their best, on the move, the great surf-fishing beaches like those in New Jersey can provide magical angling days. With your daypack—food and beverage, even something to read if you like—and your tackle, you're all set. The very best way to get into it is to hire a guide a couple of times, let him show you the gear, the techniques that work best—before you blow a lot of money on the wrong stuff. There are also many clubs and associations, or perhaps you have a friend who can show you the ropes and tools. Most of the people who are really crazy about surf fishing have found they don't have to catch a lot of fish to have a good day on the beach. Of course, catching fish is what really makes surf fishing exciting. Just beachcombing won't cut it. Two of the best books to get you into the mood of surf-fishing are David DiBenedetto's *On the Run,* Morrow (2003), and Roy Rowan's *Surfcaster's Quest,* The Lyons Press (1999).

872. Lefty Kreh's "Miracle" Saltwater Fly

"Lefty's Deceiver is now used around the world in salt water (although it is a popular fresh-water pattern as well). Without being boastful, I think it's accurate to say that the Deceiver and the old Clouser Minnow are two of the most imitated saltwater flies in the sport." [Editor's Note: Lefty Kreh's Deceiver was honored by the United States Postal Service in 1991 by being chosen to illustrate a 29-cent postage stamp. Lefty says he is very proud that the caption doesn't read, "Deceiver," but instead reads, "Lefty's Deceiver."]

—Lefty Kreh, with Chris Millard, *My Life Was THIS BIG and Other True Fishing Tales,*
Skyhorse Publishing, 2008

873. The Standard Fly Casting Method Doesn't Work

"In the standard method the angler basically brings the rod from 10 o'clock back to about 2 o'clock and then back to 10 o'clock. After trying the technique for a while I began to realize that it was not the best, most efficient way to cast a fly line."

—Lefty Kreh, with Chris Millard, *My Life Was THIS BIG and Other True Fishing Tales,*
Skyhorse Publishing, 2008

874. The Lefty Kreh Fly Casting Technique

"Through trial and error I gradually learned to take the rod way back behind me and make longer backcasts and longer forward casts. I also abandoned the high-hand vertical style of the standard method and adopted a much lower position, a more horizontal profile for my arm. As I began to refine my technique I found that I was not only making longer, more accurate casts with tighter loops, but I was doing it with far less effort than the old 10 to 2 method demanded."

—Lefty Kreh, with Chris Millard, *My Life Was THIS BIG and Other True Fishing Tales,*
Skyhorse Publishing, 2008

875. Lefty Kreh's Fly Casting Revolution

"In March 1965, I wrote an article detailing my new technique in *Outdoor Life.* Many people view that article as a landmark in the evolution of the fly cast. To this day, however, many critics see it as outright heresy, an affront to the traditions of the sport. And therein lies one of the great blessings and burdens of the sport: Tradition."

—Lefty Kreh, with Chris Millard, *My Life Was THIS BIG and Other True Fishing Tales,*
Skyhorse Publishing, 2008

876. The Importance of Casting Lefty's Way

"The old-fashioned 10 to 2 technique is adequate for that limited type of fishing [small-stream trout fishing]. . . . That technique does not work well when you are fishing for larger fish with larger flies on heavier lines over larger, windier bodies of water. As a result, most people who learn traditional casting technique while fishing for freshwater trout can't perform in other conditions."

—Lefty Kreh, with Chris Millard, *My Life Was THIS BIG and Other True Fishing Tales,*
Skyhorse Publishing, 2008

877. Mystery of the Galloping Bass

"Not infrequently a school of bass will harry bait without actually feeding. On such occasions they will often roll almost clear of the water or flip their tails way out. We call this galloping—'A galloping bass never bites'—and very disappointing it is, too."

—Wyman Richardson, *The House on Nauset Marsh,* W.W. Norton, 1947

878. A Pocket Full of Good Fishing Luck

As are all the Orvis Pocket Fishing Guides, the hand-sized *Pocket Guide to Flyfishing for Striped Bass and Bluefish,* by Lou Tabory, is a quick-read, superbly illustrated guide to the skills you need to master to fly fish the briny. Available at www.amazon.com.

879. Bluefish: Power X Two

"I'd rather have two mad bluefish on the same line in a cold ocean than catch all the sailfish and marlin ever made. The only thing I know of that's better is a frisky Atlantic salmon in a cold Canadian stream, on about six ounces of fly rod."

—The Old Man in Robert Ruark's *The Old Man and the Boy,* September Song, 1953

880. Fantastic on the Table

Of all the great fish to have on your plate—particularly fried, yes deep-fried—the snook ranks near the top of my list, with some others, of course, including crappies, bluegills, catfish, walleyes, and red snapper.

881. Why Focus on Snook?

"The snook, or robalo, is closely related to the basses, although this silvery fish with a greenish or brownish back is more streamlined than any bass and has a distinctive coal-black lateral line and a long pointed head with protruding lower jaw. . . . The snook averages about 4 pounds but the world's record weighed over 50 pounds . . . a real demon on the end of a light fishing stick."

—Col Dave Harbour, *Sports Afield Fishing Annual,* 1972

882. Fighting Qualities of Snook

"As an old snook expert who should know, Tom Bonsall described this challenging fish as 'shy as a brown trout and as powerful as a tarpon.' The snook is one fish that will find the weakness of any man or his tackle in 10 seconds."

—Col Dave Harbour, *Sports Afield Fishing Annual,* 1972

883. Those Special Boat Shoes

When you're new to saltwater fishing and going on a friend's boat for the first time, it's standard courtesy to check in advance on your footwear. You don't necessarily have to have the most popular, expensive kind, but you want to make sure yours aren't going to put skid marks all over the place.

884. Beware Those Teeth!

One thing you definitely do not want to do when fishing salt water is to join the long, long list of anglers whose fingers and hands have been slashed open by bluefish teeth. When landing and unhooking bluefish, beware those teeth! The "handle with care" sign is definitely in play.

885. Hit Those Points—Hard

"Points that protrude at an angle to the beach can be ideal fishing locations. Fish the flowing water along the bar's inside edge."

—Lou Tabory, *The Orvis Pocket Guide to Fly Fishing for Striped Bass and Bluefish,* The Lyons Press, 2001

886. Surf's Up, Fly Fishing's Down

"Conditions are ideal for fly fishing when the surf along the steep ocean beaches is less than 3 feet. An increase of 1 foot in wave size increases the fishing difficulty by three times."

—Lou Tabory, *The Orvis Pocket Guide to Fly Fishing for Striped Bass and Bluefish,* The Lyons Press, 2001

887. Favorite Place to Fish

"If I could fish only one water type, it would be a creek or small river flowing into deeper water. I like places that you can cast across when the flow spills into 6- to 10-foot drop-offs."

—Lou Tabory, *The Orvis Pocket Guide to Fly Fishing for Striped Bass and Bluefish,* The Lyons Press, 2001

888. Fishing the Right Place at the Wrong Time

"Fishing a good spot under the wrong conditions is like lacing up your ice skates in July."

—David DiBenedetto, *On the Run: An Angler's Journey Down the Striper Coast,* William Morrow, 2005

889. Striper Book Destined to Become a Classic

If you love striped bass fishing, or even have a notion that makes you want to try it, an absolute, must-have book is David DiBenedetto's *On the Run: An Angler's Journey Down the Striper Coast,* published by William Morrow (an imprint of HarperCollins) in 2005. The book is so well-written that reading it seems to transport one to DiBenedetto's side as he fishes for stripers on the great fall migration run, from Maine to North Carolina.

890. Summer Stripers Are Night Feeders

"The stripers had yet to show their fall colors, so I concentrated my efforts at peak feeding times, the happy hours of dawn and dusk and throughout the night. At these times, stripers rely on their excellent night vision to ambush unsuspecting prey."

—David DiBenedetto, *On the Run: An Angler's Journey Down the Striper Coast,* William Morrow, 2005

891. Go Slow for Stripers at Night

"To catch a striper at night, you need to reel agonizingly slowly. Old-timers like to say, 'Reel as slow as possible, then reel twice that slow.'"

—David DiBenedetto, *On the Run: An Angler's Journey Down the Striper Coast,* William Morrow, 2005

892. Bluefish and Striper Migration Differences

Striped bass basically migrate north along the Atlantic coast in the spring, then south in the fall. Bluefish migrate from Atlantic depths offshore to preferred inshore areas in the spring, then fade back into the depths in the fall and early winter.

893. The Fall Striper Migration Run

The great fall striper migration run, a virtual living river of fish along the Atlantic coast, from Maine to North Carolina, takes place within a mile or so of shore. It varies with the run of the baitfish. Where the baitfish go, the stripers follow—from areas well offshore right up to the beach.

894. Misjudging Late-Fall Fishing

As a landlubber sensitive to temperature changes and the advent of winter, you might feel that those cold late-fall, early winter days have shut down the fishing. Perhaps it has, in fresh water, but the sea temperatures take time to drop, and fishing along the coast can be red-hot just when you're thinking the weather has turned too cold.

895. The Good Old Chum Line

" . . . Dad and I also chummed grass shrimp along the coast for striped bass and tide-running weakfish . . . The trick was to drift a pair of tiny shrimp back in the chum slick at the same rate as the tide was flowing."

—Mark Sosin, *The Complete Book of Light-Tackle Fishing*, The Lyons Press, 1979

896. You'll Need a Gaff on the Jetties

"A longer gaff is important when fishing jetties, as it's often dangerous to scramble down to the water in order to land a big fish. Jetty regulars carry longer gaffs strapped to their backs so they're not impeded when walking."

—Al Ristori, *The Complete Book of Surf Fishing*, Skyhorse Publishing, 2008

897. Sand Fleas: The Kind You Like

When you hear saltwater vets refer to sand fleas, they're not talking about insects that swarm and bite like regular "fleas." As Al Ristori tells us in his excellent *The Complete Book of Surf*

Fishing, Skyhorse Publishing (2008), sand fleas are tiny crabs that scurry back and forth along the surfline and can be caught by hand. They make good bait for all kinds of saltwater denizens, particularly for that gourmet's delight, pompano.

898. Great Surf Fishing Starts Right Here

Al Ristori's *The Complete Book of Surf Fishing,* Skyhorse Publishing (2008), is the perfect starting point for getting into this rewarding and challenging fishing experience. From tackle to techniques, Ristori gives aspiring surf anglers all the solid, no-nonsense information they need to catch the fish that roam along the beaches. A legendary angler and writer from New Jersey, Ristori has fished many of the world's greatest beaches, and knows firsthand everything he writes about. When I look at his pictures of tarpon and snook in the surf beside the Parismina River in Costa Rica, I have to smile. It was there a leaping 90-pound tarpon knocked me overboard and broke my foot back in the 1970s. Al was there when it happened.

899. Rigging Up to Bottom Fish Live Bait

"The best all-purpose rig is what I call the basic bottom rig. The sinker comes off one arm of a three-way swivel on a short length of leader and the hook is attached to the other arm via a leader. The leader varies in length, but for many situations, I like at least 3 feet. You can make it shorter when necessary."

—Mark Sosin, *The Complete Book of Light-Tackle Fishing,* The Lyons Press, 1979

900. Spring Means Mackerel

They're sometimes called "little warriors," and the fishing fleets all along the Atlantic coast will be rigged and on the move for mackerel in March and early April. New Jersey, Long Island (especially Montauk), and points north usually get fantastic runs of little warriors that bring the first taste of spring to winter-weary anglers. Check your coastal listings and climb aboard. The action is fast, friendly, and rewarding.

901. Stripers in the Surf: Six Top Lure Choices

In his Fishing Column in *Field & Stream,* May 2008, John Merwin named his six top lure choices for stripers in the surf: 1) Bucktail Jigs, ¼ to ½ ounce, white tipped with red pork-rind strip, black after dark: www.basspro.com; 2) Slug-Go soft-plastic jerkbait. Available at www.lunkercity.com; 3) Kastmaster wobblers: www.acmetackle.com; 4) Bomber Magnum Long A plug: www.bomberlures.com; 5) Super Strike Super "N" Fish Needlefish Plug: www.superstrikelures.com; 6) Pencil Popper (Stan Gibbs): www.gibbslures.com.

902. Give Sea Trout Your Best Shot

Sea trout answer to many names, including spotted sea trout, speckled trout, and specks. In the mid-Atlantic saltwater regions, sea trout never achieve the box-office status of striped bass and bluefish, even though they are eagerly sought and caught at times. Head on down through the Carolinas and on around the coasts to the Gulf states and Texas, and you'll find where the sea trout really come into their own. Sea trout are outstanding on the table, one of the best. Best baits and lures include live shrimp worked over grassy flats in water 6 feet deep, over oyster bars, and at the mouths of tidal creeks.

903. The Tides Are the Key

"In salt water, the fish are on the prowl much more than they are in lakes or streams. Tides play a vital role in their existence and their body rhythms are tuned to this cycle. Saltwater angling looks much easier than freshwater sport to those who have never tried it, but figuring out where fish might be on a stage of the tide isn't always the easiest thing to do."

—Mark Sosin, *The Complete Book of Light-Tackle Fishing*,
The Lyons Press, 1979

904. Gulls and Terns Taking It Easy

Okay, you were expecting a blitz, gulls screaming and diving, showing you stripers and blues tearing the water and baitfish to pieces. Instead, all is quiet, and the only gulls you see are sitting on the water, resting. Before you head for another spot—or go home—consider that the birds may just be taking it easy for a spell while the baitfish have gone back deep, taking the blues and stripers with them. The area is definitely worth checking out on sonar or just by watching or trying some casts for a while.

CHAPTER 21

Fishing the Big Deep: Experiences with Monster Fish

905. Fishing with Zane Grey

While the name Zane Grey is synonymous with a long list of romantic westerns with titles such as *Riders of the Purple Sage,* he was also one of the true pioneers of big-game fishing around the world—adventures which he wrote about in classic books such as *Tales of Fishing Virgin Seas, Tales of Swordfish and Tuna,* and many others. Grey used earnings from his vastly popular novels to finance journeys to places where there were no guides, few boats, and little information. His stories may not help you catch more fish, but they will provide immense pleasure in your favorite reading chair as you journey to the far reaches of fishing frontiers. Among the many books available on www.amazon.com and at other booksellers and your local library, check out George Reiger's *Zane Grey: Outdoorsman,* Prentice-Hall (1972), a superb anthology that samples some of Grey's greatest fishing and hunting articles.

906. Beyond Crunch and Des

Florida writer Philip Wylie is well known for his enormously-popular Crunch and Des stories that ran in the old *Saturday Evening Post* and have been collected in several anthologies. Crunch and Des are fishing guides and heroes of tales about fishing for everything from sailfish to tarpon and sharks. Not so well known is a collection of serious nonfiction pieces Wylie did on big-game fishing for magazines like *True.* Called *Denizens of the Deep: True Tales of Deep-Sea Fishing,* the book is a collection of wonderful fishing stories that take you from fighting tuna off the New Jersey coast to billfish off Florida. Look for it wherever used books are sold.

907. Hemingway's Best Marlin

When Ernest Hemingway wrote and published *The Old Man and the Sea* in 1952, first in *Life* magazine and then in Scribner's hardcover edition, the event culminated many years of thinking about the story. Back in April 1936, in an article called "On the Blue Water: A Gulf Stream Letter" for *Esquire* magazine, Hemingway wrote: "Another time an old man fishing alone in a skiff out of Cabanas hooked a great marlin that, on the heavy sashcord handline, pulled the skiff far out to sea." Hemingway went on to describe the "old man" harpooning the fish, then losing most of it to sharks two days after hooking the great fish. One can only imagine Hemingway's years of thinking about the story, mulling over the details, learning more and more about deep-sea fishing, before finally committing the story to paper. Hemingway, by the way, was born in 1898.

908. A Big Marlin Remembered

In one of his articles for *Esquire* in 1933, "Marlin Off the Morro: A Cuban Letter," Ernest Hemingway described a marlin that had been caught by a commercial fisherman and brought to the market. The fish was said to have weighed 1,175 pounds, gutted, with the head and tail cut off, and "flanks cut away." Hemingway wrote, "All right. You tell me. What did he weigh in the water and what did he look like when he jumped?"

909. Hemingway Movie Marlin

When the movie version of Hemingway's *The Old Man and the Sea* was in production, Hemingway and others attempted to obtain new jumping marlin film sequences for the movie. Fishing included the Cabo Blanco area of Peru, which, at that time (not today, alas) was yielding marlin of mammoth size. Despite these efforts, the sequences actually shown in the movie are from the Alfred C. Glassell, Jr., world-record marlin catch of 1,560 pounds on August 4, 1953, at Cabo Blanco.

910. IGFA Fishing Hall of Fame and Museum

The International Game Fish Association Hall of Fame and Museum is a "must-visit" destination for anglers. The permanent exhibits include the film *Mighty Marlin*, all about Alfred C. Glassell's quest for the world-record marlin at Cabo Blanco. The Museum is located at 300 Gulf Stream Way, Dana Beach, Florida, and is open daily from 10:00 AM to 6:00 PM.

911. Don't Miss S. Kip Farrington, Jr.

One of the most prolific and finest writers on big-game fishing was S. Kip Farrington, Jr., who was saltwater angling editor of *Field & Stream* and author of many books on fishing and railroading. You can find his books on sites such Albris and Amazon or by using Google. One of his smallest volumes is also one of the best. *Fishing With Hemingway and Glassell*, McKay (1971), includes the great fishing at Cabo Blanco, Peru, when that area was producing record marlin catches.

912. Hemingway on Using the Boat

"You do not tow him or pull him with the motor boat; you use the engine to shift your position just as you would walk up or down-stream with a salmon."

—Ernest Hemingway, "On the Blue Water: A Gulf Stream Letter," *Esquire*, April, 1936

913. For Those Dull Days Offshore

"When the breeze dies and the weather sizzles, I won't leave the dock without two things: first a downrigger or planer, and second, a couple of small trolling feathers for bonito and other tunas. These will get you bites even when you think there's nothing out there."

—Skip Smith, "Fishing the Dog Days of Summer,"
Sport Fishing magazine, www.sportsfishingmag.com

914. Don't Miss the IGFA's Web Site

The International Game Fish Association Web site at www.igfa.org is loaded with features of interest to all anglers, but especially to saltwater fishers. Among other informative links, the site's "Go Fish" section is a wonderful fish database covering every fish you can think of, plus everything you want to know about world records.

915. Your Friendly Flying Fish

"Flying fish make good marlin baits. They are good to eat, inspiring to watch, and sometimes they indicate that bigger game is about."

—Tom Paugh, *Sports Afield*, March 1975

CHAPTER 22

Flat-Out Great:
Tips for Taking Tarpon and Bonefish on the Flats

916. Flats Fishing: Seeing Is Believing

It's said that when you hire a flats-fishing guide, you're hiring a pair of eyes. Truer words were never spoken. On every flats trip I've ever been on, it takes about two days to train my eyes into seeing those mysterious shapes and shadows the guides seem to spot so easily. Usually, on about the third and last day of my trips, I'm starting to get the hang of it. Too little, too late!

917. A Fly So Secret . . .

As one who has spent most of his professional life in magazine work, I am always interested in magazine cover lines—especially when one shouts at me with the words, "The Fly Keys Guides Don't Want You to Know About." That certainly got my attention on the cover of *Fly Fishing in Salt Waters,* March/April 2006. The article was about the Toad Fly and the success the fly has enjoyed in the Florida Keys on tarpon, redfish, bonefish, snook, and just about everything else. In autumn of 2009, I checked up on the fly by using Google and the words "Toad" saltwater flies. I got several links, including Bass Pro Shops. The fly has gone through several variations that are very interesting and still evidently catching fish. Look for its history on www.midcurrent.com and check the other links for dealers, like www.basspro.com. They sell the fresh water versions of the fly, which I have not tried but look deadly. My hunch is that they will be effective on freshwater bass as well.

© Pat Ford 2010

918. When Tarpon Strike

"If you don't spook a tarpon and you get him to eat, the most important thing you can do is just keep stripping until the line goes tight. Most people, when they finally get the chance to see a fish open that big bucket of a mouth and bite their bug, the first thing they do is raise the rod. Their instinct is to do a trout strike. The fly comes flying out."

—Former Olympic ski champion and tarpon addict Andy Mill, in an interview with Thomas Pero, Editor and Publisher, *Fish & Fly* magazine, Autumn 2004

919. The Bahamas Everything Fishing Book

If you're interested in fishing the Bahamas, the one book you must have is *The Bahamas Fly Fishing Guide,* from The Lyons Press, updated several times since originally published in 1999.

It is impossible to imagine how one book could hold more useful information about the magnificent islands of the Bahamas. Here are maps, detailed guides on where to stay, where to fish, even discussions of gear and tactics. Stephen and Kim Vletas, the authors, are cofounders of the Westbank Anglers in Jackson, Wyoming. The Westbank site, www.westbank.com, is a great site for gear, trips, and information about everything fly fishing. The book is available there, as it is at www.amazon.com and other book retailers. There are other good books on fishing the Bahamas, but this is one you *must* have.

920. Florida Keys Fishing Guide

Ben Taylor's *Flyfisher's Guide to the Florida Keys,* Wilderness Adventures Press, is a grand book of detailed how-to and where-to, and has revealing maps on fishing the Keys and the Gulf backcountry. The book includes all forms of light-tackle fishing, including spinning and bait-casting, making it a guidebook of depth. It's available from book retailers everywhere.

921. Nothing Wrong with Teamwork

"Some anglers get overly sensitive if his guide says, 'You're a little too far!' or 'You're a little too close!' They get defensive. My view is that we have to work as a team."

—Former Olympic ski champion and tarpon addict Andy Mill, in an interview with Thomas Pero, Editor and Publisher, *Fish & Fly* magazine, Autumn 2004

© Pat Ford 2010

922. Good Casts Are the Key to Success

"Once you learn to cast well, you'll start getting flies in front of tarpon. Once you start getting flies in front of tarpon, you're going to start getting tarpon bites . . . you start learning hookups . . . you are going to start learning how to battle a fish. You have to start somewhere, so I say you start with your casting."

—Florida flats guide Tim Hoover, in an interview with Thomas Pero, Editor and Publisher, *Fish & Fly* Magazine, Autumn 2004

923. Sun Protection: It's Critical on the Flats

A sure way to ruin your long-anticipated flats fishing trip is to subject yourself to sunburn. Make no mistake: It can ruin your trip the very first day. I have one friend who waded the bonefish flats all day barefooted, and ended up in the emergency room that night. Wear long sleeves, long pants, wide-brimmed hats, even those light gloves that are available from Orvis. Drink plenty of liquids. Keep fishing!

924. You Can Count on Shrimp for Bonefish

Fly fishing for bonefish is a superb angling treat and challenge, but that doesn't rule out the fun you can have with a spinning rod in your hands. My personal best bonefish ever was an 11-pounder I caught on a spinning rod and shrimp beside the Key Biscayne Yacht Club in the shadows of the Miami skyline.

925. Fish the Muds for Bonefish Action

"Frequently large schools of small bonefish will gang up and form what is known as a 'mud,' a large patch of discolored water in the center of which the fish are feeding. If the angler can locate a mud and get ahead of it, as the fish move slowly with the tide, he can catch bonefish as fast as he throws out his bait."

—Van Campen Heilner, *Salt Water Fishing*, Knopf, 1937

926. Destination: Small Tarpon, Big Action

Not all fishing for tarpon is focused on catching the biggest fish. Fantastic action awaits in the Florida backcountry, the Gulf side of the Keys, where good guides can get you into fighting, leaping tarpon that will test your light tackle and your skill to the limit. Be honest with yourself: Would you rather jump and catch forty tarpon weighing 5 to 20 pounds in three days' fishing, or jump two 100-plus pounders in three day's fishing?

927. Spinning for Bonefish

Just because you're not into fly fishing does not mean you have to give up plans for a bonefish adventure on the flats of Florida, the Caribbean, or other regions where these great fish swim. You'll find plenty of guides well versed in getting you into fish with shrimp, cut crabs, and lead-head jigs. The fly rodders you run into will probably try to act as if they're having more fun, but the truth is you'll be having just as much fun with your (or the guide's) spinning tackle.

928. Sorting Out the Bonefish Pods

Like birds of a feather that supposedly flock together, bonefish of similar sizes swim in pods or schools. There are exceptions, of course, but generally speaking you'll find 2- and 3-pound fish in one pod, 5- and 6-pounders in another pod, and so on.

929. Bow to the King!

When you're playing a tarpon, big or small, it's often easy to see the line arching to the surface as the fish prepares to jump. Don't just stand there in awe as the silver king explodes into the air. Bow forward, allowing the line to go slightly slack. You may lose him anyway, but the bow is the correct move at this time.

930. You Play Fish, but You Jump Tarpon

In tarpon fishing, you'll probably only land and release a small portion of those you hook. That's why tarpon anglers like to say, "We 'jumped' three today," instead of saying, "We had three on today."

© Pat Ford 2010

931. The Biggest Bonefish Are Loners

The largest bonefish tend to patrol the flats solo, or in pairs or groups of four or five, instead of with the large schools and pods of fish you so commonly see. When you spot a bonefish that tops 7 pounds, it probably will be alone, and you can bet your hands will start shaking in anticipation of his powerful run—if you hook him!

932. Bonefish Over 10 Pounds Are Loners

A.J. McClane, famed angler and fishing editor of *Field & Stream* for years, reported in March 1961 that in landing over twenty bonefish that topped 10 pounds, not a one had been in a school or pod of fish. Look for them to be solo, in pairs, or groups of four or five.

933. Targeting That Bonefish Pod

One of the most exciting moments in all angling is to be standing on the bow of a bonefish skiff—or wading the flats—when you spot a pod of fish moving your way. This is the moment you planned for, dreamed about in fact. Now's the time to try your best to put your fly or spinning bait somewhere in front of the pod's direction. Cast too close, and you'll spook the whole bunch in one lightning swirl of water. It's a sight that can hurt if you've been out there a long time without any action.

© Pat Ford 2010

934. Fish On! Rod Up!

When a bonefish takes off on that initial sizzling run, most veterans hold the rod high and keep the line free of the grass or coral on the bottom.

935. Another Florida Flats-Fishing Guide

Fishing Florida's Flats: A Guide to Bonefish, Tarpon, Permit and Much More, by Jan Malzler, is another of the great Florida fishing books available at www.amazon.com. This is a comprehensive, info-packed guide, one of many available on the Amazon site.

936. Where to Catch the Biggest Bonefish

Islamorada, in the Florida Keys, is not the place to catch the *most* bonefish—other locations in the Bahamas and Caribbean have that honor—but it consistently produces some of the *biggest* bonefish caught on the fly anywhere. Records are constantly changing, but fish in the 12-pound-plus range have been caught there on flies, including the monster 15-pound 1-ounce fish taken in 2006. Google the words "Islamorada Florida Bonefish Guides" and you'll get tons of booking options.

© Pat Ford 2010

937. Chico's Bonefishing Book

Chico Fernandez is one of the most well-known, experienced, and knowledgeable flats-fishing anglers to ever lean on a push pole or bow to a tarpon. His book, *Fly Fishing for Bonefish,* www.amazon.com, is a modern classic that will help any angler understand bonefish and catch more of them.

938. Florida Keys Kayak Fishing

At Big Pine in the Florida Keys, Stu Apte's base in his old guiding days, Captain Bill Keogh runs a flats-fishing, flats-touring, and kayak rental operation of considerable note. You can arrange for four hours of fishing for $150 per person, two-person minimum. It's quite a bargain. Keogh has just produced a new book, *The Florida Keys Paddling Guide,* and will send a signed copy for $22 after you call him at 877-595-2925 or 305-872-7474. The Web site for his Big Pine Kayak Adventures is www.keyskayaktours.com. [Editor's Note: We have included this same item in the Chapter 4, "Portable Angler," section.]

PART EIGHT

ON THE WATER

for Wilderness Fishing

Wilderness Fishing That Calls to the Bold: Tips for Canoe-, Backpack-, and Float-Trip Success

939. Wilderness Canoe Fishing's Top Information Source

The quarterly magazine *Boundary Waters Journal* is the ultimate source for great reading and vast information on canoe-trip fishing and camping in the B.W.C.A. and Quetico areas. You'll see articles, products, and destination information on the entire region. It covers fishing tactics and tackle, packs, canoes, cooking gear, food, canoeing safety—everything imaginable about canoe fishing and camping. For the angler and camper who wants reliable, hard-to-find facts about enjoying the wilderness experience in this region, the *Journal* is the ultimate source. I treasure every issue—March, Spring; June, Summer; September, Fall; December, Winter. The Web site is www.boundarywatersjournal.com.

Call toll-free at 800-548-7319 or write to *Boundary Waters Journal*, 9396 Rocky Ledge Road, Ely, MN 55731. As this is being written subscriptions cost $23 for one year, $43 for two years, $63 for three years, $99 for five years. All two-, three-, and five-year subs get a 24 by 36-inch planning map of B.W.C.A./Quetico. Back issues of the magazine are available.

940. Backcountry Trout in the High Rockies

Trout fishing for the adventurer—the strong, in-shape backpacker types—awaits in the high Rockies. A key book to literally opening the door to this fishing Mecca is Rich Osthoff's *Fly Fishing in the Rocky Mountain Backcountry*. Published by Stackpole in 1999, Osthoff's book is one of the most detailed on both the how to fish and where to fish. Get it and you can start planning a great high-country trout adventure. Available at www.richosthoff.com.

941. Canoe Trip Fishing: Base Camps Are Better

To each his own, but for my taste the fishing canoe trip where you're traveling every day, paddling hard to stay on a schedule, and moving from site to site isn't as much fun as setting up one or two base camps. I like to travel hard for perhaps a day and a half or two days, but then I want to be deep into good fishing country where I can set up a nice camp, stay for a spell, and catch my favorite fish—walleyes, lake trout, smallmouths, whatever. Obviously, there should be good fishing at this camp, and, hopefully, nearby waters that can be explored with day trips.

942. How to Shorten Canoe-Trip Portages

On your next canoe trip with a companion, when you have a lot of gear, consider cutting down on portage time by doing one and a half portages on those portages that usually require two trips. Your friend starts across with the canoe and one of the smaller packs. He takes this load all the way across the portage. You follow with the first load of packs. At the place where your best guesstimate says you've hit the halfway point, leave the packs and go back to the starting place for the others. Meanwhile your companion comes back along the portage to pick up the packs you left halfway. When you both reach the end of the portage, you will have made one and a half trips apiece over the entire portage length instead of two.

943. Boundary Waters/Quetico: Wilderness Canoe Fishing at Its Finest

Among fishing trips that call to the bold, wilderness canoe fishing and camping stir my senses and start me dreaming and planning like no other. I see lakes and rivers in vast forests of spruce, birch, and pine. I see battling lake trout early in the spring, and walleyes and small-mouth bass from summer to autumn. I see beautiful campsites where one can relax and fish for days, when the weather cooperates. I hear and see loons, geese, ducks, beavers galore, and sometimes moose and bear. The chirring red squirrels awaken me at dawn, the hoots of the great horned owl are the last things I hear at night.

If you've never done anything like this, take my word: Start planning now.

There are several places where you can enjoy this kind of experience, and I'm going to point you to as many as I can in this book. My favorite lies at the northeastern top of Minnesota on the Ontario border, north of the town of Ely, Minnesota. Here lies the great Boundary Waters Canoe Area (B.W.C.A.) in Minnesota and the adjoining Quetico Provincial Park in Ontario. Except for a couple of entrance stations, floatplanes and outboards are forbidden throughout the region. This is the land for the paddler and his canoe, for fishing with your preferred tackle without live bait, for enjoying wilderness solitude and using individual skills of coping with the great outdoors. You're on your own out here, just the way you want it.

Ely can rightly be called the U.S. headquarters for launching your wilderness fishing adventure into the B.W.C.A. and Quetico. You can literally arrive in Ely with nothing but a toothbrush, and the myriad outfitters there will fit you out with rented canoe, gear, and even your food. They'll plan your route if you like and provide the maps you need and the various permits. They'll take you to your departure point and meet you on your return.

There are other areas where you can launch your trip with outfitter services—and we will cover as many as we can in this book—but Ely can be considered the U.S. command post.

Begin your search with www.elycanoetrips.com or the number of sites you can find by going onto Google with "Ely Minnesota canoe trips." You'll see a lot of choices to begin learning about the area, with all sorts of literature and brochures. Or you can phone them at 800-950-2709 or write them at B.W.C.A. Canoe Trips, 2030 East Sheridan St., Ely, MN 55731.

944. Mapping Out Your Wilderness River Trip

Great maps, books of maps, and other aids for planning your river fishing trips are all available from Wilderness Adventures Press. Several states, including all of the Rocky Mountain high country, are included in their coverage. From Montana's Missouri to Georgia's Chattahoochee, you'll find great graphics and information. Check out www.store.wildadvpress.com.

945. Three Best Maps for the B.W.C.A./Quetico

Even in winter, when I'm a long way from my favorite wilderness area, the B.W.C.A./Quetico, I love poring over these great maps. And, of course, on canoe trips they're right there in front of me, in a plastic folder. Order Fisher Maps through the *Boundary Waters Journal;* McKenzie Maps at www.bwcamaps.com or through the *Boundary Waters Journal;* and Voyageur Maps at www.VoyageurMaps.com.

946. Those Very Special Mountain Brookies

"Mountain brookies are a special breed, although of the same species as the Eastern brook trout cousins of the rivers below. . . . I am advised by experts that the mountain relative of the large Labrador brookie lives but a brief four or five years. He is fragile, they say, and cannot withstand water temperatures above 75 degrees F."

—John Randolph, *Sports Afield*, "Brook Trout and Solitude
The Beaver Pond Way," February, 1975

947. Beaver Pond Brook Trout

"As I search for healthy ponds, I mark deep, dark water and cold inlet streams . . . I'll go alone when I go and come home alone and hide the path which has taken me out and in so no one else will cover my place . . . I'll talk a lot about these brookies in the high ponds, but I won't deal in revealing specifics. And other beaver pond anglers will understand why there's no invitation to come along, for they too have secret places and they too guard them closely. All know that one cannot share a beaver pond."

—John Randolph, *Sports Afield*, "Brook Trout and Solitude
The Beaver Pond Way," February, 1975

948. Finding Backcountry Hot spots

"In your research, don't overlook off-trail lakes that are close to roads. A lake that requires a 3-mile cross-country hike to reach may see fewer anglers than one 20 miles into the backcountry but right on a main trail."

—Rich Osthoff, *Fly Fishing the Rocky Mountain Backcountry*, Stackpole, 1999

949. Your Secret Backcountry Treasure

"Once you do find a good backcountry lake or stream, though, it's almost like owning private water. Just a handful of such spots can give you great angling for years to come."

—Rich Osthoff, *Fly Fishing the Rocky Mountain Backcountry*, Stackpole, 1999

950. Low Water Can Mean Canoe-Trip Nightmares

In low-water years of drought, or following such conditions, be aware that certain creeks and water courses that normally float your canoe will be muddy, boot-sucking bogs, extremely difficult to negotiate with your canoe and packs. What should have been an easy ride can turn into a nightmare in the sun, mud, sweat, and swarms of mosquitoes. On small watercourses where you were supposed to be paddling, not portaging, you'll be faced with the toughest conditions imaginable. Plan accordingly.

951. Canoe Trip's "Necessary" Extra

If you're going to paddle into a wilderness area and establish a base camp smack in the middle of good fishing, consider adding a tarp or fly to protect your cooking area or tent during periods of prolonged rain. In the spring or fall, especially, cold fronts can linger. There's not much worse than a soggy camp and gear.

952. Trolling for Your Supper

You don't have to set up camp to catch fish in the B.W.C.A. or Quetico. While on the move, troll a lure behind the canoe to pick up your walleye supper. Swimbaits such as Rapalas and others should do the trick.

953. Those Great Duluth Packs: Still With Us

The traditional canvas canoe packs from the legendary Duluth Pack folks in Duluth, Minnesota, have been around since 1911 and are still on the trail. They also have luggage. Available at Great catalog (800-849-4489) www.duluthpacks.com.

954. Trout Along the Appalachian Backbone

The name "The Appalachian Trail" brings to mind refreshing (especially to lowlanders) visions of the Blue Ridge Mountains, folded one onto another, stretching from Maine to Georgia, with hidden valleys always in shadows, and cold water flowing clear and swift, water where trout live and thrive. These aren't huge trout. A 12- to 14-incher is a trophy fish here, especially when it's a brookie, the original, pure, native-American brook trout. There are also rainbows and browns in some places. All this sounds great, and it is, but you won't find the best of it by getting in your car and driving along one of the mountain parkways and getting out to fish near the roads. From Georgia to Maine, whether you're in the Great Smoky Mountain Park or in Virginia's Blue Ridge, the most scenic streams with the best trout fishing are back in the mountains. There are books and maps aplenty to tell you exactly where they are, and even how to fish them. There are even places never written about, places that become your secret discovery. But to get into this rich, small-stream fishing opportunity, you've got to become a hiker and backpacker. If you are in decent shape and learn the skills and pull together the gear, the kind of fishing one dreams about can be yours. To get a taste of what this is all about, I read Christopher Camuto's classic book, *A Fly Fisherman's Blue Ridge,* available at www.amazon.com. If you're already convinced you want to get into this kind of rugged, individualistic fishing, that's great. But if you're thinking about it, and want to know exactly what it's like—how everything looks and feels out there off the main trails—Chris Camuto will show you the way.

955. Brook Trout Salvation

My friend Jim and I were young and strong, and we had come up to the Ontario wilderness to canoe a portion of the Drowning River, a tributary of the legendary Albany brook trout river. We took the train from Toronto to the town of Nakina, where our outfitter furnished us a canoe and packs and fly-in to a lake on the river. We were after brook trout, big brook trout, but what we found in massive quantities for our mid-July trip were mosquitoes and black flies. They nearly ate us alive, but we managed to portage the rapids, keep on paddling, and after three days and nights on the river, we spotted a tiny spring creek flowage into the river. The area was packed with big brookies, and we stayed there and caught them for two days before pushing on to the lake for our fly-out pickup. Had we not spotted that spring creek, the trip would have been a bust.

956. Brook Trout Salvation: Part Two

We were after brook trout on a canoe trip through Ontario's Algonquin Park, along the Petawawa River. Three days into the trip without a strike we found a section of the river where the water flowed from the lake through a creek-sized stream with long sets of small rapids and riffles. Brook trout charged our Mickey Finns and Edson Tigers from behind every rock it seemed. They were small fish, 10 inches or so, but they were wild trout, beautiful and tasty beyond words. We stayed there two days and the experience made our trip. Like the man said, "Size is not the measure."

957. The Smallmouth Transition

When I first began fishing the northern backcountry, I was not properly equipped with smallmouth lures. Being a good old boy, however, I had plenty of largemouth tackle, and I learned very quickly how to make it work for smallmouths: downsizing. When I went to much smaller lures and spinners, I began catching bronzebacks.

958. Don't Let the Bugs Win the Fight

Running out of insect repellant or protective net gear in the backcountry is like your airplane running out of gas: You're going to get hurt, and your trip is going to be ruined.

959. Fly Rod Posturing

We were talking about the wilderness pike we had caught that day (pike now . . . not steelhead or salmon or any other *holier-than-thou* fish), and this guy says, "Yea, but I got mine on a fly." Give me a break.

960. Sweet Dreams Guaranteed!

For some time now, I have devoted my bedtime reading to stories about the backcountry—and backcountry fishing. No current events, no controversy—all poison pills! My reading tastes constitute a sleeping pill I can count on.

961. Curly-Tailed Grubs: The Backcountry Go-To Lure

Because they are so effective and in their soft-plastic state you can carry so many of them, curly-tailed and twister-tailed grubs rank as some of the deadliest lures you can carry into the backcountry. Two-inch sizes are the most popular, and they should be rigged with jig heads of ⅛ to ½ ounces. Whatever head you choose, always rig your grub with the hook pointing up and the tail pointing down. Popular colors are white, lime-green, yellow, and pearl.

962. Don't Forget Alaska's Grayling

An Alaskan fishing adventure has so much to offer in salmon and trout action that it's sometimes easy to forget about the grayling—and northern pike too, for that matter. I am especially fond of grayling, especially the big-finned arctic grayling, which are at their best in summer fly hatches out on the Alaska Peninsula. I've had great fishing in June out of the late Bud Branham's camp near Lake Clark, flying out with Bud and the late Warren Page, shooting editor of *Field & Stream*. We'd land on lakes, hike over the small rivers, and start catching big grayling. Grayling are so much fun to catch on a dry fly that, in my opinion, a trip designed solely to focus on grayling would be a winner.

963. Where the Salmon and Halibut Play Together

Although most of my considerable Alaska fishing experience has been devoted to freshwater salmon, trout, and grayling rivers, I have managed to chalk up some quality time at the renowned Waterfall Resort on the West Coast of Prince of Wales Island. A forty-minute floatplane hop from Ketchikan, which has daily jet service from Seattle, Waterfall features top-drawer fishing all along the coast for salmon, kings, and silvers, and huge, mouth-watering halibut, both of which the resort will pack for you to take home in copious numbers. Lodging and meals are first-class. The fishing is from custom-designed North River Almar aluminum 25-foot cabin cruisers built especially for Alaska waters. In the Almars, you'll be fishing inside coves and outside on the edge of the sea if that's where they're biting best. You'll be accompanied by pods of whales, otters, walrus, and the ever-present bald eagles screaming and diving around your boat. Waterfall is an experience few others can match. Visit them at www.waterfallresort.com.

964. An Instant Fishing Guide

What do you get when you mix a smattering of local knowledge, a pickup truck, a great desire to go fishing, a baseball cap, lots of free time, and a strong dislike to shaving? Answer: A fishing guide, especially in backcountry areas. I've seen so many horror stories on blogs out of Alaska and other places that it makes me wonder sometimes what people can be thinking when they hire on these "instant" guides. Let's start with a fresh sheet of paper on the guide thing. First, the beard. That part is OK, if he's a neat guy. Just a matter of personal taste, but after that we've got to stick to some rigid requirements: A man or woman with vast experience, the latest proper equipment, tons of local knowledge, and the brains and desire to make it all work together on behalf of the client. The guide must be set up to maintain good communications with the client and the information sources along the lakes and rivers. If you can't do the homework yourself, try to use sources like "The Angling Report."

965. The Coho: Alaska's Super Salmon

The chinook salmon is called a king, while the coho salmon is called a silver. In my view, however, and one shared by a multitude of anglers, the silver is the true king of Alaskan waters.

Silvers fight harder, jump more often, and hold in the rivers at far less depth than kings. Oh, the kings are big all right, reaching awesome weights in the 30- to 60-pound class, while silvers go 8 to 15. Still, I'm a silver man, and I'll plan my trips around their runs, usually in August and September. Yes, you will still be able to get rainbows on the side when the silvers are running, although not in prime-time rainbow numbers.

966. Those Big Alaska Rainbows

If you go after the big rainbows out on the Alaska Peninsula, you'll find the fishing to be as varied as the terrain and weather. It is in late season, after the salmon runs have been progressing, that the rainbow fishing changes from traditional "fish the water" techniques to the great salmon-egg feast, with the rainbows gorging themselves on salmon eggs as they follow the runs of fish upstream. The eggs and patterns are all well-known to the guides, and the action can be furious. Sometimes the takes can be hard to spot, but, what the heck, with that many takes going on, you're bound to get your share of hookups. While fishing salmon eggs may not be as interesting as floating a dry fly or a mouse pattern over a rainbow hiding along a bank, the game is still appealing to any fly rodder.

967. Chum Salmon Get No Respect

The chum salmon, sometimes called "dog salmon" because of the native practice of feeding them to the dogs as a winter staple, usually run the rivers just ahead of the silvers, sometimes intermixing with them. They are big fish, running up to 40 pounds, and are chrome silver when they enter the streams but begin to turn very quickly. Chums are dogged, powerful fighters, and although they do not jump as frequently as silvers, they give a good account of themselves.

968. Where Alaska Gets Crowded

The word "Alaska" should be synonymous with wilderness fishing, and it is. Not all of it is uncrowded, however. Like any other wilderness fishing area, from Alaska to New Zealand, wherever roads touch the wilderness, there will be people. Alaska has few roads, and not many people, but the people who call it home love to fish. When they gang up at the end of the roads—in places like the Kenai, for instance—the scene can sometimes look like opening day in New Jersey. Even some lakes and streams reached by remote fly-out fishing camps can look like a floatplane fly-in convention at times when a particular salmon river is hot. Most everybody will be catching fish, but "uncrowded" it ain't!

969. Semi-Wild Smallmouth Fishing

I've been fortunate to do many canoe trips for wilderness smallmouths—particularly in the Boundary Waters-Quetico area and in Algonquin Park—and such trips have become personal favorites for dreaming and planning. In an attempt to mimic such fishing in areas closer to home where I live in the eastern United States, a number of years ago I began to do three-day float trips for smallmouths on the Upper Potomac river, particularly in the area from Paw Paw, West Virginia, down to Hancock, Maryland. Taking long weekends from Friday, we had two nights on the river and three days of floating and fishing. Canoes or jonboats will take you there, once you arrange your put-in and pull-out logistics. You won't feel like you're in the Quetico—more like in Deliverance country—but you'll find a nice slice of wilderness that's close to home.

970. Semi-Wild Smallmouth Fishing, Part Two

Bound for a pleasant couple of days floating a nice smallmouth stream like the Upper Potomac in West Virginia and Maryland, in mid- or late-summer you'll get your best results by wet-wading and carefully fishing the best-looking rapids, riffles, and sweeps of water. Don't race over and past them in your canoe or jonboat. It's time to get out and use your legs. This is fishing that cries out for light spinning tackle and flinging Mepps spinners across and down, working them into shadowy pockets and current seams where the fast water starts relaxing a bit. You might have a partner who insists on trying fly fishing for a time, and he's welcome to it. You'll make more casts, work more water, and catch more fish with light spinning tackle.

971. Wilderness Police and Fire-Starter Paper

We've seen an instance now of rangers in the Boundary Waters Canoe Area flagging down anglers who left scraps of paper with their kindling in their fireplace, with the intention of starting the evening fire quickly. Rangers say the paper sometimes blows all over the place, creating ugly trash. The point is, keep a clean campsite. Leave it the way you'd like to find it.

972. The Perfect Base Camp

In setting up the base camp that's to be your headquarters for a few days of backcountry fishing, be sure to avoid establishing it at the end or the beginning of a prominent portage trail.

973. The Burlap Bag Fish Cooler

Using the powers of evaporation, a simple burlap bag in the bottom of your canoe will keep your fish cooler, wetter, and fresher than a stringer hanging awkwardly over the side.

974. On-Target Wilderness Casting

In his classic and venerable *The Angler's Handbook,* Thomas Crowell (1949), the late Ted True-blood relates graphically how a good caster has an advantage over a poor caster, particularly in waters that are usually very clear. "One afternoon at a lake in New York state I caught and released sixty bass. My companion caught only two. The sole reason was that they were frightened by the boat and would not strike closer than 75 feet . . . My companion had fished all his life, but he never had learned to cast. He used a sideswipe and couldn't get his plug more than 50 to 60 feet from the boat—and he tried so hard that he was picking out backlashes fully half the time." Even though Trueblood wasn't fishing at a true wilderness destination, the importance of the lesson is clear.

975. When The Plane Does Not Come

You may not need a bail-out bag (survival kit) in backcountry or canoe-trip fishing, but you do have to give some serious thought to the bag you'll need on the day (or days) when the plane does not come to fetch you for the trip home. If you fish enough in the backcountry, it will happen.

976. Last Cast . . .

The sun is pouring pure gold through a bastion of pines cupping a cove of dark water. It's time to head for camp, strike a match, and get out the tin cups. Suddenly, up ahead in the gloom, the slap of a beaver tail resounds through the stillness. You can't see it, but there's a beaver lodge up there in the shadows—structure, cover, a smallmouth hotel. Your soft-plastic jig is rigged weedless; you don't need to see where it lands. Just one last cast . . .

PART NINE

ON THE WATER

For Ice Fishing

CHAPTER 24

Surefire Hard-Water Tactics: Fishing the Ice for Fun and Food

977. The Truth About Ice Fishing

"Ice-fishing isn't so much a sport as it is a way of positively dealing with unfortunate reality. I mean, you can wake up in the morning depressed because it will be months yet before you can fly fish in real, liquid water, or you can leap out of bed thinking, 'Oh boy! It's the height of ice-fishing season.' Or if not, 'Oh boy,' then at least, 'Okay.'"

  —John Gierach, *The View from Trout Lake*, Simon & Schuster, 1988

978. Where the Fish Are

"Fish congregate under the ice, and do not spread out over the lake as in spring, summer, and fall. The deep holes are best, but these deep holes do not necessarily have to be in the middle of the lake."

  —Charles J. Farmer, *Sports Afield*, "The Sound Approach to Ice Fishing," January 1975

979. Ice Fishing's Biggest Mistake

"The most common error I have seen in ice fishing is angling too far from shore. Think of the ice-covered lake as you would if you were covering it in a boat. Chances are you would not fish the middle of the lake, but rather you would cast to points, the drop-offs, and where streams enter the lake."

  —Charles J. Farmer, *Sports Afield*, "The Sound Approach to Ice Fishing," January 1975

980. When Panfish Move Deeper

As the winter deepens and the action slows on your favorite areas along the banks for catching panfish—bluegills, yellow perch, pickerel—you may not have to chase all over the lake looking for them. First check out the deep water just adjacent to the areas where you caught panfish in summer and then at the start of winter's ice fishing.

981. Keeping Those Precious Smelt Alive

"Smelt are hard to get and hard to keep. They can't take sloshing around in bait buckets and will not be alive just when you need them most. Some anglers put baffles in their bait buckets to stop that from happening."

—Tom Hennessey, outdoor columnist for the *Bangor Daily News*

982. Modern Ice-Fishing Gear: The Key to Having Fun

"The snowmobile and power ice auger made ice fishing what it is today. In the days before these devices came along, ice fishing only called to the strongest and most hearty. All the equipment being used today—from power augers to rods, reels, and jigs—is amazing in what it can do to help you have fun days out on the ice, instead of drudgery and plain hard work. Check out the gear on the Internet, particularly at places like www.cabelas.com, www.basswpro.com, and www.gandermountain.com."

—Tom Hennessey, outdoor columnist for the *Bangor Daily News*

983. Check Those Traps Frequently

"Checking traps frequently can produce action with the bait that leads to strikes. Lifting the bait to check it gives it movement, action, attracting fish. Once attracted, they may start biting."

—Tom Hennessey, outdoor columnist for the *Bangor Daily News*

984. The Key to Taking Landlocks

"Landlock salmon move around the lake only a foot or two below the surface. Fish for them more shallow than other species."

—Tom Hennessey, outdoor columnist for the *Bangor Daily News*

985. Catching Lake Trout Through the Ice

"Best bait for lake trout (togue, to Maine folk) is a golden shiner or sucker, about 3 to 4 inches long. Make a cut just where the gills meet at the belly where there's an artery that will bleed. Find the bottom, then lift bait about a foot off it."

—Tom Hennessey, outdoor columnist for the *Bangor Daily News*

986. Setting Drag on Ice-Fishing Reels

"Basically, you want your ice-fishing reel to have little or no drag. Often when fish mouth the bait and feel tension, they will drop it. Fishing with no drag, you can set the hook after they've run a bit and taken the bait."

—Tom Hennessey, outdoor columnist for the *Bangor Daily News*

987. Best Ice-Fishing Rigs

"Use 6 to 8 feet of leader for deep fishing, less for the salmon, which move about only a foot or so below the ice. Use a swivel connected to line and use a No. 6 hook (or 4 sometimes). Use split-shot."

—Tom Hennessey, outdoor columnist for the *Bangor Daily News*

988. Using Smelt as Bait

"Smelt will swim around and around and twist line. They will come to the top if you don't have sinker."

—Tom Hennessey, outdoor columnist for the *Bangor Daily News*

989. Better Lure Action Under the Ice

Imagine an ice-fishing lure so effective it gives you the ability to "cast" under the ice. Sounds pretty good, don't you think? So do writers Ted Takasaki and Scott Richardson, who wrote on the tactics of ice-fishing guru Dave Genz in the article "Ice Spoonin' Walleyes" in the Articles section of the Lindy Tackle Web site, www.lindyfishingtackle.com. Genz especially likes first-ice walleyes when the oxygen levels and temps are more to their liking and they're more aggressive. He goes after them with Lindy's Rattlin' Flyer Spoon, with the look, flash, and sound that brings in walleyes, especially late in the afternoon when other lures are losing their effectiveness. The design of the Rattlin' Flyer, say Takasaki and Richardson, like its predecessor, the Flyer, allows the lure to have a gliding action when dropped into a hole, covering the water much like a cast. Genz uses a stiff-tip rod (limber tips won't give the lure action) and suggests on fishing the lure: "Don't lift it and let it pendulum back below the hole. Drag it. Twitch it as you drag it. Now, you're almost fishing like you would fish in summer." If you're a serious icefisher or a serious wannabe, check out all the details in this excellent article and many others at the Lindy site.

990. Early-Ice Walleye Spots to Set Up

Points that lead to drop-offs have always been known as prime walleye spots to put your ice auger to work on. Some experts tweak this idea with a further refinement: They choose the spots where the drop-off is the steepest, and is leading to the deepest part of the lake.

991. Working the Jig

The word "jigging" seems to be synonymous with ice fishing, and everybody seems to do it differently. Common knowledge, however, says to let the spoon or jig go all the way to the bottom, then lift it with a couple of cranks on your reel and keep it at that level as you make it flutter up and down.

992. Making Your Jig Even More Deadly

Bait fishermen with their tip-ups catch a lot of fish through the ice, but the method that's the most fun is jigging with a short rod. You can sweeten your jig by adding a minnow, hooked through the lips. The same rig is very effective in crappie fishing.

993. Better Way to Fish Jigging Spoons

"Jigging spoons usually have the hook on the fatter end and you tie your line to the thinner end. Reversing that will cause the lure to flutter more and keep it from dropping too fast."

—Larry Whiteley, OutdoorSite Library,

Bass Pro Shops, www.basspro.com

994. Don't Let Those Fish Freeze

"Don't let your fish freeze out on the ice unless you have a way of keeping them frozen. If they thaw out and you refreeze them when you get home, they will lose a lot of their flavor. "

—Larry Whiteley, OutdoorSite Library, Bass Pro Shops, www.basspro.com

995. Tackle for Hard-Water Bluegills

In an excellent article on the Bass Pro Shops' OutdoorSite Library, Jason Aki explains his tackle for consistently taking bluegills. "An ultralight to light jigging pole between 2 and 3 feet coupled to a micro spinning reel with line-holding capacity of 100 feet of 4-pound test . . . "

996. Lures and Rig for Hard-Water Bluegills

Continuing recommendations from Jason Aki in his article on jigging bluegills through the ice: "First off, line your rod with the lightest fishing line you feel confident in using, and then tie on a small spoon with the treble hook removed. Onto the bottom of the spoon tie a 10- or 12-inch leader of monofilament line and a small curved-shank hook. Onto the hook spear two to three wax worms or a dorsally hooked crappie minnow. The idea here is to have the spoon attract the bluegills' attention from a distance and the scent of the bait to get the fish to bite."

—Jason Aki, "Jigging Ice for Bluegill," OutdoorSite Library,

Bass Pro Shops, www.basspro.com

997. Moving On to Better Things

"Small moves are tweaking your position on a piece of structure. They're 5- to 20-yard changes . . . Large moves are used to cover big distances. . . . Often it's better to move and try to find active fish than spend a lot of time with finicky fish. Sometimes, a few short moves will put you into biters, while some days are just tough bites."

—Tim Allard, "Ice Fishing a New Lake,"

OutdoorSite Library, Bass Pro Shops, www.basspro.com

998. Ice Fishing with Gander Mountain

We've mentioned the Gander Mountain mail-order and resource center elsewhere in this book, but their ice-fishing coverage deserves special mention. Tackle, gear, and information; it's a complete coverage. Check it out at www.gandermountain.com. The articles and tips are in their Resource Center.

999. Find the Fish with Sonar

"The sonar available to the modern ice angler is nothing short of amazing. In fact, many anglers don't even drill holes through the ice unless they first spot gamefish with their sonar. How is that possible? By simply pouring water on solid, clear ice and placing the transducer in the water, the unit can transmit and receive sound waves through the ice, allowing you to see the depth, weeds, and even fish."

—Gander Mountain article, www.gandermountain.com

1000. The Yellow Perch Challenge

Yellow perch are a universal ice-fishing joy. They're great on the table, they usually roam the waters in schools, and they are widely distributed over North America's best ice-fishing destinations. While perch can be easy to find at times, they can also be difficult, zigging while you're zagging and vice versa. Before you can catch them, you have to find them—and it's not always that simple.

1001. Yellow Perch Lures of an Expert

In an excellent article on the Bass Pro Shops Outdoor Library, angler Tim Allard says he divides his baits between "search" baits, which are relatively big jigging baits and "finesse" baits, for subtle jigging on holes where he knows there are fish. Allard tries to attract perch with relatively big jigging baits like Northland's Buckshot Spoon, Blue Fox's Rattle Flash Jig'n Spoons, Bay de Noc's Swedish Pimples, and Lindy's Rattlin Flyer. For subtle jigging he names ice jigs like Lindy Little Joe and Northland's Super Glo.

ALSO AVAILABLE

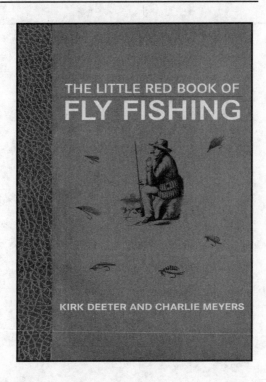

The Little Red Book of Fly Fishing
by Charlie Meyers and Kirk Deeter

Two highly respected outdoor journalists, Charlie Meyers of the *Denver Post* and Kirk Deeter of *Field & Stream*, have cracked open their notebooks and shared straight-shot advice on the sport of fly fishing, based on a range of new and old experiences—from interviews with the late Lee Wulff to travels with maverick guides in Tierra del Fuego.

The mission of *The Little Red Book of Fly Fishing* is to demystify and simplify the tricks and tips that make a great trout fisher. There are no complicated physics lessons here. Rather, conceived in the "take dead aim" spirit of Harvey Penick's classic instructional on golf, *The Little Red Book of Fly Fishing* offers a simple, digestible primer on the basic elements of fly fishing: casting, presenting, reading water, and selecting flies. In the end, this collection of 240 tips is one of the most insightful, plainly spoken, and entertaining works on this sport—one that will serve both novices and experts alike in helping them reflect on and hone their approaches to fly fishing.

Charlie Meyers was the outdoors editor for the *Denver Post*, covering various fishing and hunting angles since 1966, and was editor-at-large for *Angling Trade*. He has also contributed many fishing-related stories to magazines including *Field & Stream*, *Outdoor Life*, *Fly Fisherman*, *Flyfishing in Salt Waters*, *Southwest Fly Fishing*, *The Drake*, among others. He lived in Golden, Colorado, until his death in 2010.

Kirk Deeter is an editor-at-large for *Field & Stream* magazine and co-editor of its Fly Talk blog. He is also the editor-in-chief of *Angling Trade* and senior editor of the *Flyfish Journal*. His stories have appeared in *Garden & Gun*, *The Drake*, *5280*, *Fly Rod & Reel*, *Fly Fisherman*, *Big Sky Journal*, *SaltWater Sportsman*, and *Trout*, among other places. He lives in Pin, Colorado.

$16.95 Hardcover • 224 Pages

ALSO AVAILABLE

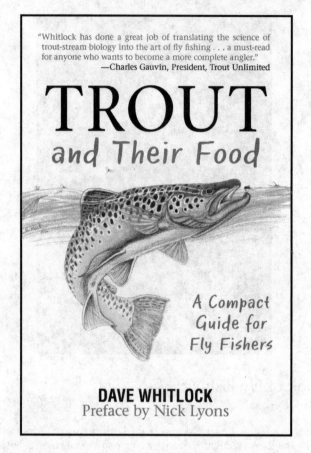

"Whitlock has done a great job of translating the science of trout-stream biology into the art of fly fishing . . . a must-read for anyone who wants to become a more complete angler."
—Charles Gauvin, President, Trout Unlimited

TROUT
and Their Food

A Compact Guide for Fly Fishers

DAVE WHITLOCK
Preface by Nick Lyons

Trout and Their Food
A Compact Guide for Fly Fishers
by Dave Whitlock

A new book by Dave Whitlock, author of some of the best books on fly fishing ever written, is a reason for fly fishermen to celebrate. The aim of this book is simple: Whitlock wants to take the guesswork out of fly fishing and pass on the wisdom he's accumulated over decades on the water. Fly tying is broken down into simple steps, and Whitlock stays grounded in the practical importance and relevance of every fly in the book. Anchored by Whitlock's own beautiful illustrations, this book provides plenty of knowledge and excitement for those hours spent at home and off the water.

Dave Whitlock's art and writing appear regularly in every major fly-fishing and outdoor publication, including *Fly Fisherman*, *Trout Magazine*, and *Field & Stream*. His books, including *Dave Whitlock's Guide to Aquatic Trout Foods* and the *L.L. Bean Fly Fishing Handbook*, have helped educate hundreds of thousands of anglers. He lives in Welling, Oklahoma.

$16.95 Paperback • 244 Pages

ALSO AVAILABLE

The Complete Book of Surf Fishing
by Captain Al Ristori

Fishing from beach or rocky coastline presents challenges not faced by anglers who head out to sea. Written to open new frontiers to the old hand and provide advice to novice surf fishermen, *The Complete Book of Surf Fishing* will be a boon to all coastline anglers. Author and licensed charter captain Al Ristori covers the basics of traditional surfcasting, with well-illustrated instruction on casting big rods in big water. He covers the gamut of tackle that does duty in the surf—conventional gear, spinning gear, fly tackle, and light tackle—and discusses the full range of bait, lures, and flies. Most importantly, he tells you how to find fish. Whether you are casting on the East Coast, Gulf Coast, or West Coast, with Ristori's tips and tricks and decades of experience, you will know where the fish are when they are most likely to bite. Everyone needs advice from an expert fisherman once in a while, and now no angler plying the surf will have to do without.

Captain Al Ristori is a Coast Guard-licensed charter captain and the saltwater fishing editor for *The Star-Ledger*.

$16.95 Paperback • 240 Pages

ALSO AVAILABLE

The Complete Book of Fishing Knots, Leaders, and Lines

by Lindsey Philpott

Whether you're fly fishing, trolling, spinning, or surfcasting, your knots must hold well, be easy to remember, and help the lure to wriggle. *The Complete Book of Fishing Knots, Leaders, and Lines* teaches anglers the best way to tie reliable, workable knots. Knots you already know and unusual special-purpose knots are depicted in color photographs tied with thick monofilament, so you don't have to guess what each knot is really supposed to look like. There are descriptions of fifty knots as well as tips to improve your tackle and simplify life for yourself—because the fish make fishing hard enough! *The Complete Book of Fishing Knots, Leaders, and Lines* also offers clear instructions for tying winning leaders, tips for selecting lines, and up-to-date information from the field that will bring you the quickest, slickest, and best catch ever.

Lindsey Philpott has been tying knots since the age of six. His father taught him how to fish without a rod, line, or hook by "tickling" trout in the Devon streams of his native England.

$9.95 Paperback • 176 Pages

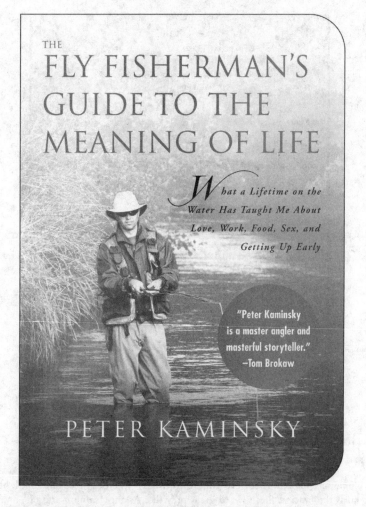

The Fly Fisherman's Guide to the Meaning of Life
What a Lifetime on the Water Has Taught Me About Love, Work, Food, Sex, and Getting Up Early

by Peter Kaminsky

The fly fisherman is a unique breed of sportsman—he loves the sparkle of sunlight dancing off a trout stream, the surreal beauty of a mayfly hatch on a spring day, and the heart-thumping eruption of a surface strike by a large trout. Here Peter Kaminsky writes about the angler's passion and his pursuit of knowledge. He explains that long days without fish can teach you how to deal with failure and releasing a caught fish can remind you about ethics. He offers inspiration to readers who love the sport as much as he does.

Peter Kaminsky is the author of *Fishing for Dummies* and has been published in dozens of mainstream and outdoor periodicals, including the *New York Times* and *Field & Stream*. He lives in Brooklyn, New York.

$9.95 Paperback • 160 Pages

ALSO AVAILABLE

The Gigantic Book of Fishing Stories
Edited and Introduced by Nick Lyons

This one-of-a-kind volume has something for everyone who fishes—whether he or she fondly remembers fishing with worms as a child, or hurls the fanciest flies toward great prey like Atlantic salmon and tarpon. Its selections celebrate fishing for bass, catfish, trout, striped bass, crappie, tarpon, muskie, Atlantic salmon, bonefish, pike, and many other species. If it swims and can be landed with a rod, line, and hook, it's featured here—as are locations all over the world, from the greatest rivers of Montana and Southern lakes to American coasts and far-off locations around the world.

Anglers will find their favorites here—writers who have made a living writing on the joys of fishing and renowned names of literature who have shared their tales and wisdom, such as James Henshall, Rudyard Kipling, G.E.M. Skues, Roland Pertwee, Bill Barich, Ted Leeson, James Prosek, Lefty Kreh, John McPhee, Zane Grey, Joan Wulff, Howell Raines, and so many more. There are also wonderful, little-known pieces by virtually unknown authors and special discoveries—like the famous painter of birds, John James Audubon, writing about cat-fishing in the Ohio River. Fishermen nationwide will love this gigantic compendium, which will make an ideal gift.

Nick Lyons has written over twenty books—mostly on fishing—in addition to hundreds of articles on the subject, which have appeared in magazines such as *Field & Stream*, *Outdoor Life*, and *Fly Fisherman*. He is also the editor of *Hemingway on Fishing*.

$24.95 Hardcover • 800 Pages

IGFA's 101 Freshwater Fishing Tips and Tricks

by Bill Dance

One of America's best-known fishermen, with more than fifty years of on-water experience, Bill Dance is also a tournament champion and a television personality. His tips will help any angler catch more and bigger fish. Even experienced fishermen may not know that dark-colored lures work best during low-light conditions; that reluctant bass often bite at smaller lures fished slowly; that 75 percent of all line failures occur at the knot, so good knot tying is essential to success; and that when waters rise, bass move shallower, and when they fall, they move deeper. Dance's knowledge is so wide-ranging that absolute beginners and crusty old veteran fishermen alike will be educated, entertained, and amazed. This book is being supported by The International Game Fish Association (IGFA), a leading authority on angling and the keeper of fishing's world record.

Bill Dance is an outdoors legend who has delivered witty fishing advice to television audiences for over thirty years. He is a member of the National Fishing Hall of Fame and has won twenty-three National Bass Titles. An avid and amusing writer, he has authored seven books on fishing and has contributed to major outdoor magazines.

$12.95 Paperback • 160 Pages

ALSO AVAILABLE

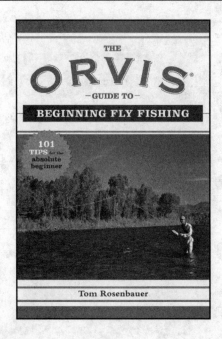

The Orvis Guide to Beginning Fly Fishing
101 Tips for the Absolute Beginner
by Tom Rosenbauer

This book, by America's oldest fishing tackle business, offers beginners a chance to learn the fundamentals of the great sport of fly fishing quickly and easily. *The Orvis Guide to Beginning Fly Fishing* can be the start of a lifetime journey of discovery that will increase your intimacy with the natural world and allow you to gain skill and finesse in your fly-fishing techniques.

Proven teaching methods and bright, helpful illustrations will enable new fly fishers to:

- Find fish in streams, lakes, and salt water.
- Select and assemble proper, balanced tackle.
- Cast a fly line with authority.
- Recognize and simulate natural fish foods.
- Tie effective knots.

Orvis concisely explains fishing ethics, offers helpful safety advice, defines basic angling terms, and convinces the new angler that fly fishing couldn't be simpler or more fun. *The Orvis Guide to Beginning Fly Fishing* is a crisp, helpful, and finely illustrated primer of the highest rank.

Tom Rosenbauer has been fly fishing for over forty years and is the vice president of marketing at Orvis. He lives in Sunderland, Vermont.

The Orvis Company, America's oldest fish-tackle business, mails fifty-five million catalogs each year. Its headquarters are in Manchester, Vermont.

$12.95 Paperback • 192 Pages